London

Recent Titles in Contemporary World Cities

Tokyo: Geography, History, and Culture
Louis G. Perez

Beijing: Geography, History, and Culture
Qian Guo

London

GEOGRAPHY, HISTORY, AND CULTURE

Victoria R. Williams

Contemporary World Cities

BLOOMSBURY ACADEMIC
NEW YORK • LONDON • OXFORD • NEW DELHI • SYDNEY

BLOOMSBURY ACADEMIC
Bloomsbury Publishing Inc
1385 Broadway, New York, NY 10018, USA
50 Bedford Square, London, WC1B 3DP, UK
29 Earlsfort Terrace, Dublin 2, Ireland

BLOOMSBURY, BLOOMSBURY ACADEMIC and the Diana logo
are trademarks of Bloomsbury Publishing Plc

First published in the United States of America by ABC-CLIO 2022
Paperback edition published by Bloomsbury Academic 2025

COVER PHOTO: Financial District of London and the Tower Bridge.
(John Kellerman/Alamy Stock Photo)

Bloomsbury Publishing Inc does not have any control over, or responsibility for,
any third-party websites referred to or in this book. All internet addresses given
in this book were correct at the time of going to press. The author and publisher
regret any inconvenience caused if addresses have changed or sites have
ceased to exist, but can accept no responsibility for any such changes.

Library of Congress Cataloging-in-Publication Data
Names: Williams, Victoria, author.
Title: London : geography, history, and culture / Victoria R. Williams.
Description: Santa Barbara, California : ABC-CLIO, LLC, [2022] |
Series: Contemporary world cities | Includes bibliographical references and index.
Identifiers: LCCN 2021024302 (print) | LCCN 2021024303 (ebook) |
ISBN 9781440877438 (print) | ISBN 9781440877445 (ebook)
Subjects: LCSH: London (England)
Classification: LCC DA677 .W535 2022 (print) | LCC DA677 (ebook) | DDC 942.1—dc23
LC record available at https://lccn.loc.gov/2021024302
LC ebook record available at https://lccn.loc.gov/2021024303

ISBN: HB: 978-1-4408-7743-8
PB: 979-8-2161-9474-3
ePDF: 978-1-4408-7744-5
eBook: 979-8-2161-1266-2

Series: Contemporary World Cities

To find out more about our authors and books visit www.bloomsbury.com
and sign up for our newsletters.

Contents

Series Foreword

In William Shakespeare's *The Tragedy of Coriolanus,* the character Sicinius poses the question, "What is the city but the people?"[1] According to the United Nations, our global cities are made up of more than half of the people in the world, with a projection that 60 percent of the world's population will be living in urban centers by 2030.[2] But diving deeper than population statistics, Sicinius was right—the heart of a city is not in its architecture or green spaces, nor is it in its stores, restaurants, Wall Streets, or red-light districts. The heart of a city is found in the people that live there, their diversity and unity, and the strong heartbeat that makes the city unique and loved by visitors and natives alike.

What is it like to live in these global centers, the main hubs of countries and regions, where industries thrive, immigrants settle, and traditions evolve? The *Contemporary World Cities* series examines the world's major urban centers—from Tokyo to Mexico City, Beijing to London, and Moscow to Paris. Each volume focuses on one major global city, incorporating information on the host country, but honing in on the urban center itself. Volumes begin with a preface and chronology of major events that have occurred in the city, followed by chapters covering the following topics:

- Location
- People
- History
- Politics
- Economy
- Environment and Sustainability
- Local Crime and Violence
- Security Issues

- Natural Hazards and Emergency Management
- Culture and Lifestyle
- The City in Pop Culture
- The Future

Chapters can be read on their own or one after another, with information suitable for researchers, general readers, and even travelers. "Did you know... ?" sidebar boxes are scattered throughout the text, providing readers with intriguing fun facts about culture, taboos, and the "unwritten" rules of the city, such as how to properly order food from a street vendor to breaking down how the subway system *really* works. Chapters are accompanied by "Life in the City" inset boxes, memoir-styled interviews with people who have lived or visited each city, including exchange students and natives. These anecdotes include stories about culture shock, typical daily customs, and life in the city during major world events.

Contemporary World Cities allows readers to fully immerse themselves in another culture by gaining a better understanding of the culture, history, and society that make up the urban nerve centers of countries.

NOTES

1. William Shakespeare. *The Tragedy of Coriolanus*. Act 3, Scene 1. Retrieved from: http://shakespeare.mit.edu/coriolanus/coriolanus.3.1.html.

2. "The World's Cities in 2016 Data Booklet." United Nations, 2016, page ii. Retrieved from: https://www.un.org/en/development/desa/population/publications /pdf/urbanization/the_worlds_cities_in_2016_data_booklet.pdf.

Preface

Why, Sir, you find no man, at all intellectual, who is willing to leave London. No, Sir, when a man is tired of London, he is tired of life; for there is in London all that life can afford.

—Samuel Johnson

That was the opinion of the English writer and lexicographer Samuel Johnson (1709–1784), and it is an opinion shared by many Londoners, who tend to be very proud of their hometown. This single-volume work covers all aspects of life in London, one of the world's most vibrant cities. The book looks at London's history from its legendary beginnings through to the modern era—through the plague, an all-consuming fire, two world wars, postwar rebuilding, the Swinging Sixties, terrorist attacks, and into the modern era. There are sections on London's geography and environment, including sustainability and transport issues, the city's role in popular culture (particularly in film, art, and literature), and chapters on the city's politics and economy.

The book has been kept as jargon-free as possible so that it may be enjoyed by general readers. Nonetheless, this book is aimed primarily at researchers. Keeping this in mind, each chapter can be read as a stand-alone item or as part of a wider examination of London. Additionally, each chapter is followed by notes giving sources for specific information and a "Further Reading" list. A "Chronology" of London's history immediately follows this preface.

Sidebars are scattered throughout the book in order to provide interesting information connected to the chapters, while the "Life in the City" boxes document the anecdotal experiences of individual Londoners during specific times in London's history. The "Life in the City" interview topics range from memories of the death of King George VI and the coronation of Queen Elizabeth II in the 1950s to what it was like to be teenager in swinging London of the 1960s, the excitement of attending the London 2012 Olympics and Paralympics, and what it is like to work in a pub during the COVID-19 pandemic. I have included my own memories of dancing in Trafalgar Square as part of a BBC television program.

I wrote this book during an extremely strange time in London's history. In March 2020, London, like the rest of the UK, went into lockdown due to the COVID-19 pandemic. This meant individuals' travel was curtailed; libraries were shut; and museums, archives, and educational establishments were closed. For this reason, it proved very difficult to access resources and interview individuals. I would like to thank all my interviewees for their help: my mother, Rosemary Williams, for her memories of royalty; my sister, Alexandra Williams, for insights into London pub life; my uncle Bill Barrett for his memories of working at Wembley Stadium; my friend, Matthew Davis, for his memories of London 2012; and his mother, Chris Davis, for reminiscing about the 1960s. I would also like to thank my former acquisitions editor at ABC-CLIO, Kaitlin Ciarmiello, for her unwavering support over the course of the writing of this book and others. As a Londoner born and bred, I feel extremely proud to have had the opportunity to write about my hometown and hope this book provides an insider's insight into London life, past, present, and future.

Chronology

1100 BCE–1000 BCE
According to legend, London is founded by Brutus of Troy.

43 CE
Romans invade Britain under Emperor Claudius.

47
The Romans establish the settlement of Londinium.

50–410
Londinium is the largest city in Roman Britain.

60
Warriors from the Iceni tribe led by Queen Boudicca sack London.

70
London's basilica is built.

90–120
London's basilica is expanded.

125
Much of London is likely destroyed by fire.

150
Parts of London are demolished to make way for a stone wall to be built.

190–225
Stone wall is built around the city.

290
Roman commander Carausius has special coins made in London.

296

Roman troops regain London.

367

London is invaded by Picts, Gaels, Saxons, and mutinous Roman troops.

410

Roman army leaves Britain.

600

Anglo-Saxon kingdoms are established in Britain.

604

St. Augustine establishes the episcopal sees of London. St. Paul's Cathedral is founded.

675

St. Paul's is damaged by fire.

700s

London is now Anglo-Saxon and known as Lundenwic.

800s and 900s

Lundenwic is raided by Vikings.

Mid- to late 800s

Raids make London virtually uninhabitable.

880–890

People start to resettle in London.

889

London has become a major trading port and market again.

961

St. Paul's is raided by Vikings.

Late 900s to 1066

Control of London passes between Vikings and Anglo-Saxons.

1042

St. Edward the Confessor, penultimate Saxon monarch of England, initiates construction of Westminster Abbey.

1050–1300

Quays are constructed on the River Thames's northern banks.

1066

Norman Conquest sees William the Conqueror crowned King of England at Westminster Abbey.

1087
Fire destroys many of London's wooden houses as well as St. Paul's.

1091
UK's largest tornado hits London.

1123
St. Bartholomew's Hospital and Smithfield meat market open.

1189
Henry Fitz-Ailwyn becomes first mayor of London. King Richard I's coronation is held at Westminster Abbey.

1212
Henry Fitz-Ailwyn dies in office.

1290
London's oldest Roman Catholic church building, St. Etheldreda's, is built.

1300
The so-called Little Ice Age begins.

1305
Scottish rebel William Wallace is hung, drawn, and quartered at Smithfield following his trial at Westminster Hall.

1320
Hanseatic League merchants establish the Steelyard in Dowgate, in the City of London.

1348
Black Death hits London.

1381
Peasants' Revolt takes place in London.

1392
King Richard II retakes control of London.

1397
Richard ("Dick") Whittington is appointed Lord Mayor of London by King Richard II.

1406
Londoners elect Whittington as their Lord Mayor.

1419
Whittington is reelected.

1476

William Caxton founds the world's first portable printing press in Westminster.

1485

King Henry VII is crowned. Yeoman Warders of His Majesty's Royal Palace and Fortress the Tower of London (the Beefeaters) is formed by the new king.

1509

King Henry VIII is crowned.

1520

Craft guilds have added and continue to add much to London's prosperity.

1529

Henry VIII starts to convert York Place into the Palace of Whitehall.

1536

Anne Boleyn is executed in the Tower of London.

1555

Relief for London's poor is organized. Royal hospitals are established.

1559

Queen Elizabeth I is crowned at Westminster Abbey.

1565

Thomas Gresham founds the Royal Exchange.

1574

Theatrical performances are legalized in London.

1576

The first London theater opens.

1580

Queen Elizabeth I takes controls of London's urban expansion. An earthquake causes a pinnacle to fall from Westminster Abbey.

1581

Explorer Sir Francis Drake is knighted aboard the *Golden Hind* at Deptford, southeast London.

1586

Conspirators in the Babington Plot to assassinate Elizabeth I and replace her with Mary, Queen of Scots, are hanged, drawn, and quartered in St. Giles Field, London.

1587

The Rose theater is built in Southwark.

1588
Elizabeth I deploys London troops against the Spanish Armada.

1599
The Globe theater opens in Southwark.

1600
The East India Company is founded.

1603
London's population has grown to 215,000.

1605
The Gunpowder Plot to blow up the King and Houses of Parliament is foiled.

1609
A reservoir is built in Islington.

1622
First English newspapers appear in the form of newsbooks printed in London.

1625
Licensed Hackney carriages are allowed to operate.

1642
Parliament orders the closure of all of London's playhouses.

1650
Claude de Jongh paints *View of Old London Bridge from the West.*

1652
The first London coffeehouse opens.

1654
Covent Garden market opens.

1659
London weather data are first recorded.

1662
Royal Mail postal service begins by carrying letters in London.

1663
Theatre Royal opens on Drury Lane and is awarded a Royal Warrant.

1664
Russian ambassador donates pelicans to live in St. James's Park.

1665–1666
Bubonic plague likely kills over 100,000 Londoners.

1666

London's streets are lit at night. The Great Fire of London destroys much of the city.

1667–1671

Most of London's houses are reconstructed.

1671

Thomas Blood tries to steal the Crown Jewels from the Tower of London while disguised as a clergyman.

1675

The Royal Observatory is founded in Greenwich.

1694

The Bank of England is instituted.

1697

Artist and social commentator William Hogarth is born in London.

1703

Storm kills between 8,000 and 15,000 people and blows roof off the Houses of Parliament.

1707

Department store Fortnum and Mason opens.

1711

The new St. Paul's Cathedral is completed.

1750

Westminster Bridge is the first of six new bridges built across the River Thames.

1759

The British Museum opens in Bloomsbury. Kew Gardens is founded by Princess Augusta, mother of King George III.

1819

Burlington Arcade opens to become England's oldest and longest shopping arcade.

1821

King George IV comes to the throne.

1829

London's first centralized police force (the Metropolitan Police) is established.

1832
A major cholera outbreak occurs. The Cholera Morbus Prevention Act allows the authorities to perform compulsory housecleaning.

1834
Fire destroys part of the Houses of Parliament.

1837
Charles Dickens's first novel, *The Pickwick Papers*, is published.

1842
Report on the Sanitary Condition of the Labouring Population of Great Britain is published.

1848
The establishment of the Metropolitan Commission of Sewers makes London's sewer infrastructure the responsibility of a single public body.

1848–1849
Cholera kills over 14,000 Londoners.

1849
Dr. John Snow suggests cholera is spread through contaminated water.

1851
The Great Exhibition is held.

1852
The Victoria and Albert Museum is founded.

1855
The Metropolitan Board of Works is established.

1857
The Science Museum is founded.

1858
The Great Stink prevents politicians from sitting in Houses of Parliament.

1859
The bell known as Big Ben chimes for the first time.

1863
Metropolitan Railway opens between Paddington (then Bishop's Road) and Farringdon Street. It is the world's first underground railway.

1866
Another major cholera outbreak occurs.

1869
The Holborn Viaduct is built.

1870
The School Board for London is established under the Education Act of 1870. Outbreak of Franco-Prussian War causes many French painters to move to London.

1871
Greater London's population reaches 3,840,595.

1875
London's new sewer system is completed. Liberty department store opens.

1879
The Thames Flood Act is enacted.

1881
Hamleys, the world's largest and oldest toy shop, opens.

1885
W. T. Stead's multipart article "The Maiden Tribute of Modern Babylon" is published.

1888
Mary Ann Nichols is generally considered the first victim of Jack the Ripper.

1890
The world's first electric underground railway opens, running from King William Street in the City of London to Stockwell.

1897
The first gasoline-powered omnibus service begins.

1898
The world's first escalator is unveiled at the Harrods department store.

1899
London County Council is supplanted by the Metropolitan Board of Works.

1901
Greater London's population reaches 6,506,889.

1902
London water companies merge into a publicly owned Metropolitan Water Board. Ealing Studios (the world's oldest continuously working film studio) makes its first film.

1908
A suffragette rally takes place in London.

1909
Selfridges department store opened by American businessman Harry Gordon Selfridge.

1910
"Black Friday" sees around 300 suffragettes head to the Houses of Parliament.

1911
London-based artistic group the Camden Town Group is founded.

1913
Suffragettes rally in London.

1914
World War I begins.

1915
German air force bombs London.

1916
Prime Minister Herbert Asquith declares his support for women's suffrage.

1918
The Representation of the People Act grants some women the right to vote.

1924
The first British Empire Exhibition opens in Wembley.

1925
The first British Empire Exhibition closes at a loss.

1928
British women are granted equal suffrage. The last severe tidal flooding occurs in London.

1936
Jarrow March sees 200 men from Jarrow head to London to protest against unemployment and poverty.

1939
World War II begins, and the British government organizes mass evacuations from London.

1940
The Blitz is on. Nazi Luftwaffe bomb London.

1941
Nazi nighttime bombing of London ends.

1943–1944
The Greater London Plan proposes radical plans to rebuild London.

1946
The New Towns Act proposes locations to relocate many Londoners outside the city.

1948
London hosts the Summer Olympics.

1949
London's first multistory council housing apartment block opens in Holborn.

1951
The Festival of Britain is held.

1952
The world's longest-running play, *The Mousetrap*, opens in London's West End.

1953
Queen Elizabeth II's coronation takes place. A North Sea flood forces the UK's authorities to consider building the Thames Barrier.

1954
A tornado blows the roof off Gunnersbury Underground station.

1956
London's smog is improved by the Clean Air Act.

1968–1981
London's docks close as they are unable to compete with ports in continental Europe.

1970
London's earliest modern pub theater, the King's Head in Islington, opens.

1973
Camden Market opens.

1976
Severe heat wave affects London.

1980s
London Docklands Development Corporation urges major changes to the Docklands.

1982
Thames Barrier opens.

1983
Harrods is bombed by the IRA.

1985
Live Aid concert is held at Wembley Stadium.

1987
Extreme weather event known as the Great Storm hits the UK, including London.

1988
Damien Hirst's *Freeze* exhibition is held in East London.

1996
IRA bombs Canary Wharf.

1997
Sensation exhibition is held at Royal Academy of Arts.

2000
Londoners become the first British citizens to directly elect a mayor when Ken Livingstone comes to power on May 4.

2003
London Congestion Charge is introduced. UK's highest temperature, 101.6 F, reached during a 10-day heat wave.

2004
Ken Livingstone is reelected as mayor.

2005
On July 6, 2005, London is selected as host of the 2012 Olympic and Paralympic Games. The next day, London suffers a series of coordinated terrorist attacks.

2008
Boris Johnson becomes mayor of London.

2009
Heavy snowfall disrupts flights involving Heathrow Airport, London City Airport, and Luton Airport.

2010
Iceland's Eyjafjallajokull volcano erupts, grounding flights involving Heathrow Airport.

2011

UK Census finds more than 100 languages spoken in almost every London borough. Widespread rioting breaks out in London.

2012

London hosts the Olympic and Paralympic Games.

2014

The Zoological Society of London records 2,000 seals living in River Thames. Ex-Hurricane Bertha causes widespread travel disruption across London.

2015

Cleaner Thames Campaign is launched by the Port of London Authority.

2016

Sadiq Khan becomes the first Muslim to serve as mayor of a Western capital city when he becomes London mayor. UK votes to leave the EU in "Brexit" referendum.

2018

London is named the world's most sustainable city. The city experiences the "Beast from the East" cold weather event.

2019

Boris Johnson becomes British prime minister. London becomes world's first National Park City. The Ultra Low Emission Zone (ULEZ) is introduced.

2020

COVID-19 pandemic begins with London becoming the epicenter of the pandemic in England. According to the Office for National Statistics (ONS), in the four weeks to April 24, 5,901 people in London were killed by COVID-19—more people than died in London during the worst four-week period of the Blitz aerial bombardment.

2021

Sadiq Khan reelected mayor. Wembley Stadium holds the final of the delayed UEFA Euro 2020 soccer tournament final. Major drive to vaccinate Londoners against COVID-19—as of June 2021, London had the UK's lower rates of vaccine take-up because of the size, diversity, and comparative youth of the city's population.

ENGLAND

SCOTLAND

NORTHERN
IRELAND   Isle of Man

• Durham

North
Sea

NORTHERN
IRELAND

Irish
Sea

York •

Leeds •

Liverpool •   • Manchester

IRELAND

Nottingham •

• Leicester   • Norwich

ENGLAND

WALES

Oxford •

London •

Celtic
Sea

Bristol •

Southampton •

Newquay •   • Plymouth

St Ives •

English Channel

FRANCE

LONDON

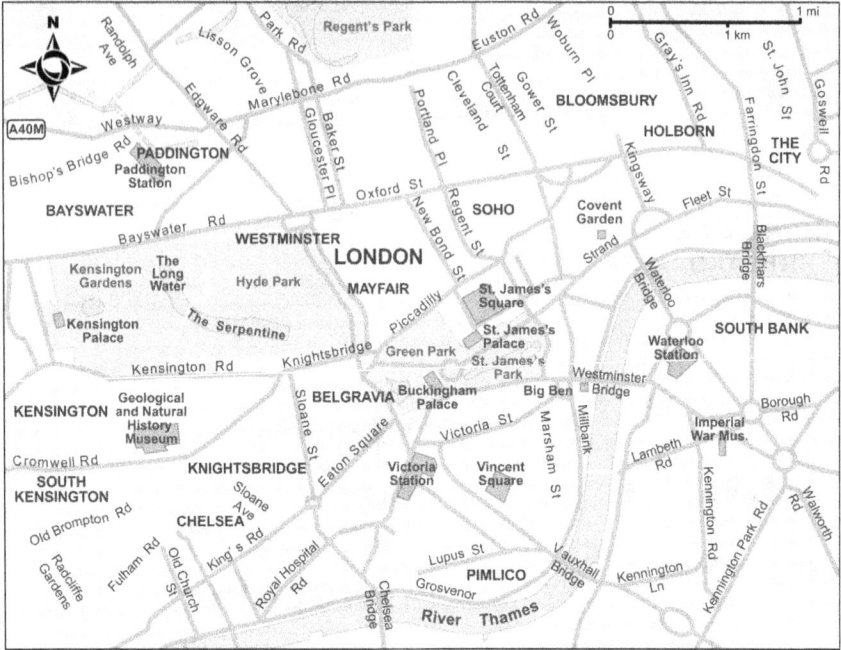

N

Randolph Ave
Lisson Grove
Park Rd
Regent's Park
Euston Rd
Woburn Pl
Gray's Inn Rd
St. John St
Goswell
1 mi
0
0
1 km
Westway
Edgware Rd
Marylebone Rd
Cleveland
Tottenham
Court
Gower St
Kingsway
Farringdon St
Goswell Rd
A40M
Bishop's Bridge Rd
PADDINGTON
Paddington Station
Baker St
Gloucester Pl
Portland Pl
BLOOMSBURY
HOLBORN
THE CITY
BAYSWATER
Bayswater Rd
Oxford St
Regent St
SOHO
New Bond St
Covent Garden
Fleet St
Blackfriars Bridge
WESTMINSTER
LONDON
Strand
Waterloo Bridge
Kensington Gardens
The Long Water
Hyde Park
MAYFAIR
St. James's Square
Kensington Palace
The Serpentine
Piccadilly
St. James's Palace
Waterloo Station
SOUTH BANK
Kensington Rd
Knightsbridge
Green Park
St. James's Park
Westminster Bridge
Big Ben
Borough Rd
KENSINGTON
Geological and Natural History Museum
Sloane St
BELGRAVIA
Buckingham Palace
Victoria St
Marsham St
Millbank
Imperial War Mus.
Cromwell Rd
Eaton Square
Lambeth Rd
Kennington Rd
Kennington Park Rd
Walworth Rd
SOUTH KENSINGTON
KNIGHTSBRIDGE
Sloane Ave
Victoria Station
Vincent Square
Old Brompton Rd
CHELSEA
King's Rd
Royal Hospital Rd
Lupus St
Vauxhall Bridge
Kennington Ln
Radcliffe Gardens
Fulham Rd
Old Church St
PIMLICO
Grosvenor
Chelsea Bridge
River Thames

1

Location

London is the capital city of the UK. The city has the coordinates N 51.5074°, W 0.1278°, meaning London lies farther north than almost all of the United States and farther north than Vancouver, Montreal, and Toronto, in Canada. However, despite London's northerly latitude, the city has a temperate oceanic climate that is drier than that of New York City, Miami, and Mexico City.[1] London is located in southeastern England and straddles the River Thames some 50 miles upstream from the river's estuary on the North Sea (the body of water that divides England and Scotland from Continental Europe).

LONDON GEOLOGY

The landscape of southeastern England is wrought from an undulating bed of white chalk and clay. In the bed's upper sections, the chalk comprises pure limestone flecked with flint. Beneath the chalk is an intermittent layer of Upper Greensand (a Cretaceous rock that is up to 145 million years old) and a thick impermeable layer of Gault clay (pale to dark gray or blue-gray clay or mudstone that has a sandy base). Beneath these layers is a stable layer of hard rocks dating from the Paleozoic age that are between 250 million and 540 million years old. This layer of rock acts as London's geologic foundation, for it lies some 1,000 feet below London.[2] It slopes southward to below the English Channel (an arm of the Atlantic Ocean that divides southern England from northern France).

London lies above the London Basin, an elongated, roughly triangular declivity (a downward inclination). The basin formed as a result of thrust tectonics related to the Alpine orogeny (the building of mountain ranges in parts of Europe and Asia) during which the earth's crust shortened and thickened. The London Basin is bordered to the south by the chalky North Downs hills and to the north by the chalky Chiltern Hills. The basin's chalk floor features a series of clay and sand sections dating from the Neogene and Paleogene periods that occurred between 2.6 million and 65 million years ago. The predominant clay found in the basin is the stiff, gray-blue clay known as London Clay. London Clay is formed from seabed sediment that accumulated between 34 million and 56 million years ago. In some places the London Clay layer is 150 centimeters thick.[3] Though London Clay is unsuited to farming on account of its heavy nature, it is easy to tunnel through. Consequently, most London Underground tunnels have been dug through areas of London Clay. For this reason, North London is served by more Underground lines than South London, for south of the Thames there are fewer London Clay deposits than north of the river, making it harder to create Underground tunnels. The London Clay also supports the majority of London's deeper foundations and makes a good material for brick making (the yellow building bricks known as London Stock are made of London Clay). London's subsoil is topped with a layer of granite that comprises mainly flint, quartz, and quartzite. London's soil also contains patches of brick earth. This is a mixture of clay and sand that is often used as a construction material. Many of modern London's buildings lie atop deposits formed by centuries of human habitation that have accumulated beneath the oldest parts of the City of London and Westminster.

Over time, London grew and spilled across a roughly symmetrical valley area shaped by shallow ridges of gravel and clay that rise to around 450 feet on the north at Hampstead and about 380 feet at Upper Norwood some 11 miles south. Between these two points, the landscape drops via a sequence of gravel terrace plateaus. The terraces are highest at a section called the Boyn terraces that reach between 100 and 150 feet high in Islington, Putney, and Richmond. A second, larger level, called the Taplow terraces, reaches heights of between 50 and 100 feet. It is on the Taplow terraces that the City of London, the West End, the East End, Peckham, Battersea, and Clapham sit. The lowest terrace lies only just above high-tide level and forms the valley's large floodplain.

The natural lay of London is evident from several vantage points around the city that are open to the public. For example, from Hampstead Heath (a large, ancient heathland in North London that sits on a ridge of London

Clay to form one of the highest points in London), the central basin of the London metropolis can be viewed. Meanwhile from Shooters Hill and Alexandra Palace in North London, and Upper Norwood in South East London, it is possible to look inward to the skyline of the City of London and the West End or outward to the so-called Home Counties (the English counties that surround London and are now entirely or partially subsumed by the Greater London metropolis: Berkshire, Buckinghamshire, Essex, Hertfordshire, Kent, Surrey, and Sussex), as well as the Thames estuary, the South Downs, and the Weald.

THE RIVER THAMES

As the River Thames meanders toward the North Sea, it erodes the terraces located north and south of the valley. The Romans founded London where the northernmost meander undercuts the higher gravel terrace to form a steep bluff (a wide, rounded cliff), as this was a good location from both a defensive and trading perspective. Much of London has grown from this early settlement, extending along the northern terraces, as these drained better than the southern terraces. Settlement on the alluvial soil south of the River Thames remained difficult to inhabit until tidal embankments were constructed in the nineteenth century.

An aerial view of the River Thames taken from the London Eye, a revolving observation wheel located on London's South Bank. At 443 feet tall, the London Eye is one of the world's tallest Ferris wheels. The wheel features 32 viewing pods representing the 32 London Boroughs. (Seemice/Dreamstime.com)

The River Thames is the main river of southern England. The river rises in the Cotswolds (a ridge of limestone hills extending roughly 50 miles across south-central England) with its source likely found at Thames Head, some 3 miles southwest of the town of Cirencester. The basin of the River Thames measures approximately 6,178 square miles and is the most densely populated river basin in the world, for at its most densely populated center, the basin supports 13 million people.[4] The River Thames is about 205 miles long and travels some 140 miles from its source to the tidal waters limit at Teddington Lock near Twickenham in southwest London. As an estuary, the river runs a further 65 miles from Teddington Lock to the Nore, a sandbank (i.e., a submerged bank of sand) that marks where the river changes from an estuary to the open sea.

The basin of the River Thames has a complex structure. In its upper course, the river drains a triangular area defined by the chalk escarpment of the Chiltern Hills and the chalky downlands of the Berkshire Downs in the east and south, with the rolling hills of the Cotswolds to the west, and the uplands of Northamptonshire to the north. At Goring Gap (a valley that sees the River Thames pass between the North Wessex Downs and the Chiltern Hills), the Thames cuts through a chalk escarpment and then drains the land that lies north of the slope formed by the North Downs (chalk hills that stretch from the town of Farnham in Surrey to the White Cliffs of Dover on the English Channel in Kent). The Thames's great tributary, the River Medway, drains much of the low-lying Weald area of Kent and Sussex that is located south of London.

THE THAMES'S TRIBUTARIES

London is home to several tributary streams of the River Thames that run north and south. Many of the tributary streams rise from springs in the gravel terraces. The tributaries in central London have been covered by culverts (structures such as pipes embedded into surrounding soil that allow water to flow under an obstruction) or serve as ornamental water features in one of London's many parks (e.g., the Serpentine in Hyde Park). The names of these tributary streams survive in several London place names—for example, Fleet Street and Walbrook.

Away from central London, many larger tributaries exist and are used for navigation, as water sources, for gravel quarrying, as ornamental water features, or for recreational purposes. For example, to London's northwest are the River Colne, which joins the River Thames at Staines, and the River Crane, which joins the River Thames at Isleworth. Another tributary of the River Thames, the River Brent is found in West and North West London. The River Brent rises in the Borough of Barnet and flows southwest before joining the tidal River Thames at Brentford. To the northeast flows the River Lea, a large river that drains much of the county of Hertfordshire before entering the River Thames near the Isle of Dogs at Blackwall. The River Roding joins the River Thames approximately four miles downstream at Barking. South London is home to many smaller rivers that lead north to the River Thames. The rivers of South London include the Ravensbourne, which flows through Bromley, Lewisham, and Deptford before entering the tidal Thames at Greenwich; and the River Wandle, which originates near Croydon before continuing on to Merton and Tooting and then to Wandsworth where it joins the River Thames. The Beverley Brook rises in Sutton and flows to the foot of Wimbledon Common, through Richmond Park, and on to Barnes Common before emerging from a culvert at Barn Elms. The Hogsmill River runs from the Epsom Downs (chalk uplands in Surrey that form part of the North Downs) to Kingston upon Thames, while the River Mole drains the Surrey Hills to join the River Thames at Hampton Court, a palace in the London Borough of Richmond upon Thames.

THE SHAPE OF LONDON

The Metropolitan Green Belt (more commonly referred to by Londoners as simply the Green Belt) is a ring of countryside in which the expansion of London's urban sprawl is prohibited. London's Green Belt comprises parts of Greater London (the ceremonial county that makes up most of London), as well as the Home Counties. The Green Belt extends along the hills of the London Basin, along a lengthy ridge toward London's south, and north to the higher land that runs from Iver Heath (near Heathrow Airport) clockwise through Ruislip Common, Bushey Heath, Enfield Chase, Epping Forest, Hainault Forest, and South Weald.

London's main ring road is the M25 motorway that encircles the city at a radius of about 20 miles from the city center. Since the 1950s, London's sprawl has been halted by strict town-planning controls. The physical limits of London correspond roughly with the administrative boundaries that separate Greater London from the Home Counties. Much of Greater London to the south of the River Thames is located in the county of Surrey, while most of Greater London north of the River Thames is in the historic county of Middlesex.

While much of the land surrounding London was once owned by the aristocracy, the church, or other organizations, the city's expansion was driven largely by the need for housing. Consequently, over time, villages and small towns near London were gradually engulfed as the city grew and transport improved. All the while, Londoners in general became wealthier, meaning they had greater purchasing power to buy houses. During World War II, London suffered extensive damage due to bombing raids. The destruction wrought by the war proved a pivotal time in London's history, because it ended the expansion of London's suburbs. Post–World War II, the British government decided that London had grown too large for its own good and so initiated the Green Belt. In time, London's administrative boundaries were modified to include virtually all of the physical entity of London, resulting in modern Greater London. Today, London's historical growth is reflected in a concentric ring pattern of growth. The center of the ring is the City of London, a small municipal corporation and borough of London that houses many important buildings. Surrounding the City of London is the suburban belt often referred to as Inner London, which evolved from the late eighteenth century through to the beginning of World War I. In Inner London, houses tend to be terraced except for where original houses were replaced by higher-density housing built by local councils in areas that were destroyed by wartime bombing or during postwar land clearance. Outer London equates to the third ring of London. This area comprises mostly suburban housing built mainly during the period from 1925 to 1939. The majority of houses in Outer London are semidetached (often abbreviated to "semi"), a distinctively British type of housing that takes the form of a single house joined to a similar house on only one side as a compromise between row housing and freestanding homes. The Green Belt constitutes the last of the concentric rings and therefore defines the shape of London.

The shape of London's settlement is governed largely by the city's topography, which divides into three basic patterns. First, the meandering River Thames separates North London from South London. Historically, the majority of London's most important locations are situated north of the river. Settlement in South London is essentially a patchwork of inhabited areas united by roads. There is also a west-east divide of London, for the River Thames and prevailing winds both flow eastward. As a result, shipping, heavy haulage, manufacturing, and working-class districts developed in London's East End. Contrastingly, London's wealthier classes tended to live on London's west side. This social divide was reinforced by the fact that the royal residences of Westminster, Kensington, Richmond, and Windsor (which is just beyond London) all lie in the west. West London's affluence means the area contains many elegant open spaces located on either side of the River Thames, stretching from St. James's Park through Hyde Park, Kensington Gardens, Battersea Park, Wimbledon Common, Richmond Park, the Royal Botanic Gardens at Kew, Richmond Park, Hampton Court Park, and Bushey Park. Traditionally, the West London borough of Ealing is nicknamed "Queen of the Suburbs" on account of its many parks and proximity to the countryside surrounding London.

The relatively green landscape of West London mitigates somewhat the noise pollution caused by its location under the flight path of Heathrow Airport, though in part, West London's nearness to one of the world's busiest airports attracts many people to live and work in the area. London's east-west divide is instilled in the psychology of Londoners, but in recent years the social divide has diminished: the East End's port activity and manufacturing industry have declined, and the working classes who traditionally lived there have been replaced by people who work in white-collar jobs. In the 1980s and 1990s, this process of gentrification quickened, for London's derelict docklands in the east (including such areas as Wapping, Limehouse, the Isle of Dogs, Beckton, and Bermondsey Riverside) were regenerated as the London Docklands, an area now known for its skyscrapers, riverfront homes, shops, and restaurants.

LONDON'S WEATHER

London's location means the city has a temperate oceanic climate that, like the rest of southeastern England, enjoys cool (though not cold) winters and mild summers with few extremes of temperature and precipitation spread evenly throughout the year. London's weather has been recorded continually since 1659, with wind-direction data available since 1723 and precipitation data noted since 1697. London's average daytime air temperature is 52 degrees Fahrenheit with an average January temperature of 42 degrees Fahrenheit and an average July temperature of 65 degrees Fahrenheit. Though London has a reputation for being overcast, weather statistics show that London experiences sunshine on five days out of every six. London's prevailing wind direction is west-southwest.

The Chiltern Hills and North Downs shelter London to a degree, meaning London experiences slightly less rain than the surrounding Home Counties. According to the Met Office, on average over a 30-year period, London experiences 106.5 days of rainfall per year (i.e., days on which at least 1 millimeter of rainfall fell). This means that London has rainfall on 29 percent of the days of the year and no rain on 71 percent of the days per year. By way of contrast, every year, the Florida cities of Miami and Orlando experience 135 and 117 days, respectively, on which rain falls.[5] In addition to rain, London can also experience hail, sleet, and snow occasionally, though such weather varies greatly from year to year: some years, London experiences no snow at all. When snow does fall in London (usually between January and March), the snow does not tend to accumulate to any great depth. For this reason, semihardy plants can be overwintered in London gardens. Some more sheltered London gardens are able to grow plants such as vines and figs that are normally associated with warmer climes.

A farm located near the Chiltern Hills. The Chiltern Hills take the form of a chalk escarpment that shelters London, resulting in the city receiving less rainfall than surrounding areas. (Chris Lofty/Dreamstime.com)

London has an urban heat island created by the city's concentration of buildings, vehicles, and heating and air-conditioning units. Consequently, temperatures are higher and the air drier toward the center of London. London's urban heat island is most noticeable at night and is mainly associated with the rate at which heat is stored and then released from urban surfaces. The heat island's effect is most intense when the weather is warm, winds are light, and skies are clear. City life also influences London's precipitation: heavy rain tends to be more intense in London than the surrounding countryside because pollution particles in city air act as condensation nuclei for water vapor.

NOTES

1. Tibi Puiu, "Why Does It Rain So Much in London? Well, It's Not That Much Really," *ZME Science*, July 24, 2019, https://www.zmescience.com/ecology/climate /rain-much-london-well-not-much-really.

2. *London's Foundations: Protecting the Geodiversity of the Capital* (London: Greater London Authority, March 2009), 25, http://londongeopartnership.org.uk /wp/wp-content/uploads/2018/08/Londons-Foundations-2009.pdf.

3. "Geology of London," London Natural History Society, June 27, 2020, http:// lnhs.org.uk/index.php/articles-british/249-geology-of-london.

4. "Overview of the Thames Basin," British Geological Survey, 2020, https://www.bgs.ac.uk/research/groundwater/waterResources/thames/overview.html.

5. Puiu, "Why Does It Rain So Much in London?"

FURTHER READING

Brenchley, Patrick J., and Peter F. Rawson. *The Geology of England and Wales*. 2nd edition. Bath, UK: Geological Society, 2006.

Dangerfield, Andy. "The Lost Rivers That Lie beneath London." *BBC News*, October 4, 2015. https://www.bbc.co.uk/news/uk-england-london-29551351.

"Geology of London." London Natural History Society, June 27, 2020. http://lnhs.org.uk/index.php/articles-british/249-geology-of-london.

London's Foundations: Protecting the Geodiversity of the Capital. Greater London Authority, March 2009. http://londongeopartnership.org.uk/wp/wp-content/uploads/2018/08/Londons-Foundations-2009.pdf.

"London's Natural Signatures." Natural England: Access to Evidence, January 31, 2011. http://publications.naturalengland.org.uk/publication/6540238365130752.

"Overview of the Thames Basin." British Geological Survey, 2020. https://www.bgs.ac.uk/research/groundwater/waterResources/thames/overview.html.

Puiu, Tibi. "Why Does It Rain So Much in London? Well, It's Not That Much Really." *ZME Science*, July 24, 2019. https://www.zmescience.com/ecology/climate/rain-much-london-well-not-much-really.

Weinreb, Ben, Christopher Hibbert, John Keay, and Julia Keay. *The London Encyclopaedia*. 3rd ed. London: MacMillan, 2000.

2

People

EARLY POPULATION GROWTH

By far the largest settlement in the UK, London is a vibrant, sophisticated city. During Roman times, London had a population of roughly 60,000 residents. Following the collapse of the Roman Empire, however, London experienced several centuries of population decline, and by the eighth century, its population was only 8,000.[1] Nonetheless, by the tenth century, London's economic importance grew, and the city became the political center of Britain. Despite its importance, at the start of the twelfth century, London's population was likely only around 20,000 people. But over the next 200 years, London's population grew rapidly. Then, in the fourteenth and fifteenth centuries, many Londoners died of bubonic plague.

In the sixteenth century, England became a colonial power, and London became the center of the burgeoning British Empire. In the eighteenth and nineteenth centuries, London grew quickly again as the center of the British Empire and as one of the birthplaces of the Industrial Revolution. By the late eighteenth century, Britain had come to dominate the global economy, and as the capital of the empire, London became one of the most important, as well as one of the largest, cities in the world. London also began to expand beyond its traditional boundaries; today, a large majority of people residing in the London metropolitan area live outside the traditional city limits.

DID YOU KNOW?

PEARLY KINGS AND QUEENS

The tradition of the Pearly Kings and Queens (also called Pearlies or Pearly Royalty) was instigated by a nineteenth-century, orphaned street sweeper named Henry Croft, who worked at the Somers Town market located between London's Euston and St. Pancras stations. Croft wanted to collect money for charity on London's streets and, inspired by the Costermongers (a group of London street traders selling fruit and vegetables who were able to recognize each other by the buttons sewn onto their clothes), Croft donned a suit covered in pearl buttons to attract attention while collecting. It is said that originally a Costermonger sewed pearl buttons to the hem of his black trousers after a cargo of pearl buttons arrived in London from Japan during the 1860s. Soon, demand for Croft's charity became too great, and Croft asked the Costermongers for help with this charity work. In time, the Costermongers became some of the first Pearly families.

The tradition of being a Pearly King or Queen is handed down through families. The arrival of the Pearly King and Queen in a decorated donkey cart, wearing pearl button–encrusted suits, is one of the great sights of Derby Day, held at the Epsom racetrack to the south of London. The Pearly Royals are still important society figures in various parts of London, for they give their time for free to raise funds for charities.

Currently, London's main demographic challenge is how its authorities will manage to keep up with the city's population growth, which has contributed to high housing prices. Local authorities as well as businesses and nonprofit organizations may struggle to supply enough affordable housing and services to a growing number of people. Additionally, some commentators report that in light of the COVID-19 pandemic, many Londoners aim to relocate from the city by moving to nearby towns such as Aylesbury in Buckinghamshire, which has a population density of 222 people per square kilometer as opposed to the average London borough density of 7,845 people per square kilometer.[2] The Londoners looking to move out of London tend to be more affluent and able to work from home, prompting fears that the middle classes will leave the city, thereby exacerbating existing inequalities and leaving only households with low-paid jobs in London.

MODERN LONDON DEMOGRAPHICS

In 2018, London's population was estimated to comprise around 8.9 million people, having expanded by 1 percent that year, an increase of 83,000 people. The 1 percent population growth was a slightly higher rate of growth than the year before,[3] though from 2011 to 2015, London's population growth rate was 5.7 percent, almost twice that of the UK's national average of 2.9 percent.[4] It is likely that by 2036, London's population will have increased to 10 million.[5]

The increase in London's population was driven by both international migration and natural demographic change. While the number of people moving out of London to live elsewhere in the UK has risen slowly over the last few years, the number of people leaving London has been offset by the number of people migrating to London from across the UK. Generally speaking, London's population trends show that the population of Outer London has increased at a slower pace than the population of Inner London has done. At the same time, the boroughs that have experienced the most population growth are not necessarily the most densely populated. Also, while London's population is aging, it remains the UK's youngest region.

London's population growth occurs for several reasons. First, London experiences high net international migration. For instance, between June 2017 and June 2018, 113,000 people moved to London from abroad, a figure that was 35 percent higher than the year before. Additionally, London experienced a 6 percent rise in the number of foreign immigrants as well as a 17 percent fall in the number of Londoners moving abroad.[6] From

---

TREVOR BAYLIS (1937–2018): THE ESCAPOLOGIST INVENTOR

DID YOU KNOW?

Born in North London, Baylis left school without any qualifications. He was, however, a gifted swimmer and, as a boy, won many swimming competitions. Later, Baylis worked as a salesman for a swimming pool manufacturer. In this role Baylis suggested that the firm's sales would improve if he dove into the pools. Eventually, this led to Baylis being employed as a swimming stuntman and in 1970, he starred in a German circus as an aquatic escapologist. In 1964, Baylis devised a futuristic chlorination system and also constructed a water tank for use by British comedians Peter Cook and Dudley Moore. Baylis saw his most famous invention—the Baygen Freeplay wind-up radio—as a response to the HIV/AIDS crisis, for he believed people living in developing countries without access to batteries could use the radio to receive information. Baylis also invented more than 250 products, of which over 200 were "Orange Aid" products aimed at the disabled. Baylis knew many disabled people from his time working as a stuntman. In 1997, Baylis received an OBE for his inventions. Later, Baylis founded Trevor Baylis Brands, a company aiming to assist other inventors with turning their inventions into successful products. In 2015, Baylis was appointed CBE for services to intellectual property. However, despite this honor, Baylis died penniless.

2011 to 2015, London's population also grew because people in their 20s moved to London from elsewhere in the UK at a rate of around 35,000 per year. During the same period, births in London outnumbered deaths in the city, something that contributed to a 4 percent increase in London's overall population.[7] More recently, the number of people moving to London from the rest of the UK rose by 1 percent (to 340,500 in mid-2018), but this was counterbalanced by that fact that during the same time period, 240,000 more people moved to London, resulting in a net 1 percent fall in internal migration. England's southeastern and eastern regions remain the most popular destinations for people moving out of London to resettle.[8]

Greater London cannot expand outward because of the presence of the Metropolitan Green Belt, the protected zone that rings the city. For this reason, the Greater London Authority, London Boroughs, and other bodies have to work out how to provide increased housing and services within the permitted amount of space. For instance, it is likely that by 2025, London

---

DID YOU KNOW?

ADA LOVELACE (1815–1852): THE FIRST COMPUTER PROGRAMMER

Born in Ealing, Ada Lovelace was a mathematician considered to have written the first ever computer program. Lovelace was the daughter of poet Lord Byron and his wife, Lady Byron. At her mother's insistence, Lovelace was taught mathematics and science, subjects that were not typically studied by girls of the time. As a teenager, Lovelace became friends with the mathematician Charles Babbage, often considered the father of computing. Lovelace was fascinated by Babbage's ideas and was asked to translate a foreign language article on his analytical engine for a Swiss journal. Lovelace not only translated the original text, but also added her own comments on the engine. Subsequently Lovelace's comments were published in an English science journal. In her comments, Lovelace noted that codes could be created that would allow a device to handle letters, symbols, and numbers. Lovelace also suggested a method for a device to repeat series of instructions, a process called looping that is used in modern computer programming. However, Lovelace's journal article attracted little attention during her lifetime, and in later life, she was reduced to using her mathematical talents to develop methods for winning at gambling. The gambling schemes proved unsuccessful, however, and Lovelace faced financial hardship as a result. Lovelace's contributions to computer science were not recognized until her notes were published in 1953, almost a century after she died in Marylebone.

Lovelace taught at the Ealing Grove Industrial School founded by her mother, which was the first school of its kind for underprivileged children. Since 2009, the annual international Ada Lovelace Day, a celebration of women in science, technology, engineering, and math, has been held on the second Tuesday in October.

will have to accommodate 60,000 new primary (elementary) school students plus 10,400 secondary school students to meet demand.[9]

London also has an aging population because people are living longer than before. However, London's population is aging at a slower rate than in the rest of the country. From mid-2001 to mid-2018, the average age of Londoners increased by 5 percent, compared to a UK average of 6 percent. Consequently, London is the youngest region in England, with an average age of 35.3 years, whereas Greater Manchester's population has an average age of 37 years, and the populations of Tyne and Wear and Merseyside have an average age of 40 years.[10]

In recent years, population change in London's outer boroughs has occurred at a slower rate than in Inner London. In the ten years ending June 2018, Outer London Boroughs' population experienced an average increase of 12 percent. Over the same period, the population of boroughs in Inner London grew by 17 percent. The central and Inner East London Boroughs of Tower Hamlets, Newham, and Camden experienced the most population growth, for their populations grew by 37 percent, 27 percent, and 25 percent, respectively.[11]

In contrast, Kensington and Chelsea was the only London borough to experience a fall in its population (of 4 percent). Nonetheless, while Kensington and Chelsea is London's second-smallest borough after the City of

---

Sir William Perkin (1838–1907)

DID YOU KNOW?

Perkin was a chemist born in London's East End. As a teenager, Perkin entered the Royal College of Chemistry (now part of Imperial College London), where he accidentally discovered a process for creating the first synthetic dye. Perkin called his dye mauveine, though it is also known as Perkin's mauve, or as aniline purple, because it incorporates molecules of the organic compound aniline. Later, Perkin continued to research the replacement of natural dyes by artificial textile dyes. In 1857, Perkin opened a chemical factory called Perkin and Sons near the Grand Union Canal in Greenford, West London. In 1862, Queen Victoria wore a dress dyed with mauveine to the Royal Exhibition, but by the late 1860s, mauveine had fallen out of fashion. Undaunted, Perkin went on to discover new dyes, including Britannia Violet, Perkin's Green, and Alizarin (a red dye). It is said the water of the Grand Union Canal turned a different color every week depending on which dye Perkin's factory was producing at the time. Following his retirement in 1874, Perkin continued his research into organic chemistry. As part of his research, Perkin synthesized coumarin, an organic chemical compound that smells like vanilla. Coumarin went on to form the basis of the synthetic perfume industry. In recognition of his work, Perkin received nine honorary degrees and a knighthood. The uniform of Greenford's William Perkin C of E High School is colored mauve in his honor.

DID YOU KNOW?

COCKNEY RHYMING SLANG

Cockney rhyming slang is a form of English slang that originated among London's Cockneys. Traditionally, Cockneys are working-class natives of East London who are born within the sound of Bow Bells (the bells of St. Mary-le-Bow Church in the City of London). Many Cockney rhyming slang expressions have passed into common usage among non-Cockney Londoners. Rhyming slang works by replacing the word to be masked with the first word of a phrase that rhymes with that word. For example, if you wanted to obscure the word "face," you would say "boat" because "face" rhymes with "boat race." Sometimes Cockney rhyming slang uses a whole phrase, such as "currant bun" to mean "sun"; as a phrase, one might say "the old currant bun's shining" ("the sun's shining"). Below is a list of other commonly used rhyming slang terms:

- Apples and pears = stairs
- Brahms = Brahms and Liszt (classical composers) = pissed (drunk)
- Brass Tacks = facts
- Brown bread = dead
- China = china plate = mate ("my old china = my old friend")
- Cobblers = cobblers' awls = balls (meaning testicles, but taken to mean "rubbish," as in "You're talking cobblers" = "You're talking rubbish")
- Cream crackered = knackered (exhausted)
- Dog and bone = phone
- Ginger = ginger beer = queer
- Hampton Wick = prick (penis)
- Have a butcher's = butcher's hook = have a look
- Loaf = loaf of bread = head ("use your loaf" = "use your head")
- Mince pies = eyes
- Mutton = Mutt and Jeff = deaf (named after early comic-strip characters)
- Plates of meat = feet
- Porkies = pork pies = lies ("You're telling porkies" = "You are lying")
- Ruby = Ruby Murray = curry (named after a 1950s singer)
- Skin = skin and blister = sister
- Titfer = tit for tat = hat
- Tom and Dick = sick ("I feel Tom and Dick" = "I feel sick")
- Treacle = treacle tart = sweetheart ("Hello treacle" = "Hello sweetheart")
- Trouble = trouble and strife = wife
- Whistle = whistle and flute = suit
- "Would you Adam and Eve it?" = "Would you believe it?"

London, it is among London's most densely populated boroughs, with 13,000 residents per square kilometer. Only Islington, Tower Hamlets, and Hackney have higher population densities (16,000, 15,900, and 14,000 people per square kilometer, respectively). In the ten years ending in mid-2018, the North London borough of Barnet experienced 15 percent population growth and thus became London's most populous borough, with 392,000 residents. However, Barnet is one of the London Boroughs with the least dense population, with just 4,500 residents per square kilometer.[12]

LONDON MIGRATION

London has long been a melting pot of different cultures and nationalities as people from across the world settled in the city. In the twentieth century, bankers and investors who worked for international banks and finance houses moved to London, joining the merchants and seamen who had already settled there.

London also became home to European peoples seeking both economic opportunities and an end to political and religious persecution. Between the end of the nineteenth century and the first decade of the twentieth, the two motivating forces combined to momentous effect such that by 1914, London was more cosmopolitan than it had probably ever been. From 1880

SIR JOHN SOANE (1753–1837)

DID YOU KNOW?

Soane was one of the leading architects of the Regency era and a professor of architecture at London's Royal Academy. Born the son of a bricklayer, Soane's family connections to architects together with his innate artistic talent allowed him to train as an architect. In 1768, Soane began working for George Dance the Younger, surveyor to the City of London. From 1772, Soane attended the Royal Academy of Arts schools, where he received the Royal Academy's prestigious Gold Medal for architecture. Soane was also granted a travel scholarship by King George III that allowed him to undertake a grand tour of Europe. The tour allowed Soane to travel throughout Italy and inspired his lifelong interest in Classical art and architecture. Soane would go on to experiment with Classical architectural forms as well as the use of light and space in architecture. In 1788, Soane was appointed surveyor to the Bank of England. During his career, Soane designed many important London buildings, including the Bank of England, Dulwich Picture Gallery, and the Sir John Soane's Museum in Lincoln's Inn Fields. In 1801, Soane bought Pitzhanger Manor, in Ealing, as a country home, having first worked on the house as a teenager. Following his appointment as professor of architecture at the Royal Academy in 1806, Soane expanded his collection of artifacts to create a museum.

onward, London attracted young people from across Britain as well as increasing numbers of Europeans, especially Russians and Russian Poles, the majority of whom were Jewish and settled in London's East End. Indeed, by 1911, 68,000 Russians and Russian Poles lived in London (not counting those born in Britain).[13] The next largest migrant group comprised natives of Germany, 30,000 of whom lived in the County of London (a now-defunct English county that corresponded to the area of Inner London) and around 5,000 in Outer London. There were also roughly 10,000 Austro-Hungarians who also spoke German. London's oldest established European minority was, however, the French. In 1911, 14,000 French people lived in the County of London, as did 12,000 Italians.[14] By 1914, Americans had started to settle in London, with American investors and entrepreneurs helping to modernize various aspects of the city. Notable Americans included Henry Gordon Selfridge, who moved to London in 1906 and founded the Selfridges department store on Oxford Street, and transport tycoon Charles Tyson Yerkes, who was involved in the creation of the London Underground. American writers and artists were also attracted to London. By 1911, London was home to around 6,000 Americans, most of whom worked in professional roles, retail, or city commerce.[15] The growth of London's retail and commercial sectors created a two-tier middle class consisting of a more well-to-do middle class and a lower-middle class of clerks and shop assistants. The middle class drove the creation of suburban London in the late nineteenth and early twentieth centuries. Meanwhile, the city's elite became increasingly wealthy and more powerful until the outbreak of World War I in 1914.

Today, both internal and international migration shape London's migration patterns. Inner London tends to attract migrants from outside the UK, while people who live in Inner London are more likely to resettle in Outer London than vice versa. In contrast, people from Outer London are more likely to leave London for other parts of the UK than are people who live in Inner London. Migrants from elsewhere in the UK are evenly split between Inner and Outer London.

The official 2011 UK census recorded that 36.7 percent of London's population was born outside of the UK. In 2015, the number of foreign-born people living in London was 3.2 million, meaning London accounted for 36.8 percent of the UK's total immigrant population.

In 2015, 267,000 Londoners were born in India, and 135,000 were born in Poland, Pakistan was the birthplace of 113,000 Londoners, Bangladesh 126,000, and Ireland 112,000 Londoners.[16] In the UK, National Insurance (NI) is a very important element of the welfare state because individuals' payment of NI contributions helps them access certain state benefits. In the first quarter of 2019, 72,500 foreign nationals in London had registered for a National Insurance Number (NINo) that would enable them to work

Selfridges department store, located at the westernmost end of Oxford Street. The store was opened in 1909 by the American businessman Harry Gordon Selfridge. (Amanda Lewis/Dreamstime.com)

or to claim benefits. This number represents a 24 percent increase over the same quarter in 2018 and the highest number of overseas nationals registering for a NINo since the last quarter of 2016. At the start of 2019, 45,400 (or 63 percent) of all NINo registrations in London were nationals from European Union (EU) member states. However, registrations by EU nationals for the year ending at March 2019 were 6 percent lower than for the same time the year before, as EU nationals felt uncertain about living in London in the run-up to Brexit (the UK's withdrawal from the EU). In contrast, at the beginning of 2019, non-EU NINo registrations were at their highest level since 2011, at 27,000. This was a 21 percent increase over the year before. Between 2009 and 2019, there has been a decline in the number of NINo registrations from all parts of the world except for East Asia. Indeed, East Asia is the largest regional contribution to London's NINo registrations from outside Europe. The sharpest decline in NINo registrations between 2009 and 2019 were from people from sub-Saharan Africa (65 percent fewer registrations), Oceania (56 percent fewer), and Central and South America (54 percent fewer).[17] In contrast, registrations for Indian nationals rose by 77 percent in the year ending at March 2019 when compared with the year before. This increase reflects the number of Indian nationals moving to London to take jobs in the National Health Service and the information technology sector.[18]

LIFE IN THE CITY   BEING A TEENAGER IN LONDON DURING THE SWINGING SIXTIES

I was a teenager in London during the 1960s, which was an incredibly exciting time because there was a sense of change in the air, and the London music scene was really taking off. Artists like the Beatles, Billy Fury, and Cliff Richard were emerging. At the time, girls tended to be more into the Beatles, while boys seemed to prefer the Rolling Stones, as the Stones seemed more rebellious. I bought a lot of clothes from Biba; I practically lived in their shop—as did most teenage London girls in the mid-1960s. I loved Biba because there had never been anything like their clothes: they were so different from anything else and not expensive. They also came in the most gorgeous colors: I especially liked their plum, mulberry, and grape colors and their pink, knee-high suede boots. The atmosphere in the Biba shops on Kensington High Street and Kensington Church Street was amazing: the lighting was dark, and music played in the background, so it felt like being in a nightclub. The clothes were presented on old-fashioned hat stands, and there were sofas dotted around the shop so that boyfriends could sit down while the girls shopped. There were also vases filled with dusky-colored ostrich feathers. These were so popular with shoppers that eventually the shop sold feathers so people could re-create the look at home. I used to travel to the shop by Tube. Usually I would visit during my lunch hour because I worked in the head offices of the retailer Marks and Spencer on Baker Street, but sometimes I would visit on weekends traveling from my home in Yiewsley, near Uxbridge in Outer West London. This was a much longer journey, though, so I tended to go from work. At the time, most of my friends wanted to work in Outer London where we lived, but I wanted to work in central London, as it was so exciting to be in the middle of everything.

I kept my Biba clothes for a long time but over the years I have cleared them out. Although I wouldn't fit in the clothes now, I wish I had kept them for the memories. All I have left are two Biba badges. I also lived in London when England won the 1966 World Cup soccer tournament. It was such as exciting time. When England won, I jumped in the air and split my trousers!

—*Chris Davis*

NOTES

1. Toni Mount, *Everyday Life in Medieval London: From the Anglo-Saxons to the Tudors* (Stroud, UK: Amberley Publishing, 2014).

2. Robert Booth, "Covid-19 Sparks Exodus of Middle-Class Londoners in Search of the Good Life," *The Guardian*, June 24, 2020, https://www.theguardian.com/uk-news/2020/jun/24/covid-19-sparks-exodus-of-middle-class-londoners-in-search-of-the-good-life.

3. Silviya Barrett and Erica Belcher, "Demography," *London Intelligence*, issue 9, July 25, 2019, https://www.centreforlondon.org/reader/the-london-intelligence -issue-9/demography/#components-of-population-change.

4. Sara C. Jorgensen, "London, United Kingdom: Facing the Challenges of Population Growth," in *Cities of the World: Struggles and Solutions to Modern Life, Volume 1*, ed. Jing Luo. (Santa Barbara, CA: ABC-CLIO, 2019), 274.

5. Ibid.

6. Barrett and Belcher, "Demography."

7. Jorgensen, "London, United Kingdom," 274.

8. Barrett and Belcher, "Demography."

9. Jorgensen, "London, United Kingdom," 275.

10. Barrett and Belcher, "Demography."

11. Ibid.

12. Ibid.

13. Stefan Goebel and Jerry White, "London and the First World War," *London Journal* 41, no. 3 (2016), https://www.tandfonline.com/doi/full/10.1080/03058034 .2016.1216758.

14. Ibid.

15. Ibid.

16. Jorgensen, "London, United Kingdom," 275.

17. Barrett and Belcher, "Demography."

18. Ibid.

FURTHER READING

Barrett, Silviya, and Erica Belcher. "Demography: Components of Population Change." *London Intelligence*, issue 9, July 25, 2019. https://www.centrefor london.org/reader/the-london-intelligence-issue-9/demography/#components -of-population-change.

Booth, Robert. "Covid-19 Sparks Exodus of Middle-Class Londoners in Search of the Good Life." *The Guardian*, June 24, 2020. https://www.theguardian .com/uk-news/2020/jun/24/covid-19-sparks-exodus-of-middle-class -londoners-in-search-of-the-good-life.

Goebel, Stefan, and Jerry White. "London and the First World War." *London Journal* 41, no. 3 (2016): 199–218. https://www.tandfonline.com/doi/full/10 .1080/03058034.2016.1216758.

Jorgensen, Sara C. "London, United Kingdom: Facing the Challenges of Popula- tion Growth." In *Cities around the World: Struggles and Solutions to Urban Life, Volume 1*, edited by Jing Luo, 274–79. Santa Barbara, CA: ABC-CLIO, 2019.

Mount, Toni. *Everyday Life in Medieval London: From the Anglo-Saxons to the Tudors*. Stroud, UK: Amberley Publishing, 2014.

Shelley, Fred M. *The World's Population: An Encyclopedia of Critical Issues, Cri- ses, and Ever-Growing Countries*. Santa Barbara, CA: ABC-CLIO, 2015.

3

History
___

LONDON'S LEGENDARY BEGINNINGS

According to legend, as set out by the British cleric Geoffrey of Monmouth's pseudohistorical chronicle *Historia regum Britanniae* (*The History of the Kings of Britain*, ca. 1136), London was founded between 1100 BCE and 1000 BCE by Brutus of Troy, a descendant of the legendary Trojan hero Aeneas. According to both *Historia regum Britanniae* and British legend, Brutus took control of Britain (or Albion, as it was then called) when he overcame Gogmagog, the last survivor of a mythical race of giants that ruled the island. According to legend, after the fall of Troy, Brutus and the Trojans arrived on Albion and found it very much to their liking but were unable to defeat the island's native giants, who were much bigger than they were. The Trojan captain Corineus was able to match the giants for strength, however, and one day, Corineus killed Gogmagog. The defeat meant freedom from giants for Albion, allowing Brutus to divide the land among his Trojan captains. Consequently, Brutus became the founder and first overall king of Britain and, according to legend, founded a new Troy on the banks of the River Thames. This new Troy would go on to become London and was the seat of numerous legendary kings, including Lud, who is reputed to have named early London *Caer Ludein*. According to several medieval writers, legendary Lud is buried at Ludgate in central London.

THE REAL FOUNDING OF THE CITY: ROMAN LONDINIUM

Recent archaeological discoveries indicate there were likely some very early settlements around the River Thames, for timber structures dating from the Bronze Age (roughly 2100 BCE to 650 BCE) have been found near Vauxhall Bridge, in central London. However, London's true history begins with the Romans, who invaded Britain under Emperor Claudius in 43 CE. In 47 CE, the Romans established the settlement of Londinium to the north of the River Thames's boggy valley. From around 50 CE to 410 CE, Londinium was the largest city in Roman Britain, serving as both the province's administrative and commercial center and as an international port. At that time, the city's population comprised a mixture of civilians, Roman soldiers, and slaves. Many of Londinium's inhabitants came from other areas in the Roman Empire, but most were indigenous Britons from various tribes. Indeed, Londinium was a melting pot of cultures, as Roman officials were sent there from across the Roman Empire to help run the new Roman province of Britannia. Administrators, traders, artisans, and soldiers were all required to make Britannia successful, and so they moved to Londinium, bringing with them their families and other members of their households. Most of Londinium's civilian population comprised native Britons attracted to the city in the hope of working as laborers, artisans, and shopkeepers, for Londinium's populace needed not only food but also everyday items such as clothes, shoes, and tools, all of which were produced by local makers. Roman London had a social hierarchy: at the top were citizens (who could hold administrative positions and enjoyed certain legal privileges), followed by noncitizens (people who were not citizens but who could become citizens), and then slaves. Some Roman slaves rose to relatively high positions in administration by working for the provincial government or treasury and were also allowed to buy their own slaves.

Most buildings in Roman London were built along busy roads that ran through the city. The roads were made of gravel and ran parallel to drainage ditches that people could cross by covering them with wooden planks. Houses were tightly packed but separated by narrow alleyways. Houses tended to have small backyards and outhouses in which animals lived, while shops and workshops were also often attached to houses. The houses of the wealthiest Londoners were usually located away from the city center and were furnished with underfloor heating and fashionable details such as mosaic floors and wall paintings.

For leisure, early Londoners visited public baths, where they could exercise and clean themselves, or they went to performances held at amphitheaters (open-air venues used for entertainment, theatrical performances, and sports). London also had many shops and marketplaces where Londoners could buy from artisans, among them, potters, glass-workers, carpenters, leather workers, and shoemakers. London's artisans worked from home or in industrial areas located next to running water away from the main settlement. Military and financial staff worked in government offices, while wealthy merchants and bankers worked at forums (public meeting places), in shops, or from riverside warehouses.

On religious feast days, Roman Londoners celebrated at the temple of the deity whose feast they were celebrating. The Londoners would pray to the deity and make sacrifices to ensure the deity's favor. At this time, most Londoners worshipped the official gods of the Roman Empire, such as Jupiter (king of the gods and god of sky and thunder), Minerva (goddess of wisdom, medicine, the arts, poetry, and crafts), and Mars (god of war). Other deities, such as Mithras (the Indo-Iranian god of friendship, light, and order) and Isis (the Egyptian goddess of women, death, life, magic, and healing), were also worshipped by Londoners. In Roman London, the secretive cult of Mithraism, which centered on Mithras and also served as a cult of loyalty toward the emperor, was very popular among soldiers, merchants, and administrators. Over time, however, Christianity and other religions gained in popularity in London.

EARLY REBELLION AND PROSPERITY

The earliest documented mention of London refers to the year 60 CE and occurs in *Annals*, written by the Roman senator and historian Tacitus (56–ca. 120). In *Annals*, Tacitus describes London as being a noted business center. The year 60 CE was important in the history of Roman London, because in that year tribesmen from the Iceni tribe from eastern England, led by Queen Boudicca (also called Boadicea) sacked the city. The Iceni rebelled against the Romans while the Roman governor of Britain, Gaius Suetonius Paulinus, was absent, leading a military campaign in northern Wales. During the rebellion, Boudicca's warriors defeated the Roman Ninth Legion and destroyed Colchester, the then capital of Roman Britain. The Iceni went on to sack London and Verulamium (now called St. Albans, a city about 20 miles north of central London). Tens of thousands of people were killed in the rebellion. Ultimately, the Iceni were defeated by a Roman army led by Paulinus, while Boudicca is reputed to have committed suicide in order to avoid capture. Today, a bronze monument to Boudicca, *Boadicea and Her Daughters*, stands at the western end of Westminster Bridge facing the Palace of Westminster.

Boudicca's defeat allowed the Romans to restore their rule over London and reinstate a fortified garrison that had been located in London until the arrival of the Iceni forced its abandonment. The Romans rebuilt London as a planned settlement, and within about a decade, the city was fully reconstructed with new buildings, including a great basilica. Built in 70 and then expended between 90 and 120, London's basilica formed one side of a forum that acted as a public meeting place and market. The basilica served as a civic center and housed administrators, law courts, an assembly hall, a treasury, and religious idols. Today, London's Leadenhall Market, an ornate, covered market built in 1881, stands on the site once occupied by the basilica. The size of the basilica, then one of the largest buildings in northern Europe, cemented London's place as a major city.

Over the course of the later decades of the first century, London expanded rapidly to become Britain's largest city. However, archaeological remains found in London suggest that around 125, much of London was destroyed by fire. The fire prompted the Romans to rebuild London once again. Following the reconstruction, London remained an important Roman city, but it did not expand further. Rather, London supported a small, but stable, settled population.

The first half of the second century saw London prosper. Around 150, areas of London's houses and workshops were demolished, and a stone wall was built around the city between 190 and 225. The wall was not solely defensive, however; its size symbolized London's status as a great city. Originally, the wall included four city gates as well as an entrance into the fortress situated at Cripplegate, in the northern section of the wall. Cripplegate was almost entirely destroyed in the Blitz bombardment of World War II, and today it is the site of the Barbican Center, one of Europe's largest performing-arts centers. In front of the eastern section of the wall was a large ditch. This stretch of the wall stood near the southeast corner of a trench that now lies inside the Tower of London. Today, remains of the Roman wall are visible at the Barbican (close to the street called London Wall) and on Tower Hill. The wall was partially remade and extended during medieval times, which meant additional gates were built to accompany the six Roman gates.

In 289, the Carausian Revolt (286–296) saw the Roman naval commander Carausius appoint himself emperor of Britain. In order to highlight his independence from Rome, Carausius had special coins made in London from gold, silver, and copper. In this way, the London Mint was established in 290. Ultimately, Carausius was assassinated by his subordinate Allectus, however, and in 296, Britain was regained by Emperor Constantius I, when Roman troops massacred Allectus's fighters in London. Following the Romans' regaining of London, the Diocletian Reforms (during which the Roman Empire was divided and reorganized) saw the Roman administration of Britain restructured. It is probable that London became the capital of one of the reorganized Roman provinces, but it is unclear which one. During the twelfth century, the writer and clergyman Gerald

A surviving fragment of the original third-century Roman wall in Cooper's Row near Tower Hill Underground station. The wall protected Roman London, but over time, many sections of the wall have been destroyed to make way for new buildings. (Raluca Tudor/Dreamstime.com)

of Wales listed "Londonia" as the capital of the province of Flavia, but modern academics believe London was the capital of the province of Maxima Caesariensis, located in southeastern England.

In 367, a coordinated invasion by Picts (a confederation of Celtic-speaking peoples from Scotland), Gaels (an ethnolinguistic group from Ireland, Scotland, and the Isle of Man), and Saxons (inhabitants of central and northern Germany) joined with mutinous Roman troops to attack the London wall. Over the next few years, the senior Roman military officer Count Theodosius, who used London as his base, thwarted the attack. At the start of the fifth century, Roman legions were called back to Rome, leaving many London properties vacant. In 410, the Roman army left Britain to defend other parts of their empire and never returned. As a result of the Romans' withdrawal, Britain was invaded by Germanic tribes from northern Europe called the Jutes and Angles, as well as by the Saxons.

ANGLO-SAXON LONDON: THE CREATION OF LUNDENWIC

The British tried to fight off the invaders but, by about 600, Anglo-Saxon kingdoms had been established in Britain, with most of the kingdoms located in what is now England. It is not known exactly how the

Anglo-Saxons took control of London, but it is thought that by the end of the fifth century, London was all but deserted following the withdrawal of the Romans. Virtually no artifacts from London's early Anglo-Saxon period (410 to 1066) have been discovered within the city's wall. As of 597, however, London was still considered a major city, as emphasized when Pope Gregory I sent St. Augustine from Rome to England. In 604, St. Augustine established the episcopal sees of London for the East Saxons, with St. Mellitus (d. 624) as its bishop. This appointment made St. Mellitus the first bishop of London, and it was probably St. Mellitus who founded St. Paul's Cathedral (also in 604), thereby laying the foundation for one of London's most iconic buildings. The earliest St. Paul's buildings were relatively short-lived, however, for they were damaged by fire in 675 and then by Viking raids in 961.

By the late seventh century, it is likely that London had regained its position as a major trading center, for while much about this period of London's history is unknown, archaeological excavations around Covent Garden and the Strand have revealed artifacts (evidence of buildings, industry, trade, personal possessions, graves, roads, and a harbor) that suggest London was a successful center of commerce. By the eighth century, London was home to a large, densely packed population and was known as Lundenwic. This name is significant for in Anglo-Saxon, the suffix "wic" referred to a trading town. The exact location of Lundenwic was unclear for many years, but it is now known that it did not correspond directly to the Roman settlement of Londinium (which was located in what is now the site of the modern City of London). Rather, Lundenwic was located around one mile west of Londinium, around the Strand and Covent Garden, near the mouth of the River Fleet. This location meant that Lundenwic sat at the boundary of three Anglo-Saxon kingdoms; Mercia, Wessex, and East Anglia and so was an important site of trade by water as well as land. Lundenwic's trade made it wealthy. During the ninth and tenth centuries, however, this wealth prompted waves of attacks on Lundenwic by raiders from Sweden, Norway, and Denmark. Lundenwic was extremely vulnerable to attack because, like many Anglo-Saxon ports, the city was not encircled by protective walls and the buildings were made of wood. Anglo-Saxon writers refer to the invaders under the umbrella term "Danes" (or "Norsemen"), though today they are called the Vikings. The waves of assaults meant Lundenwic was virtually uninhabited from the mid- to late ninth century. By this time, the Danes not only made raiding trips to Britain but had also started to make temporary winter camps there. Eventually, various Danish raiding parties united to invade Britain under the rule of the King Guthrum. By the 880s, Guthrum had gained control of all Anglo-Saxon kingdoms except for the Kingdom of Wessex, which was ruled by King Alfred.

LUNDENBERG: KING ALFRED'S LONDON

King Alfred fended off Danish assaults and established a system of "burhs" (defensive forts), two of which he set up in London: one within the stone walls of what had been Roman Londinium and the other in Southwark to protect London Bridge. The London burhs became known as Lundenberg. Alfred established a new town inside the burhs in order to protect the area's important trading activities. In so doing, Alfred founded the City of London. In 879, Alfred defeated the Vikings whose leader, Guthrum, agreed a treaty with Alfred that decreed the area west of the River Lea, including London as belonging solely to Alfred. Under Alfred, London became an important defensive site and trading town with people beginning to resettle in Lundenberg as early as 880. Although the defeat of the Vikings initiated a fragile peacetime, Danish raids continued on areas surrounding Lundenberg and the area north of Lundenberg, known as the Danelaw, remained under Danish control. Many Danes settled in the Danelaw as well as in trading towns, including Lundenberg. By 889, Lundenberg had become a major trading port and market. The city's Roman walls and London Bridge were restored, and a new grid system of streets was implemented as the city's settlement pattern. Houses were built with plots of land attached so that inhabitants could rear animals.

Over time, Lundenberg grew in size and significance to become an important center for trade as well as a center of government. By the tenth century, Lundenberg had become a bustling settlement full of houses, shops, markets, and workshops with trade revolving around such crafts as woodwork, fabric making, and metalworking. By the end of the century, Lundenberg was the focus of Anglo-Saxon activities, something that prompted the Danes to resume their regular attacks on the city, this time under Sweyn Forkbeard (king of Denmark from 986 to 1014). From the end of the tenth century through to 1066, control of Lundenberg passed between the Danes and Anglo-Saxons. Nevertheless, Lundenberg continued to serve as a major trade hub. By the end of the Anglo-Saxon period and the start in 1066 of the Norman period of British history, Lundenberg had become a cultural melting pot again, thereby laying the foundation for the London of the future.

MEDIEVAL LONDON: TRADE, RIOTS, AND THE BLACK DEATH

London's future importance as a financial, military, and political center became clear following the Norman Conquest (1066), for one of the initial acts of the first Norman king of England, William the Conqueror (William I, ca. 1028–September 9, 1087) was to create a charter that promised

London's citizens the same laws as they had enjoyed under Edward the Confessor (1003–1066, one of England's last Anglo-Saxon kings). Just beyond London's walls, William established a keep called the White Tower, which formed the center of the fortress-castle now called the Tower of London. The White Tower is the central tower of the Tower of London and the castle's strongest point. Originally, it provided accommodation and a chapel used by both the king and his staff. When King Richard I returned from the Third Crusade (an 1187 attempt by the leaders of England, France, and the Holy Roman Empire to regain the Holy Land following Jerusalem's capture by the Muslim leader Saladin), he brought with him new ideas about how to defend London. One idea was to surround London's keep with concentric walls and towers. This defense project was completed by King Henry III (r. 1216–1272). The Norman kings chose Westminster as their permanent base. This was where Edward the Confessor (r. 1042–1066) had constructed a church dedicated to St. Peter. It would eventually become known as Westminster Abbey.

Around 1087, a fire destroyed many of London's wooden houses as well as the centuries-old St. Paul's Cathedral. In the ensuing reconstruction, London's wooden houses started to be replaced by those made of stone and tile, though wooden homes remained the norm. At the same time, streets became cleaner through the introduction of open sewers. Between 1050 and 1300, quays were constructed on the River Thames's northern banks. Here German merchants established a trading enclave called the Hanseatic Steelyard. The steelyard flourished and came to dominate trade in London, leading to rising hostility from Londoners. Ultimately, in 1598, Queen Elizabeth I (1558–1603) would have the Germans expelled from London. Although the steelyard would reopen under King James I (1556–1625), it never regained its economic dominance, and much of the structure was destroyed by the Great Fire of London in 1666. But along with the early German merchants, other foreign trading groups were operating in London, having migrated from Gascony (now in France), Flanders (in France and Belgium), and Italy. Over time, these European populations assimilated into the melting pot that comprised London.

The vitality of medieval London came to a sudden end with the outbreak of the Black Death. The Black Death was most likely the bubonic plague, a disease of rodents—especially black rats—that is passed between animals by bites from their fleas. When a rat died from the plague, its fleas found a new host on which to live; if this new host was a human, the disease could infect the human too. The main symptoms included headaches, fever, vomiting, coughing up blood, swelling in the lymph nodes, gangrene, and blistering. The Black Death arrived in London in the autumn of 1348. In the ensuing 18 months, the disease killed half of all Londoners, possibly as many as 40,000 people, most of whom were buried in mass graves. A serious outbreak of the Black Death struck London approximately every 20 to 30 years, each time killing roughly 20 percent of London's population. Lesser outbreaks alternated with major outbreaks, and sometimes a lesser outbreak could last for several years.[1]

Over time, London experienced several political and organizational changes. For example, in 1189 King Richard I installed businessman Henry Fitz-Ailwyn as the city's first mayor (Fitz-Ailwyn held office until his death in 1212.) In order to prevent unrest, London's authorities supported strong government. This was particularly true at such times as the depositions of King Edward II, in 1327, and Richard II, in 1399, and the Peasants' Revolt of 1381 (the earliest major popular rebellion in English history and a response to the imposition of an unpopular tax). The Peasants' Revolt began in Essex, but the rebels, led by Wat Tyler, marched to London. At Black-heath in southeast London, the rebels met with government representatives, who tried to persuade them to return home. Meanwhile, the 14-year-old English king, Richard II, retreated to the Tower of London. The rebels soon joined with many Londoners to attack prisons, destroy the Savoy Palace (then the grandest house in London), set fire to the Temple (London's legal heartland), and kill members of the royal government. King Richard II met the rebels at Mile End in East London and agreed to most of their demands, including the abolition of serfdom. However, in the meantime, some rebels entered the Tower of London, where they murdered the Lord Chancellor and the Lord High Treasurer. The Archbishop of Canterbury, Simon of Sudbury, was seized by the rebels after they stormed the Tower of London. The rebels dragged him to Tower Hill northwest of the Tower of London, where he was beheaded.

The rebels' rampage prompted the king to meet Wat Tyler and the rebels at Smithfield in the City of London. Soon fighting erupted, and the king's men killed Tyler. Meanwhile, London's mayor, William Walworth, gathered together a London militia to disperse the remaining rebels, allowing Richard to reestablish order in London and revoke the promises he had made to the rebels. Unrest continued until the defeat of a rebel army at the Battle of North Walsham, in Norfolk (1381), and the intervention of a large mobilization of soldiers by the king that quelled a rebellion elsewhere in England.

In 1397, a wealthy mercer, Richard ("Dick") Whittington, was appointed the Lord mayor of London by King Richard II. Since he had no heirs, Whittington used his wealth to establish numerous charitable organizations—for example, an almshouse for the poor, and a ward for unmarried mothers at London's St. Thomas' Hospital—to repair Newgate Prison, to establish and finance various drainage systems, and to establish a library at the Guildhall (an imposing municipal building in the Moorgate area of the City of London). Londoners elected Richard Lord mayor of their city in 1406 and again in 1419. In this way, Whittington famously became "thrice Lord Mayor of London," a feat that was extremely rare for the era. Over time, Whittington became a legendary London figure and inspired the English folktale *Dick Whittington and His Cat*. Even today, the fictionalized exploits of Dick Whittington are related every winter in pantomimes performed across Britain.

TUDOR LONDON: CRAFT, TRADE, AND REFORMATION

By 1520, London had become even more prosperous through the rise of craft guilds (associations of artisans or merchants who oversaw the practice of their craft or trade). London also became the seat of new industries, including silk weaving, glass production, and the manufacturing of majolica (a type of earthenware pottery). The production of such items tended to occur outside of the city gates, as this enabled manufacturers to avoid the restrictive rules set out by livery companies (the successors to the craft guilds). Similarly, the most polluting industries and slaughterhouses were located outside of London's walls, usually to the east.

Around the mid-1500s, London enjoyed a surge in trade that was boosted by the founding of such bodies as the Muscovy Company (or Russia Company), which was a body of English merchants that traded with Russia. The company was established in 1555, and it held a monopoly on Anglo-Russian trade. In 1581, the Levant Company (or Turkey Company) was established by royal charter that gave the group monopoly rights to trade between England and the Ottoman Empire. The company was not a trading organization; rather, its members were independent merchants who traded subject to the rules imposed by the Levant Company. Perhaps the most important of the monopoly organizations was, however, the East India Company, which was founded in 1600. The East India Company was an English company that was granted a royal charter to exploit England's trade with Asia, especially India. The company began as a monopolistic trading body but gradually became involved in politics, serving as an agent of British colonial rule in India during the eighteenth and nineteenth centuries. The company also helped the British gain influence over nineteenth-century China.

While London's economy grew, so did the city's population. In 1509, London's population was approximately 60,000 people, meaning the city was far larger than any other English city, containing as it did Westminster, the City of London, and Southwark. A subsequent population explosion across England naturally affected London as well, and by 1603, the city's population comprised 215,000 people.[2] Indeed, such was London's population growth that the City Fathers (members of the Court of

Common Council) attempted to stop the custom of subdividing London's houses into smaller, closely packed dwellings (a practice known as "pestering") in order to prevent more people from settling in the city. Nonetheless, at times London's population was so large that people lived on the grounds of religious buildings seized during the Protestant Reformation (a series of events in the sixteenth century that saw the Church of England break away from the Roman Catholic Church). King Henry VIII, who had been instrumental in the Reformation, began a massive construction program. The dissolution of the monasteries in 1536 (the process by which Henry VIII disbanded monasteries in England, Wales, and Ireland, appropriating their income and disposing of their assets) resulted in some of the most momentous changes ever to occur to London's property, for many religious buildings were destroyed and the remainder adapted for secular use.

The Reformation left a gap in the provision of charity and alms to Londoners, so in 1547 London's authorities organized poor relief, providing grain during food shortages and promoting the establishment or reconstruction of London's five royal hospitals (hospitals that enjoyed royal patronage): St. Bartholomew's, Christ's, Bethlehem (an asylum known informally as Bedlam), St. Thomas's, and Bridewell. Many private charities were also established at this time.

Prior to the rise of the House of Tudor and the Reformation, however, the British monarchy and government had been reforming gradually for some time. But the pace of change hastened after King Henry VII ascended the throne in 1485. To strengthen his control over the country, Henry VII introduced measures that centralized the government in London while reducing the influence of regional powerbases. Meanwhile, London's port contributed greatly to the city's development, for it allowed London merchants access to markets in continental Europe while also providing the City of London with a thriving market within which London's guilds could operate. By the end of the fifteenth century, England had come to dominate the world's wool market, while by the time Henry VIII became king in 1509, London was ready to become both the most prosperous and most powerful city in England.

During the reign of Henry VIII, London's landscape was ever changing. For instance, the establishment of Henry VIII's naval dockyard at Deptford, in southeast London, occurred alongside the creation of low-quality waterfront homes along the River Thames's north bank at Wapping, in East London. The City of Westminster began to become more defined in shape when in 1529, Henry VIII started to convert York Place (the residence of the Archbishop of York) into the Palace of Whitehall while also building St. James's Palace, Bridewell, and Hampton Court. Between Westminster and the City of London, the houses of nobles were constructed with gardens that stretched down to the Thames, each with its own gate allowing access to the river. Opposite these grand houses, along the Strand were high-quality lodgings for gentlemen who were attending legal sittings in London.

By the start of the seventeenth century, the name "London" had come to encompass the City of London and the City of Westminster as well as the land in between. It was during the reign of Elizabeth I that London's domination over England arguably peaked, for Elizabeth based her power on London's might and wealth. Indeed, London provided many of the soldiers that defended England against the 1588 Spanish Armada (an enormous Spanish naval fleet that aimed to overthrow the Protestant queen Elizabeth I and in so doing restore Catholic rule over England).

LONDON IN THE SEVENTEENTH CENTURY: COFFEE, PLAGUE, AND FIRE

The construction program that began under Henry VIII continued into the seventeenth century, as exemplified by the building of London's Banqueting Hall, in Whitehall, and the Covent Garden Piazza, designed by famous architect Inigo Jones (1573–1652). Despite the growth of the city, the rate of urbanization could not keep up with the speed of London's population growth. Indeed, on July 7, 1580, Elizabeth I demanded controls on London's urban expansion by forbidding the construction of new buildings within three miles of the city's gates. The official reasons for the proclamation included an influx of poor, unskilled people to London, inconvenience caused by congestion, house price inflation caused by increasing demand for homes, and danger to public health caused by overcrowding. At this time, London's house prices rose so fast that no buildings were demolished, and increasing numbers of them were built even upon ditches, which were filled in and covered over to provide land for construction. As London grew, so did the infrastructure required to serve the ever-enlarging city. To this end, in 1609 a new reservoir was completed in Islington (in North London), while from 1662, the Royal Mail postal service effectively began when the carrying of letters in London was declared a monopoly of the king. By 1666, London's streets were lit at night, and journeying around the capital started to resemble travel as known in London today, for licensed Hackney carriages (vehicles for hire in the way of taxi cabs) driven by Hackney-coachmen were permitted to trade starting in 1625. Additionally, wherries (river buses) operated by watermen ran regular passenger services.

Much of London's population increase of the seventeenth century was due to internal migration, for people came to London from across Britain.

At the same time, though, London was also becoming increasingly multicultural, for traders arrived constantly from across Europe. For example, London was home to brewers from the Low Countries (Belgium, the Netherlands, and Luxembourg), French tailors, and Italian fabric dyers. Gradually, different areas of London became associated with particular trades, for example, opticians on Ludgate Street, goldsmiths on Foster Lane, and booksellers on St. Paul's Churchyard. Following William Caxton's founding of the world's first portable printing press in Westminster in 1476, printers became associated with Fleet Street. The political and religious divisions evident during the Reformation created a readership for polemical pamphlets and so, in May 1622, the first true English newspaper appeared in the form of newsbooks printed in London by Nicholas Bourne and Thomas Archer. London's press operated despite government censorship that occurred throughout the reign of King Charles II (1630–1685). England's publishing laws were relaxed after the Glorious Revolution (1688–1689, during which the Catholic king James II, was replaced by his Protestant daughter Mary and her Dutch husband, William of Orange), and Fleet Street soon became the main location for the country's press.

London's importance was enhanced by its position as the focus of the country's money for it was from London that English traders and financiers, together with those from Italy, Denmark, France and Germany, traded with the world. London's Worshipful Company of Goldsmiths gave rise to numerous bankers, for the role of the goldsmith banker was created to see London goldsmiths expand their services to include the storing of wealth, provision of loans and bills of exchange (akin to checks), and the transfer of money. The goldsmith bankers also created a system of banknotes and checks that led eventually to the creation of the Bank of England. Ultimately, the Bank of England was instituted in 1694 when City of London merchants grouped together to support the War of the Grand Alliance (1689–1713, a war between France and various European factions, including England). Thereafter, the City of London's money market became central to affairs of state. In the latter half of the seventeenth century, London's insurance market developed from bankers' meetings held in the city's numerous new coffeehouses, the first of which was opened in 1652 by a Greek servant named Pasqua Roseé in Cornhill, in the heart of London's financial district. Such was Londoners' love of coffee that by 1663, the City of London alone was home to 82 coffeehouses. It was at the coffeehouses that London's traders, bankers, and insurance underwriters met to conduct business, such as insuring ships for a fee. One of the first London underwriters, Edward Lloyd, published the shipping gazette *Lloyd's News*. Ultimately Lloyd gave his name to London's insurance and reinsurance market, Lloyd's of London (usually referred to by Londoners as simply Lloyd's).

The theater was another London industry in its infancy during the seventeenth century. In 1574, regular theatre performances were legalized, with the first venue, named simply "The Theatre," opening in 1576. Numerous theaters opened subsequently, including the Curtain, the Rose, the Swan and the Globe (where William Shakespeare debuted the majority of his plays), and thrived until they were shut during the Interregnum (the period between the execution of King Charles I in 1649 and accession of his son King Charles II in 1660). King Charles II was a huge fan of the theater (his most famous mistress was the acclaimed actor Nell Gwyn), and after his Restoration (when the king returned to England from exile in Europe in 1660), a grand revival of London's theatrical tradition began. As part of this revival, in 1665 the Theatre Royal on Drury Lane near Covent Garden was awarded a Royal Warrant, that is, a prestigious mark of recognition that an institution supplies goods or services to the royal family. The granting of the Royal Warrant cemented the theater's place in the heart of London life.

Two dark shadows would soon threaten London, however: the bubonic plague and the Great Fire of London. During the period from 1665 to 1666, 68,596 deaths were recorded in London as being due to bubonic plague, though in truth, it is likely that over 100,000 Londoners died as a result of

Shakespeare's Globe Theatre, located on London's South Bank. The theatre is a reconstruction of an Elizabethan playhouse for which William Shakespeare wrote plays. The roofless theater looks circular but actually takes the form of a 20-sided icosagon. (Alexandre Fagundes De Fagundes/Dreamstime.com)

the illness. At a minimum, this would mean the plague killed around 15 percent of London's population. The earliest plague cases occurred in early 1665 in St. Giles-in-the-Fields, a parish outside of London's city walls. During the ensuing hot summer, the death rate from the disease started to climb, peaking in September, when 7,165 Londoners died in just one week.[3] The wealthiest Londoners left London to escape the disease, while Charles II and his court left for Hampton Court initially and then Oxford. Parliament and law courts also moved to Oxford, though London's lord mayor and aldermen (the town councillors) stayed behind in order to try to stop the plague from spreading. Healthy but poor Londoners had little choice but to remain in the city alongside plague-infected rats and the sick. During this period, official watchmen locked the houses of infected Londoners to prevent the inhabitants from leaving, while parish officers provided sick people with food. Other officials scoured London for corpses, which were transported to plague pits and buried there. While the plague ravished London, all trade between infected towns (including London) and noninfected areas ceased, meaning many Londoners became unemployed and lost money. Eventually, the coming of cold weather slowed the rate of plague cases in London.

The Londoners who survived the plague soon faced another disaster, for on September 2, 1666, a fire started in a bakery in Pudding Lane near London Bridge that was owned by the king's baker Thomas Farriner (also spelled Farynor). Normally, fires that occurred in London were extinguished fairly easily, but that summer had been very hot and dry, so London's wooden buildings burned easily. The dry conditions, coupled with a strong easterly wind, allowed the fire to take hold and spread quickly to destroy 300 houses.[4] The fire swept through London, because at this time the upper stories of London's houses almost touched across the narrow, winding streets. The size of the fire meant that it was not brought under control by dousing it with buckets of water (the usual method of extinguishing a fire), and soon panic spread throughout London. As the fire raged, Londoners tried to escape the inferno by taking to boats on the River Thames. The famous diarist and politician Samuel Pepys (1633–1703) informed King Charles II of the fire, prompting the king to order that all the houses in the path of the fire should be razed to create a firebreak. The firebreak proved ineffective, however, and by September 4, half of London was ablaze. As a last resort, houses that lay in the path of the fire were destroyed en masse using gunpowder, in an attempt to create a bigger firebreak. As Londoners left their city in droves, St. Paul's Cathedral caught fire, causing its lead roof to melt and the great structure to collapse. Eventually the fire was brought under control and by September 6 was extinguished completely. By this time, only one-fifth of London had survived; almost all the civic buildings had been destroyed as well as around 90 churches and 13,000 homes.[5] The destroyed buildings included the Guildhall, the Royal Exchange, prisons, markets, bridges, gates, and company halls. Remarkably, however, only six people were officially recorded as having died in the fire. Some modern historians doubt the low death toll, citing evidence housed in the Museum of London (melted glass, iron, and pottery) that suggests the temperatures that occurred during the fire were far higher than those necessary to incinerate a human body. They speculate that any bone fragments resulting from incineration could have been crushed by falling debris or cleared away after the fire. However, there is also evidence that many Londoners did manage to escape the fire, taking with them any possessions they could carry. It is also known that the fire left around 100,000 Londoners homeless.[6]

A monument that was erected on Pudding Lane to commemorate the Great Fire is still visible today. Another monument, called the Monument to the Great Fire of London (usually referred to by Londoners as simply the Monument), is a Doric column situated near the northern end of London Bridge to the west of Pudding Lane. The Monument was built between 1671 and 1677 on the site of St. Margaret's church, Fish Street, which was the first church to be destroyed by the fire. Another monument, the Golden Boy of Pye Corner, located near Smithfield in the City of London, marks the spot where the Great Fire stopped.

While the Great Fire of London was a disaster, it also cleansed the city's overcrowded, disease-ridden streets, allowing a new London to emerge. The mathematician, astronomer, and architect Sir Christopher Wren, who

THE GREAT LONDON FIRE.

A depiction of the Great Fire of London. The fire began in a bakery on Pudding Lane near London Bridge. The fire destroyed most of London's civic buildings as well as 13,000 homes but killed only six people. (Ridpath, John Clark, *Ridpath's History of the World*, 1901)

St. Bride's: The London Church That Inspired the Wedding Cake

The multitiered wedding cake popular today was invented by nineteenth-century English bakers, for the triple-layered shape was inspired by the silhouette of St. Bride's Church steeple in the City of London, which features tiers of decreasing size. Originally, there existed several types of three-tiered wedding cakes, each intended for different social classes and wedding budgets. St. Bride's was destroyed during the Great Fire of London. The new St. Bride's was designed by Sir Christopher Wren and is the second tallest of all Wren's churches, with only St. Paul's Cathedral having a higher pinnacle. On the night of December 29, 1940, St. Bride's was gutted by firebombs dropped during the Blitz. Due to the church's location on Fleet Street, St. Bride's has long been associated with journalists and newspapers; hence it is known as "the journalists' church." For this reason, after World War II, St. Bride's was rebuilt at the expense of newspaper owners and journalists. Today, the church is a Grade I–listed building, meaning it may not be demolished, extended, or altered without special permission.

was one of the designers of the Monument, was tasked with reconstructing London. As part of the rebuild, Wren designed a new St. Paul's Cathedral, which was completed in 1711. Wren also rebuilt another 51 churches including St. Mary-le-Bow, in Cheapside; St. Clement Danes, on the Strand; and St. Stephen Walbrook, in the City of London. Many of Wren's designs are still visible in modern London, though the creative responsibility for many of the churches is now sometimes attributed to others in Wren's office, chiefly Nicholas Hawksmoor.

Wren's other distinguished buildings include the Royal Naval College, at Greenwich; the Royal Hospital, in Chelsea; and parts of Kensington Palace and Hampton Court Palace. Since the city's reconstruction program had to be achieved quickly, London's existing street plan was retained, but the city's streets were widened and straightened. From 1667 to 1671, most of London's houses were reconstructed from brick, as half-timbered buildings were outlawed. London continued to grow following its reconstruction. At that point, however, most of London lay outside the boundaries of the City of London, where previously most Londoners had lived within the walls.

THE COMING OF MODERNITY: DEVELOPMENT, REFORM, AND WAR

Starting with Westminster Bridge in 1750, six new bridges were built across the River Thames. The new bridges allowed construction to occur in areas of South London. At the same time, London expanded northward, in the fashionable west of the city, and around its eastern docks.

King George IV came to the throne in 1821, by which time many of the villages that had served as summer retreats from London during the seventeenth and eighteenth centuries had been consumed by the metropolis. For example, West London's Bedford, Portman, and Grosvenor estates were founded on land once owned by noble families. Meanwhile to the east, parts of Stepney and Bethnal Green were built on the site of former cottages. The rapidly expanding city was governed by numerous authorities. While the City of London authority was fully in charge within its jurisdiction, other areas of London were governed by numerous administrations, meaning their services and communications were disjointed. Additionally, developers were able to impose charges from which an area's paving, lighting, and cleaning were financed. Since the popularity of a developer's streets was dependent partly on the provision of these services, the streets in areas run by successful developers tended to be well administered. Contrastingly, lesser developers neglected the areas that they developed, creating a legacy of slums that would last for generations.

From the late eighteenth century to the start of World War I, in 1914, London was not just the social and financial heart of the UK but also the center of the global economy, having assumed the role previously held by Amsterdam, in the Netherlands. Powered by the profits of global trade (especially with the East Indies, the West Indies, and the Americas), London led the arts world particularly in the areas of the theater and literature. For example, eighteenth-century London was home to the hugely influential English actor, playwright, stage manager, and theater producer David Garrick, the Irish novelist and playwright Oliver Goldsmith, the writer and lexicographer Samuel Johnson (often referred to as Dr. Johnson), and the portrait painter Sir Joshua Reynolds, who founded London's Royal Academy of Arts. London was also frequented by numerous furniture makers, silversmiths, and famous foreign musicians and composers, including the German (but later British) George Frideric Handel and the Austrians Joseph Haydn and Wolfgang Amadeus Mozart.

Throughout the nineteenth century, Greater London's population continued to expand. According to official census figures, the population grew from 1,096,784 in 1801 to 2,651,939 in 1851, the year of the Great Exhibition.[7] The Great Exhibition, which was the first in a series of world's fairs, was staged at London's Crystal Palace as a way to celebrate the commercial might of Britain and the British Empire. The Great Exhibition ran from May to October and during this time attracted 6 million visitors. The event, which was one of the most successful exhibitions ever staged, proved to be a defining point of the nineteenth century. Indeed, the event returned a large enough profit to allow for a complex of educational and cultural institutions to be built in South Kensington; these include present-day London's Science Museum, Natural History Museum, and Victoria and Albert Museum. The museums can all be found on South Kensington's Exhibition Road, which takes its name from the Great Exhibition.

By 1871, Greater London's population had reached 3,840,595, while by 1901 6,506,889 people lived in London,[8] meaning one-fifth of the population of England and Wales lived in the metropolis. London's increasing population caused numerous problems. For example, while new hospitals opened that reduced Londoners' mortality, London also needed new civil authorities, modes of communication, and sanitation, all of which were introduced fairly haphazardly between 1820 and 1914. Innovations experienced by London around this time included a centralized London police force (the Metropolitan Police), which was established in 1829 under the control of the Home Secretary, thereby replacing the uncoordinated parish police that had operated previously, and gas streetlamps, which supplanted the feeble oil lamps that had previously been the source of London's lighting.

In 1842, the most important nineteenth-century publication on social reform was released: *Report on the Sanitary Condition of the Labouring Population of Great Britain.* This was an inquiry into the country's sanitation by Edwin Chadwick (1800–1890). While studying in London, Chadwick's interest in political and social reform led him to become one of the century's most important public health activists. As such, the British government commissioned Chadwick to investigate the country's public sanitation and suggest ways in which it could be improved. Chadwick linked poor living standards to the spread and growth of disease and recommended that the government provide people with clean water, improve drainage, and make local councils remove refuse from homes and streets. Chadwick's report led to the Public Health Act 1848, which saw the British government take responsibility for the health of the British populace for the first time. Subsequently, the General Board of Health (Britain's central health administration) was created, led by Chadwick. Chadwick's report was prescient, for London experienced four major outbreaks of cholera between 1832 and 1866 that killed tens of thousands of people. The first case of cholera was recorded in Britain in 1831, having spread from the Indian subcontinent. The disease caused symptoms including stomach cramps, diarrhea, vomiting, limb pain, and severe dehydration that, if left untreated, could kill within hours. At that time, there was no known cure for the disease, which caused people to panic. London's rapid expansion had not been matched by improvements to the city's sewage system, and it was usual for sewage to come into contact with the city's drinking water, thereby contaminating the water drunk by Londoners. Since cholera-infested sewage was entering London's water supply, the disease spread easily through London. At the time, it was commonly believed that cholera was an airborne illness transmitted by vapor, a theory that appeared to be proven by the fact that many cholera victims lived in London's overcrowded slums, where the air was very polluted. In actuality, London's poor were the biggest victims of cholera because they were surrounded by their own waste, for slum dwellings contained basement cesspits that overflowed due to the city's inefficient sewage system. The British government realized something needed to be done about the interrelated issues of overcrowding and poor sanitation and asked Chadwick to tackle the issue of public sanitation. Though Chadwick believed cholera was transmitted through a toxic miasma, he went against the prevailing discourse that the urban poor suffered as a result of being lazy or immoral. Rather, Chadwick believed the poor were falling sick because of their living conditions.

In early 1832, the Cholera Morbus Prevention Act was passed that allowed the authorities to perform compulsory housecleaning for the first time. However, the law was passed too late to have much impact on the 1832 cholera outbreak. In 1848, the Nuisances Removal and Diseases Prevention Act was passed to help stop the spread of another cholera epidemic and saw property owners encouraged to clean their houses in order to cleanse the atmosphere of disease and remove human waste from beneath their premises. In 1848, the establishment of the Metropolitan Commission of Sewers made London's sewer and drainage infrastructure the responsibility of a single public body and declared that properties should be cleaned and connected to sewers. However, when homes were cleaned, it was usually the case that any waste was dumped into the River Thames, thereby exacerbating the problem of water contamination. London's middle classes also contributed to the problem, for the increasing popularity of the flushing water closet (lavatory) added to the amount of sewage entering the river. For this reason, a cholera epidemic of 1848 and 1849 killed over 14,000 Londoners.[9] The Metropolitan Board of Works, established in 1855 following the Metropolis Management Act, took control of London's sewers in order to improve London's health. Nonetheless, despite the focus on water, the theory that cholera was transmitted through the air persisted. However, in 1849, John Snow, a doctor, suggested in his paper "On the Mode of Communication of Cholera" that cholera was spread through ingesting contaminated water rather than inhaling infected air. Snow came to this conclusion after realizing that a water pump located on Broad Street in the particularly overcrowded and unsanitary Soho area of London was the source of a cholera outbreak that had killed more than 500 people in 10 days.[10] Despite the evidence Snow presented to the medical establishment, public health officials were reluctant to back his theory completely. Nevertheless, Snow had impressed upon the authorities that it was imperative to clean up the pollution of the River Thames once and for all. When the "Great Stink" occurred during the hot summer of 1858, politicians were unable to stand the smell of the River Thames flowing past their offices in the Houses of Parliament and became determined to clean up the river. On June 15, 1858, Prime Minister Benjamin Disraeli tabled the Metropolis Local Management Amendment Bill that within a record 18 days was signed to bring into law improvements to London's drainage, sewage collection, and river pollution. The engineer Sir Joseph Bazalgette then developed a systematic plan for London's sewers. As the chief engineer of London's Metropolitan Board of Works, Bazalgette was responsible for designing an extensive network of sewers beneath central London that diverted waste to the Thames Estuary. The sewer project was completed in 1875, with the sewers still in use today. In 1902, various London water companies were combined into a publicly owned Metropolitan Water Board.

The Metropolitan Board of Works also undertook other major initiatives of the late 1800s, including slum clearance. The momentum for these changes was created by such reformers as Sir Robert Peel (two-time British prime minister and founder of the Metropolitan Police) and Anthony Ashley Cooper (the Seventh Earl of Shaftesbury), and it continued throughout the century. New churches, schools, pedestrian tunnels under the River Thames, improved law and order, and care for social outcasts were just some of the changes brought about by the reformers. The most visible legacy of the reforms was the creation of Trafalgar Square, the Embankment, and such streets as Shaftesbury Avenue and Charing Cross Road that were driven through the worst London slums. Meanwhile, the School Board for London, established under the Education Act of 1870, was tasked with providing elementary education for all of London's children. Changes in local government also occurred, for in 1899 the London County Council was supplanted by the Metropolitan Board of Works. The same year, areas overseen by vestries (local secular and ecclesiastical authorities) were restructured into metropolitan boroughs by the London Government Act. London continued to evolve through a combination of public and private enterprise, for an abundance of initiative, money, and raw materials plus an abundant workforce combined to allow technical progress to shape the lives of Londoners as well as the appearance of the city. For example, on January 10, 1863, the Metropolitan Railway opened between Paddington (then Bishop's Road) and Farringdon Street and in so doing became the world's first underground railway. Other transport innovations included the construction of Holborn Viaduct in 1869, the building of new bridges across the River Thames, and the rebuilding of Battersea, Westminster, and Blackfriars bridges. Additionally, major railway terminals were built in what was then Outer London (Paddington, Euston, St. Pancras, King's Cross). Meanwhile, London's road bridges outside of the City of London came into public ownership with the removal of private tollgates. Cheap train services enabled artisans and clerks to live in suburban areas and commute to work. The then prince of Wales (later King Edward VII) opened the world's first electric underground railway on November 4, 1890 (it ran from King William Street in the City of London to Stockwell in South London). Moving from suburban London to the center of the city became even easier with the advent of the first gasoline-powered omnibus in 1897. Around this time, additional underground railway lines (mostly north of the River Thames) were constructed, while the surface railway lines serving South London were electrified. Ultimately, the improved transport links between central and Outer London resulted in the great suburban development known popularly as Metroland, along the Metropolitan railway to London's northwest. The improvements in transport were accompanied by rising land values in central London, as well as by the building of large offices, factories, and warehouses.

More extensive transport links meant that London's traffic soon became a problem, an issue examined in detail by the Royal Commission on London Traffic's 1903–1906 report. Between 1903 and 1913, London passenger journeys by railway, tram, and omnibus rose from 972.5 million to 2,007.3 million.[11] A third of the journeys were made by omnibus, the mode

---

DID YOU KNOW?

ISAMBARD KINGDOM BRUNEL (1806–1859)

Brunel was a pioneering engineer whose first significant achievement was helping his father plan the Thames Tunnel from Rotherhithe to Wapping, in East London, which was completed in 1843. In 1833, Brunel was appointed the chief engineer for the Great Western Railway's network of tunnels, bridges, and viaducts that linked London to Bristol. Brunel's important achievements for the Great Western Railway include the Wharncliffe Viaduct across the Brent Valley between Hanwell and Southall, in Ealing. Brunel was also responsible for the design of many famous ships including the *Great Western* (launched 1837), which was the first transatlantic steamship; the *Great Britain* (launched 1843), which was the world's first iron-hulled, screw propeller–driven, steam-powered passenger liner; and the *Great Eastern* (launched 1859), the biggest ship ever built up to that time. Brunel also redesigned and constructed many of Britain's major docks. Brunel's last project was the Three Bridges (or Windmill Bridge) crossing of bridges near Southall. Here, the bridges are arranged so that three transport routes (the Grand Junction Canal, Great Western and Brentford Railway, and Windmill Lane) are built directly on top of each other. A statue of Brunel is located on London's Victoria Embankment, and Brunel University, based in West London, is named after him. In 2002, Brunel came second to Winston Churchill in a BBC poll to select the greatest Briton.

of transport most vulnerable to increasing congestion because the omnibuses had to compete for space with the rising numbers of private wagons, carriages, and motor vehicles. By 1914, tramways were used mostly by lower-class workers, causing some wealthier suburbs in West London to refuse to allow tram tracks to be laid in their districts. In contrast, the railways and omnibuses carried people from all classes, though rail travel was segregated by ticket price and time of travel (in the early morning the city's local railways were used mainly by working-class workmen, for at this time fares were cheaper). Initially, omnibuses were favored by the middle classes but by 1914 were generally popular with all Londoners, accounting for more than a third of 1913's metropolitan passenger journeys.[12] Nevertheless, despite the large number of people using London's public transport, many Londoners could not afford to travel to work and so had to live as close as possible to their place of employment. Indeed, at this time many Londoners were desperately poor, with an estimated 1.3 million (30.7 percent of all inner-city Londoners) living below the poverty line.[13] Differences in social class were prevalent in London, leading to tensions that erupted occasionally, chiefly as strikes (labor disputes) or the threat of strikes. On the eve of the outbreak of World War I, it seemed possible that London's class issues might boil over into revolution, but widespread rebellion failed to materialize.

Another source of social conflict in London at the time was the burgeoning women's suffrage movement, for London became the focus of the nationwide movement that was spearheaded by Emmeline Pankhurst of the Women's Social and Political Union. The suffragettes led numerous protests and rallies that peaked in intensity between 1912 and 1914 as the movement became more militant. Hyde Park in central London hosted two major suffragette rallies in 1908 and 1913, with the 1908 rally attracting over 250,000 attendees.[14] London was the site of seminal events in the movement, including the notorious event known as Black Friday. On this day, Friday, November 18, 1910, around 300 suffragettes headed to the Houses of Parliament, where they came into conflict with the police. The leading suffragette, Sylvia Pankhurst, recorded that 115 of the women were arrested, and many were sexually assaulted.[15] The start of World War I in 1914 led to the temporary cessation of the suffrage movement, as suffragettes reduced their focus on achieving women's suffrage in support of the British war effort. The war work of many of the suffrage groups during World War I helped their cause greatly and led, in 1916, to Prime Minister Herbert Asquith declaring his support for female suffrage. The 1918 Representation of the People Act granted women over 30 years of age the right to vote as long as they were married to or a member of Local Government Register. The Act also extended men's suffrage to all men ages 21 and over. Eventually, British women were granted equal suffrage under the Representation of the People (Equal Franchise Act) 1928.

While it would not be as deeply imprinted in Londoners' collective memory as the Blitz that London experienced during World War II, World War I (1914–1918) nonetheless left a deep and lasting imprint on the city. In 1914, Greater London had a population of 7.25 million people, the largest urban population of any city in the Western world.[16] London was not only impressive in size but also in wealth, for it was the world's financial center: the city's merchant banks lent capital to governments and infrastructure projects across the globe, and the Bank of England was considered an international symbol of sound financial acumen. Additionally, the Port of London was one of the world's busiest ports, for much of Britain's exports went through London, and the port served as a center for transatlantic, European, and Dominion trade. London's success made it a target of systematic aerial bombing during World War I. Indeed, the city's size made it an easy target to see from above. On the night of May 31, 1915, the German air force sent 90 incendiary bombs and 30 grenades down on London, causing Londoners to panic.[17] Following the initial strike, German zeppelins (large, long-range, hydrogen-filled airships that flew slowly but at high altitude) continued to hit London with impunity, timing raids to coincide with cloudless skies. On September 8, 1915, a zeppelin traveled over St. Paul's Cathedral to drop a three-ton bomb on London's financial center. At the time, this was the largest bomb ever dropped. The bomb caused massive damage, killing 22 civilians, including 6 children.[18] In response to the bombing raids, the British authorities introduced blackouts, installed massive searchlights, and set up antiaircraft defenses that were positioned around the capital. By mid-1916, Britain had developed aircraft capable of reaching higher altitudes. The airplanes could also fire explosive bullets that could rip into a zeppelin's outer skin as well as incendiary bullets that could set the zeppelins ablaze. Nonetheless, Londoners themselves could do little to see off the raids, and in order to escape the bombings, people huddled in basements or hid deep in London's Underground stations. Eventually, the tide turned, for British pilots achieved greater success in shooting down the zeppelins. The bombings continued but were far less frequent until, by 1917, Germany switched to bombing London using biplanes instead of zeppelins. In total, the zeppelin raids had killed nearly 700 Londoners and seriously injured 2,000.[19]

The First British Empire Exhibition, a huge exhibition intended to highlight the industry and natural resources of the British Empire, was held at Wembley Park in northwestern London from 1924 to 1925. The concept of the event was first suggested before World War I, and by 1921, former pleasure gardens at Wembley Park had been selected as the venue for the exhibition. There were four main objectives to holding the exhibition: to tell the British public about the raw materials of the British Empire, to improve trade links within the Empire, to open new international markets for both British and imperial goods, and to foster interaction between the different cultures of the Empire. The exhibition also showed that Britain and its colonies had recovered from the ravages of World War I. Wembley Park was chosen as the venue because it was in one of the most easily accessible parts of London, with two mainline stations and a new station inside the exhibition grounds. The exhibition showcased produce, manufactured goods, crafts, and historical artifacts from across the British colonies and was accompanied by a cultural program highlighting the cultures of the Empire. The exhibition attracted 17 million visitors from Britain and beyond,[20] but nonetheless, when the exhibition closed in October 1925, it had incurred losses of £1.5million.[21] Although it was not profitable, the exhibition resulted in London's improved suburban infrastructure, for an outfall sewer was built to serve the exhibition, and many new roads and bus services were introduced in northwestern London. The exhibition introduced visitors to the Wembley area, and subsequently, some visitors moved to Wembley.

WORLD WAR II AND BEYOND: THE BLITZ, EVACUATION, AND RECONSTRUCTION

London avoided the worst effects of the Great Depression (1929–1939, the worst economic downturn in the history of the industrialized world) because, unlike parts of Britain that relied on heavy industry (such as mining, iron and steel production, and, shipbuilding), London had relatively little business in that sector. London was, however, the site of the famous Jarrow March (October 5–31, 1936): when the coal mine, steelworks, and shipyard closed in Jarrow, northeastern England, 200 men from Jarrow headed to London to protest against unemployment and poverty and seek help from the government. While the Jarrow March garnered considerable public sympathy, the march made little immediate impact. Despite the government's lack of response to the march, in 1938 a ship-breaking yard and engineering works were established in Jarrow, and a steelworks opened there in 1939. Nevertheless, in areas such as Jarrow, widespread unemployment and poverty continued until World War II, when industry flourished as a result of Britain's need for armaments.

During World War II, London suffered widespread damage as a result of an aerial bombardment referred to by the British as the Blitz. The word *Blitz* (German for "lightning") was first used by the British press to describe the heavy, frequent bombing raids carried out over Britain in 1940 and 1941. The bombing targeted industrial and civilian centers, with particularly heavy raids focused on London. The bombing was intended to destroy British morale ahead of a planned invasion. The Blitz, began on September 7, 1940, with London bombed heavily and systematically by the Luftwaffe (the aerial warfare branch of Nazi Germany's military forces). The first raids came in the afternoon and were concentrated on London's densely populated East End. Around 300 bombers attacked London for over an hour and a half, and once darkness fell, the resulting firelight guided a second wave of bombers to bomb London for another eight hours.[22] Throughout the bombing, London's civil defense workers moved people to temporary shelters. All the while, in the air, ferocious dogfights developed as the British Royal Air Force (RAF) strove to repel German aircraft that were flying up the Thames Estuary. Most notoriously, a large daylight attack against London occurred on September 15, 1940. On this day, the Luftwaffe embarked on its largest, most concentrated bombing raid on London; it called for the whole of the RAF to scramble to defend London and the rest of southeastern England. The raid was seen off in a decisive British victory that proved a turning point in the war, in favor of Britain. The September 15 bombings are seen as the climax of the Battle of Britain (the military campaign in which the RAF defended the UK from the Luftwaffe), and the date is known today as Battle of Britain Day. Following the defeat, the Luftwaffe decided to focus its might on targeting London during nighttime bombing raids that lasted until May 1941.

The British had been warned in advance to expect air attacks on cities, so civil defense preparations had begun sometime before the Blitz started. These preparations included the building of Anderson shelters: corrugated steel shelters dug into gardens and covered with soil. Larger civic shelters built of brick and concrete were also erected in British towns, and blackouts were enforced rigorously. Another prewar preparation that affected London was Operation Pied Piper. On September 1, 1939, the British government initiated the program, which saw over 1.5 million people (including 800,000 children) evacuated from urban areas, including London.[23] This would prove to be the biggest movement of people in British history. Evacuees were divided into four groups deemed "nonessential to war work": school-age children, the infirm, pregnant women, and mothers with babies or preschool children (these were evacuated together). The evacuees were taken to safer areas, typically in the British countryside. The evacuation incorporated another plan designed by the London County Council (LCC), and by the summer of 1939, the LCC had requisitioned buses and trains in preparation for the mass evacuation. On August 31, 1939 (three days before war broke out), an evacuation order was given for the following day prompting children to assemble in their schools in preparation for Operation Pied Piper to begin. In order to succeed, the mass evacuation required thousands of volunteers, for London alone had 1,589 assembly points. In order to evacuate London's children, most children boarded special evacuation trains at their local stations. Other London children were evacuated by ship from the River Thames and taken to ports around England. When World War II ended, the evacuees returned to their homes, though some found their homes had been destroyed, their families had moved without them, or that years living in the countryside caused them to feel alienated from their urban surroundings. For the most part, though, family reunions brought an end to a period of confusion and separation. The evacuations impacted an entire generation of London youngsters, yet without the mass evacuations, London's death toll during World War II would undoubtedly have been much higher.[24]

Meanwhile, the night raids of the Blitz became so frequent that they were practically continuous, leaving many people to take up residence in shelters. Thousands of other Londoners moved into the city's Tube stations. Initially, the British government discouraged this move, but popular action held sway, and it was common in wartime London to see people living in the Underground stations alongside their remaining possessions.

Ultimately, the deprivations of the Blitz gave rise to a new spirit of solidarity and community among Londoners—the so-called Blitz spirit. The Blitz period of London's history has become part of British folklore. Today, Londoners still refer to the Blitz spirit as a way to describe their collective stoicism, defiance, and resilience in a difficult situation.

After May 1941, the bombings diminished as Germany focused its attention on Russia. However, sporadic bombing raids on London continued for several more years. During the course of the Blitz, London's docks, many historic buildings, and industrial, residential, and commercial districts were heavily damaged or destroyed, while roughly 30,000 Londoners died with a further 50,000 injured.[25] The end of hostilities brought not only the return of evacuees but also the large-scale reconstruction of London, even though building materials were in short supply.

During World War II, the Greater London Plan (1944) had been prepared as a blueprint for the city's reconstruction. The Plan also set out ideas for relocating Londoners and their jobs to new towns surrounding the capital as well as to areas in the English provinces. Post–World War II, London was in desperate need of large-scale reconstruction, leading town planners such as Patrick Abercrombie (1879–1957) to draw up plans to rebuild the capital in such a way as to create a balance between the need for new housing, industrial development, and open spaces. Abercrombie proposed radical plans (the County of London Plan of 1943 and the Greater London Plan of 1944) to rebuild postwar London. Among Abercrombie's proposals was that London's physical growth be halted by the Green Belt (the strip of land encircling the city) and that London's urban sprawl be combated by resettling many Londoners into separate communities connected by an improved

---

DID YOU KNOW?

THE TRAFALGAR SQUARE CHRISTMAS TREE

Every year since 1947, the Norwegian people have given Londoners a Christmas tree as a symbol of their gratitude for Britain's support for Norway during World War II. Typically, the Trafalgar Square Christmas tree is a Norwegian spruce (*Picea abies*) that is 50 to 60 years old and reaches a height of over 66 feet. The tree is chosen with great care from the forests around the Norwegian capital, Oslo, several months, sometimes even years, in advance. The tree is felled in November during a ceremony in which the lord mayor of Westminster, the British ambassador to Norway, and the mayor of Oslo take part. The tree is then shipped to the UK before completing its journey by lorry. A specialist rigging team then erects the tree in Trafalgar Square. Once erected, the tree is decorated in typical Norwegian style using vertical strings of energy-efficient fairy lights topped by a large, lit star. The tree remains in Trafalgar Square until just before Twelfth Night (January 5), when it is taken down, chipped, and composted to make mulch. In 2008, television presenter Andy Akinwolere made the news when he accidentally dropped the star that had topped the tree for ten years while attempting to attach it to the tree for a piece on the children's program *Blue Peter*. The star was left slightly damaged but still usable.

---

road network. Abercrombie also proposed the construction of an Outer Country Ring of London satellite towns. Subsequently many Londoners relocated to the "New Towns," such as Basingstoke, Stevenage, and Harlow, that were proposed by the New Towns Act (1946) as new settlements outside the metropolis. Abercrombie also suggested that high-rise housing could solve the issue of how to house London's growing population, for the blocks could replace both the houses lost during the war and London's slum districts. London's first multistory council housing apartment block opened in Holborn in May 1949.

Three years after the end of World War II, London hosted the 1948 Olympics (officially called the Games of the XIV Olympiad), which opened on July 29 at Wembley Stadium. Since wartime rationing was still in effect and the British economy was still recovering from the war, the 1948 Olympics exhibited a "make-do and mend" spirit (akin to today's "reduce, reuse, recycle" ethos). Although Britain was battle scarred, the country put itself forward to host the world's biggest sporting event because it was an opportunity to demonstrate to the world that the worst impact of the war was in the past. The 1948 Olympics cost just £730,000 (today this equates to around £20 million or $25.2 million) to put on; with the Games' tight budget, it became known as the "Austerity Games."[26] No new sporting venues were built for the Games, nor was there an Olympic village to accommodate athletes. Rather, sportsmen were housed in military camps in Uxbridge, West Drayton, and Richmond, while sportswomen were housed in London colleges. British athletes had to stay at home, with many commuting to their venues using public transport. Additionally, since clothing was still rationed, competitors were encouraged to make their own outfits. Despite the austere nature of the Games, the prestige of hosting the event greatly boosted British morale. Ultimately, the 1948 Olympic Games generated profits of £29,000 or ($36,566).[27]

In 1951, London hosted another prestige event, the Festival of Britain, which aimed to promote the sense of postwar recovery by celebrating British industry, arts, and science. The festival's main venue was built on an area of London's South Bank that had been left untouched since it had suffered bombing in World War II. The festival was the perfect way to showcase the elements of urban design that would become prominent in the postwar reconstruction of London.

Over subsequent decades, London experienced vast investment as slums were cleared, new homes built, and the city's service infrastructure improved. Urban planning became generally accepted together with the recognition that it was necessary to divert some employment and housing to areas beyond London's built-up area in order to reduce the pressure from a growing population. In the 1950s, the port of London, which had been devastated during World War II, was restored. From 1968 to 1981, however, the docks were closed because they were unable to compete in size or efficiency with the major ports of continental Europe. During the 1980s, the London Docklands Development Corporation urged major changes be made to the Docklands (the former docks), including the construction of new housing and offices, most famously Canary Wharf, London's secondary central business district. By this time, London had experienced deindustrialization, as the industries of old had collapsed. London could cope with the impact of losing its industry because, increasingly, the city's economy was geared to financial dealing and other services. In the mid-1980s, London's financial and services sectors were strengthened by legislative reforms. The growth of London's financial sectors resulted in the landscape of many areas of the City of London and the West End transforming as office blocks were built, including Broadgate, London Bridge City, next to the River Thames, and the new Lloyd's Building, home to Lloyd's of London. London's Heathrow and Gatwick airports also expanded, while a large new airport opened at Stansted some 30 miles north of London, with a smaller airport operating in the Docklands. The completion of the M25 freeway allowed vehicles to travel around London rather than move through the city. At the start of the twenty-first century, London's notable construction projects included the new British Library, the creation of Underground lines through the Docklands, and the building of the pedestrian Millennium Bridge, which connects Tate Modern on the River Thames's south bank with the north bank at St. Paul's Cathedral. Downriver from the Millennium Bridge, the Millennium Dome (now called the O2) was built at Greenwich as a major exhibition space.

In 2000, Londoners became the first British citizens to directly elect a mayor, electing veteran left-wing politician Ken Livingstone to the position. Livingstone's first term was marked by the controversial imposition of a fee-based traffic-management plan called the Congestion Charge. The Congestion Charge sees a fee charged on most motor vehicles moving within the Congestion Charge Zone (CCZ) in central London between 7:00 a.m. and 10:00 p.m., everyday except Christmas Day. The charge is intended to reduce London's traffic flow and minimize air and noise pollution while also raising funds for London's transport system. Despite the controversy surrounding the Congestion Charge, in 2004 Livingstone was reelected as London mayor. In 2019, London Mayor Sadiq Khan introduced the world's first Ultra Low Emission Zone (ULEZ) in central London, which sees drivers of older, or more polluting, vehicles charged to enter the congestion zone at any time. The initiative has proven controversial, for while Transport for London (TfL, the government body responsible for Greater London's transport system) believes ULEZ will reduce the number of polluting vehicles in London, the Federation of Small Businesses (FSB) fears the charge will be an extra financial burden on small firms. It has proven somewhat difficult for London's authorities to judge the success of ULEZ for it is hard to distinguish between the impact on traffic and pollution levels of successive COVID-19 lockdowns (when Londoners were ordered not to travel save for essential reasons) and the introduction of the ULEZ scheme. That said, improvements in London's air quality reported in 2019 were maintained when lockdown restrictions were eased in London over summer 2020.[28]

On July 6, 2005, London was selected as host of the 2012 Olympic and Paralympic Games. The following day, the city suffered a series of coordinated terrorist attacks by Islamist extremists who exploded three bombs on Underground trains and another on a double-decker bus. The attacks killed 52 people and injured some 700 others.[29] The bombings, usually referred to collectively in the UK as 7/7, shook London, though many Londoners were used to terrorist incidents, having lived through the years of IRA (Irish Republican Army) terrorist activity: the bombing of Harrods and the John Lewis department stores in 1983 and 1992, respectively, the London Stock Exchange in 1990, and the South Quay area of Canary Wharf in 1996.

In 2008, Livingstone failed to win a third term as London mayor, for he was beaten by the flamboyant if controversial Conservative candidate Boris Johnson (who would become British prime minister in 2019). Johnson retained several projects previously overseen by Livingstone, such as Crossrail (a new west-east London Tube line) and the 2012 Olympics. Johnson also introduced so-called Boris Bikes (a public cycling plan), commissioned the development of hybrid New Routemaster buses ("Boris Buses") for central London, and ordered a cable-car system be built across the River Thames between Greenwich Peninsula and the Royal Docks.

In 2011, London faced a wave of rioting after police shot dead a man who was suspected of involvement with gun-related crimes. Over the following days, numerous violent clashes between rioters and the police ensued that saw the destruction of vehicles, homes, and businesses. Looting and vandalism also occurred. The rioting soon spread from Tottenham in North London to other parts of the city, as well as other areas of England.

The London 2012 Olympic Games were a resounding success attended by sellout crowds. The Games began with a spectacular opening ceremony held on July 27 at a specially built stadium in Stratford, East London. Olympic events took place across London, with, for example, tennis held at Wimbledon, archery held at Lord's cricket ground, and equestrian events at Greenwich Park. The year's Paralympic Games were successful too. The year 2012 also saw the 60th anniversary of Queen Elizabeth II's rule, with London the venue for many of the festive events celebrating the milestone.

The 2016 mayoral election was again combative. Johnson chose not to run for reelection and in his place, Conservative candidate Zac Goldsmith—an environmentalist, journalist, and politician—was accused of practicing the politics of division as he tried to link his opponent, Muslim politician Sadiq Khan, to Islamist extremism. Ultimately, Khan won and in so doing became the first Muslim to serve as mayor of a Western capital city. The London mayoral elections planned for May 2020 were postponed for a year due to the ongoing global coronavirus that has greatly disrupted life in London. During the COVID-19 pandemic, London recorded 21 percent of all the COVID-19 deaths in England and Wales up to May 1, 2020.[30] Indeed, according to the Office for National Statistics (ONS) in the four weeks up to April 24, 2020, 5,901 deaths attributed to COVID-19 occurred in London; this is a higher figure than the number of deaths that occurred during the worst four-week period suffered by Londoners during the Blitz. Newham, Brent, and Hackney were the London Boroughs that suffered the worst COVID-19, age-standardized mortality rates during this period.[31] In May 2021, Sadiq Khan won a second term as mayor of London, beating the Conservative candidate Shaun Bailey. Khan entered a run-off with Bailey after neither candidate secured a majority in the first round of voting. Although Bailey increased the Conservative share of the mayoral vote by 1.6%, ultimately Khan won 55.2% of the popular vote to become mayor once more.[32]

LIFE IN THE CITY

ROYAL MEMORIES

When King George VI died in February 1952, I remember my father taking me and my brother to Jacob's Ladder, a bridge over the railway line at West Ealing. He took me there because the train carrying the king's coffin would pass underneath the bridge. Quite a crowd had gathered to watch the train and pay their last respects to the king; my father had to lift me up in the air so I could see what was going on. As the train passed by, all the men in the crowd removed their hats, which at that time were flat cloth caps, as a sign of respect.

When Queen Elizabeth II was crowned in 1953, very few people had televisions on which to watch the ceremony. I remember being taken to a house, along with lots of other local children, to sit in the living room of someone who had a tiny black-and-white television on which we could watch the proceedings. Adults sat on chairs at the back of the room, while the children were arranged in height order, with the smallest at the front nearest the television, so that everyone had the best possible view. Children who wore glasses were also allowed to sit near the front but had to sit at the sides because they were a bit taller. Unfortunately, not all the children liked each other, so there were some arguments about who had to sit next to whom! On the plus side though, all the children were given a cake to enjoy during ceremony. This was very special because wartime rationing was still in effect, so we rarely had any cakes to eat. I was also taken to a special color-film screening of the coronation on the big screen at our local cinema. This screening was just for schools, and all the children were given a propelling pencil with a little crown attached to it and a picture book about the queen as mementos of the occasion. When Princess Margaret (the queen's sister) got married in 1960, all the children were given the day off school to watch the wedding, as this was the first televised royal wedding in the UK. I remember thinking how lovely Margaret's wedding dress was and, being a young teenager at the time, I was impressed that a royal had married a bohemian photographer.

—Rosemary Williams

NOTES

1. "London Plagues 1348–1665," Museum of London: Pocket Histories, 2011, https://www.museumoflondon.org.uk/application/files/5014/5434/6066/london-plagues-1348-1665.pdf (site discontinued).

2. Bruce Robinson, "London: Brighter Lights, Bigger City," *BBC*, February 17, 2011, http://www.bbc.co.uk/history/british/civil_war_revolution/brighter_lights_01.shtml.

3. "Great Plague of 1665–1666," National Archives, https://www.nationalarchives.gov.uk/education/resources/great-plague.

4. "The Great Fire of London: What Happened?" National Archives, https://nationalarchives.gov.uk/documents/education/fire-of-london.pdf.

5. Ben Johnson, "Survivors the Great Fire of London," Historic UK, https://www.historic-uk.com/HistoryMagazine/DestinationsUK/Survivors-of-the-Great-Fire-of-London.

6. "What Happened in the Great Fire of London?" Museum of London: Pocket Histories, 2011, https://www.museumoflondon.org.uk/application/files/6514/5511/5493/what-happened-great-fire-london.pdf.

7. Michael Ball and David Sunderland, *An Economic History of London 1800–1914* (London: Routledge, 2001), 42.

8. Ibid.

9. TSO, "Cholera Epidemics in Victorian London," *The Gazette*, February 1, 2016, https://www.thegazette.co.uk/all-notices/content/100519.

10. Ibid.

11. Stefan Goebel and Jerry White, "London and the First World War," *London Journal* 41, no. 3 (2016): 199–218, https://www.tandfonline.com/doi/full/10.1080/03058034.2016.

12. Ibid.

13. Ibid.

14. Rebecca Myers, "General History of Women's Suffrage in Britain," *The Independent*, May 28, 2013, https://www.independent.co.uk/news/uk/home-news/general-history-of-women-s-suffrage-in-britain-8631733.html.

15. Alwyn Collinson, "How Black Friday Changed the Suffragette Struggle," Museum of London, November 14, 2018, https://www.museumoflondon.org.uk/discover/black-friday.

16. Goebel and White, "London and the First World War."

17. Christopher Klein, "London's World War I Zeppelin Terror," History, August 31, 2018, https://www.history.com/news/londons-world-war-i-zeppelin-terror.

18. Ibid.

19. Ibid.

20. Philip Grant, "The British Empire Exhibition, 1924/25," Brent.gov.uk, https://www.brent.gov.uk/media/387533/The%20British%20Empire%20Exhibition.pdf, 3.

21. "1924 British Empire Exhibition," Open University: Making Britain, http://www.open.ac.uk/researchprojects/makingbritain/content/1924-british-empire-exhibition.

22. "1940: London Blitzed by German Bombers," BBC: On This Day 1950–2005, http://news.bbc.co.uk/onthisday/hi/dates/stories/september/7/newsid_3515000/3515708.stm.

23. Grace Huxford, "Child Evacuees in the Second World War: Operation Pied Piper at 80," History of Government Blog, August 30, 2019, https://history.blog.gov.uk/2019/08/30/child-evacuees-in-the-second-world-war-operation-pied-piper-at-80.

24. "The Evacuation of Children during the Second World War," History Press, https://www.thehistorypress.co.uk/articles/the-evacuation-of-children-during-the-second-world-war.

25. Michael Williams, *Steaming to Victory: How Britain's Railways Won the War* (London, Random House, 2013), n.p.

26. Janie Hampton, *The Austerity Olympics: When the Games Came to London in 1948* (London: Aurum Press, 2008), n.p.

27. Ibid.

28. Greater London Authority, "Central London Ultra Low Emission Zone – 2020 Report," March 2021, https://www.london.gov.uk/sites/default/files/ulez _evaluation_report_2020-v8_finalfinal.pdf P4.

29. Charles A. Lieberman and Serguei Cheloukhine, "2005 London Bombings," in *A New Understanding of Terrorism: Case Studies, Trajectories and Lessons Learned*, eds. M. R. Haberfeld and Agostino von Hassell (London: Springer, 2009), 233.

30. Chris Morris and Oliver Barnes, "Coronavirus: Which Regions Have Been Worst Hit?" *BBC News*, June 9, 2020, https://www.bbc.co.uk/news/52282844.

31. Ibid.

32. "London Elections: Sadiq Khan Wins Second Term as Mayor," May 9, 2021, *BBC*, https://www.bbc.co.uk/news/uk-england-london-56997137.

FURTHER READING

Angel, Schlomo (Solly). "The Urban Expansion of London." Marron Institute of Urban Management *Blog*, September 14, 2012. https://marroninstitute .nyu.edu/blog/the-urban-expansion-of-london.

Archer, Ian W. "The Charity of Early Modern Londoners." *Transactions of the Royal Historical Society* 12 (2002): 223–44. https://www.jstor.org/stable /3679345?seq=1.

Collinson, Alwyn. "How Black Friday Changed the Suffragette Struggle." Museum of London, November 14, 2018. https://www.museumoflondon.org.uk /discover/black-friday.

"The Evacuation of Children during the Second World War." History Press, 2020. https://www.thehistorypress.co.uk/articles/the-evacuation-of-children -during-the-second-world-war.

Goebel, Stefan, and Jerry White. "London and the First World War." *London Journal* 41, no. 3 (2016): 199–218. https://www.tandfonline.com/doi/full/10.1080 /03058034.2016.1216758.

Grant, Philip. 2012. "The British Empire Exhibition, 1924/25." Brent.gov.uk. https://www.brent.gov.uk/media/387533/The%20British%20Empire%20 Exhibition.pdf.

"Great Plague of 1665–1666." National Archives. https://www.nationalarchives .gov.uk/education/resources/great-plague.

Hampton, Janie. *The Austerity Olympics: When the Games Came to London in 1948*. London: Aurum Press, 2008.

Huxford, Grace. "Child Evacuees in the Second World War: Operation Pied Piper at 80." History of Government Blog, August 30, 2019. https://history.blog .gov.uk/2019/08/30/child-evacuees-in-the-second-world-war-operation -pied-piper-at-80.

Jenkins, Simon. *A Short History of London: The Creation of a World Capital*. London: Penguin, 2019.

Klein, Christopher. "London's World War I Zeppelin Terror." History, August 31, 2018. https://www.history.com/news/londons-world-war-i-zeppelin-terror.

Kynaston, David. *City of London: The History.* London: Vintage Books. 2012.

Lieberman, Charles A., and Serguei Cheloukhine. "2005 London Bombings." In *A New Understanding of Terrorism: Case Studies, Trajectories and Lessons Learned,* edited by M. R. Haberfeld and Agostino von Hassell, 233–48. London: Springer, 2009.

"London Plagues 1348–1665." Museum of London: Pocket Histories, 2011. https://www.museumoflondon.org.uk/application/files/5014/5434/6066/london-plagues-1348-1665.pdf (site discontinued).

Morris, Chris, and Oliver Barnes. "Coronavirus: Which Regions Have Been Worst Hit?" *BBC News,* June 9, 2020. https://www.bbc.co.uk/news/52282844.

Myers, Rebecca. "General History of Women's Suffrage in Britain." *The Independent,* May 28, 2013. https://www.independent.co.uk/news/uk/home-news/general-history-of-women-s-suffrage-in-britain-8631733.html.

"1940: London Blitzed by German Bombers." BBC: On This Day 1950–2005. http://news.bbc.co.uk/onthisday/hi/dates/stories/september/7/newsid_3515000/3515708.stm.

"1924 British Empire Exhibition." Open University: Making Britain. http://www.open.ac.uk/researchprojects/makingbritain/content/1924-british-empire-exhibition.

Richardson, John. *The Annals of London: A Year-by-Year Record of a Thousand Years of History.* London: Cassell & Co., 2001.

Robinson, Bruce. "London: Brighter Lights, Bigger City." *BBC,* February 17, 2011. http://www.bbc.co.uk/history/british/civil_war_revolution/brighter_lights_01.shtml.

TSO (The Stationery Office). "Cholera Epidemics in Victorian London." *The Gazette,* February 1, 2016. https://www.thegazette.co.uk/all-notices/content/100519.

"What Happened in the Great Fire of London?" Museum of London: Pocket Histories, 2011. https://www.museumoflondon.org.uk/application/files/6514/5511/5493/what-happened-great-fire-london.pdf (site discontinued).

"What Was Life Like in Medieval London?" Museum of London: Pocket Histories, 2011. https://www.museumoflondon.org.uk/application/files/1614/5442/8566/what-was-life-like-medieval-london.pdf (site discontinued).

Williams, Michael. *Steaming to Victory: How Britain's Railways Won the War.* London: Random House, 2013.

4

Politics

Greater London is divided into 73 parliamentary constituencies that are further divided into borough constituencies. The Greater London Authority (GLA), which was created in 2000 to improve coordination between London's Boroughs, is the devolved regional governing body of London. The GLA derives much of its power from the Greater London Authority Act 1999 and the Greater London Authority Act 2007 and has jurisdiction over Greater London and the City of London. The GLA comprises an elected mayor and the elected London Assembly, which consists of 25 members. The mayor and the London Assembly serve fixed terms of four years.

The GLA has authority over London's transport, policing, economy, and fire and emergency planning. Transport for London (TfL), the Mayor's Office for Policing and Crime, and the London Fire Commissioner are responsible for the delivery of London's transport, policing, and emergency services. TfL is controlled by a board appointed by the mayor of London. The GLA consists of two branches. The top tier is called the Mayoralty, which is led by the mayor of London, who serves as the GLA's head. The mayor is responsible for policies concerning London's transport and environment, land use, construction and regeneration, economic development, and the arts. The mayor is also responsible for promoting good health among Londoners. The mayor has some control over the police, for the mayor can make appointments to the police's governing body, the Metropolitan Police Authority. The second tier of the GLA is the London

Assembly, which consists of 25 elected members and has the power to scrutinize the mayor's activities, modify the mayor's annual budget, and reject ideas proposed by the mayor.

The GLA receives most of its funding from a central government grant as well as money collected from Council Tax (an annual tax paid by households to pay for their local authority services). The GLA is a precepting authority, which means the organization does not collect Council Tax directly but rather instructs billing authorities (the London Boroughs) to do so on its behalf.

London is an unusually difficult place to govern, as evinced by the fact that in recent years the city has experienced four systems of governance. In contrast, New York City has had one form of governance since 1898.[1] The frequency with which London's system of governance changes is likely due to a combination of the city's growing population, history, and geography. Since 2016, the GLA has been controlled by the London Labour Party (or London Labour), the devolved part of the Labour Party in London.

THE PALACE OF WESTMINSTER

As the focus of UK politics, London is the location of the Palace of Westminster. This is the site of both the House of Commons and the House of Lords, the two parts of the UK's parliament. Commonly referred to by the British as the Houses of Parliament, the Palace of Westminster is situated on the north bank of the River Thames in Westminster, central London. The Palace of Westminster is a striking example of neo-Gothic architecture that has been included on the UNESCO World Heritage Site list since 1987. The Palace of Westminster has an iconic silhouette that includes the Elizabeth Tower, a clock tower that is often referred to as Big Ben although the name Big Ben actually refers to the clock tower's main bell. The earliest parts of the Palace of Westminster date from 1097 through 1099, but much of the rest of the complex, including the Houses of Parliament (or New Palace of Westminster) was built between 1835 and 1860 by Sir Charles Barry, with interior design by Augustus Pugin. The offices by the side of Westminster Hall were rebuilt after they were bombed in World War II. Due to a lack of office space in the Palace of Westminster, supplementary House of Commons offices can be found in London's Portcullis House, a modern building in Westminster that opened in 2001. During the Middle Ages, the Palace of Westminster was both the main residence of the British royalty in London and home to the law courts (located in Westminster Hall) as well as being the site of numerous government departments. In the fourteenth century, Westminster became

Located on the north bank of the River Thames, the Palace of Westminster serves as the meeting place for both the House of Commons and the House of Lords. The Palace of Westminster is often referred to informally as the Houses of Parliament. (David Steele/Dreamstime.com)

Parliament's permanent location. The House of Lords has sat in the Palace of Westminster since the thirteenth century.

The House of Commons is the lower house and main chamber of the UK Parliament. The House of Commons consists of 650 elected representatives known as members of Parliament (MPs). Members are voted into power by their constituencies through a first-past-the-post system. The House of Lords, which is often referred to in the UK as simply the Lords, is the UK Parliament's upper house. Membership of the House of Lords is usually granted by appointment or by heredity, and members of the House of Lords are known as peers. In the past, all hereditary peers were entitled to membership of that House of Lords, but under the House of Lords Act 1999, the right to membership by heredity was restricted to 92 hereditary members. The role of the House of Lords is to scrutinize, review, and amend bills that have already been approved by the House of Commons. While the House of Lords cannot usually prevent a bill from passing into law, members of the House of Lords can delay bills and force MPs to reassess their decisions. Members of the House of Lords can serve as government ministers, but most high-ranking Cabinet officials are drawn from the House of Commons.

Traditionally, the House of Lords is the site of the Queen's Speech, a speech that the monarch reads out in the Lords chamber in the presence of MPs, peers, and others in the House of Lords. The Queen delivers "the

---

DID YOU KNOW?

THE POLITICIANS VERSUS THE JOURNALISTS PANCAKE RACE

Every year since 1988, the Rehab Parliamentary Pancake Race has taken place in which British politicians from the House of Commons and the House of Lords compete against a team of political correspondents from the British media. During the race, competitors run around College Green, a small grassy area opposite the Houses of Parliament in Westminster.

The race aims to raise awareness of the work that the Rehab organization does in helping people who are socially excluded or have disabilities. The first Rehab Parliamentary Pancake Race took place in 1988, and since then the event has unsurprisingly achieved a large amount of press coverage, appearing in reports on television news broadcast by the BBC, ITN, and CNN. The Rehab Parliamentary Pancake Race takes the form of a relay race in which a team pancake (rather than a traditional baton) is passed between competitors over a course of roughly 27 yards. During the race, competitors wear an apron and a chef's hat over their work clothes. The competitors must run carrying a frying pan and toss their team pancake three times so that the tossed pancakes reach a minimum height of 3 feet. If a competitor drops the pancake, the competitor must return to the starting line and restart the race. Each team member must run the course, and the team pancake must remain intact.

Queen's Speech" as part of the annual State Opening of Parliament ceremony that marks the start of the parliamentary year. The origins of the State Opening of Parliament hearken back to the sixteenth century, but the ceremony in its current form has occurred since 1852, when the Palace of Westminster was rebuilt following a major fire. As such, the Queen's Speech is a mechanism that allows the UK government to highlight its priorities for the coming months as well as set out the laws that the government wants Parliament to approve. The State Opening of Parliament ceremony begins with a procession that sees the queen travel by horse-drawn carriage from Buckingham Palace to the Palace of Westminster. An official known as the "Gentleman Usher of the Black Rod" (usually referred to as simply Black Rod) then summons the MPs to the House of Lords. Once the queen is ready, Black Rod enters the House of Commons to summon the MPs to the House of Lords. However, as Black Rod approaches the House of Commons, the door is slammed shut in order to symbolize that the House of Commons acts independently of the monarch. Next, Black Rod bangs the door of the House of Lords three times with his mace before he is invited inside. The MPs then walk in pairs into the House of Lords.

Typically, the Queen's Speech takes place once per year, but in 2019 the Queen's Speech occurred twice. In 2019, Boris Johnson became prime minister in July and wanted a Queen's Speech to occur, but this wish was

---

SPENCER PERCEVAL (1762–1812): THE ONLY BRITISH PRIME MINISTER ASSASSINATED WHILE IN OFFICE

DID YOU KNOW?

Perceval was born in London as the second son of the Second Earl of Egmont. In 1796 Perceval entered Parliament as a Pittite/Tory MP and was soon appointed solicitor general. Perceval was appointed solicitor general under Prime Minister Henry Addington (1801–04). From 1802 and through to William Pitt's second administration (1804–06) Perceval served as attorney general. In 1807, Perceval became an unpaid chancellor of the exchequer. He also supported William Wilberforce's antislavery campaign and, in 1807, cofounded the African Institute in order to safeguard the Abolition of the Slave Trade Act. In 1809, Perceval succeeded the Duke of Portland as British prime minister. Perceval's strong evangelical Anglican beliefs underpinned his administration, and he was a vehement supporter of family (Perceval and his wife, Jane, had twelve children), private philanthropy, and personal morality. Perceval's major act while prime minister was the Regency Bill 1810, which made the Prince of Wales regent during King George III's illness. Perceval was unable to make a lasting mark on British politics, however, for in 1812, he was shot dead in the House of Commons by a merchant with a grudge against the government. Subsequently, a monument to Perceval was erected in Westminster Abbey. All Saints Church in Ealing was built in Perceval's honor on the site of his former home.

---

blocked by the Supreme Court. Controversially, Johnson was, however, allowed a Queen's Speech in October that year. Then, once the 2019 general election was held, the new Conservative government needed another Queen's Speech to take place so that the new government could set out its plans.

LONDON'S CHANGING POLITICAL STRUCTURE

In 1963, the London Government Act saw the creation of the area of Greater London. In order to create Greater London, the Act allowed the counties of Middlesex and London to be abolished, while parts of the counties of Kent, Essex, and Surrey became part of the Greater London conurbation. The Act reduced the number of local government districts within the region, resulting in local councils taking responsibility for large areas. The Act reformed the upper tier of local government to encompass all of Greater London, while the responsibility of the upper and lower tiers of local government were reorganized. The Act also divided London's Boroughs into inner and outer boroughs. London's Boroughs included new boroughs that were formed out of a combination of Inner London metropolitan boroughs, as well as Outer London municipal boroughs and urban districts in addition to the three county boroughs of Croydon, West Ham, and East Ham. Today, Greater London is made up of 32 London Boroughs plus the City of London. The Inner London Boroughs consist of Camden, Greenwich, Hackney, Hammersmith and Fulham, Islington, Kensington and Chelsea, Lambeth, Lewisham, Southwark, Tower Hamlets, Wandsworth, and the City of Westminster. London's Outer London Boroughs are Barking and Dagenham, Barnet, Bexley, Brent, Bromley, Croydon, Ealing, Enfield, Haringey, Harrow, Havering, Hillingdon, Hounslow, Kingston-upon-Thames, Merton, Newham, Redbridge, Richmond upon Thames, Sutton, and Waltham Forest. Borough councils are responsible for providing residents' education, housing, highways, fire services, social services, leisure, and libraries. Boroughs also organize waste collection and waste disposal, oversee environmental health regulations and collect Council Tax. Council Tax is the local taxation collected in England, Scotland, and Wales. The tax is levied on domestic properties, each of which is assigned to one of eight bands in England and Scotland (A to H), or nine bands in Wales (A to I). The band to which a property is assigned is based on a property's value as judged by the Valuation Office Agency, a division of the Inland Revenue. Each Council Tax band is set at a fixed amount, and the more valuable a property, the higher the tax band to which it is assigned. The level of Council Tax paid to each council is paid by local residents to finance a borough's services. In London, part of the Council Tax paid by residents include one precept that goes toward the Greater London Authority and another that contributes to adult social care.

In London, Council Tax comprises around a third of all local government funding.[2] Since 2013, any London council that wants to raise Council Tax above the threshold set by the national government must hold a local referendum. London councils are responsible for administering the Council Tax. The "full" Council Tax bill is based on the assumption that a property is inhabited by at least two adults. However, discounts are available for Council Tax. For example, properties occupied by an individual are eligible for a single-person reduction of 25 percent. Similarly, if a property is furnished but is not an individual's primary residence, then the individual may receive a second-home discount at the discretion of the local council. Households consisting of full-time students are exempt from paying Council Tax.

Each of London's Boroughs is divided into areas called wards. Typically, each ward is represented by three councillors, who are elected every four years. Councillors do not receive a salary but do receive an allowance as recompense for the work they do. Under the Government and Public Involvement in Health Act 2007, every London council must implement one of two forms of political structure. The first possible structure is to choose a leader and cabinet (or executive). Under this model, the council leader is elected by a council for a term of four years. The leader chooses a deputy leader, the size of the council cabinet, and the person who in turn selects the cabinet members. A council cabinet may comprise members chosen from one or more political parties. Most London councils employ this political structure. The London Boroughs of Hackney, Lewisham, Newham, and Tower Hamlets employ an executive mayoral system of governance. Under this system, local residents vote for local wards representatives as well as a mayor, who serves as the council leader. The directly elected mayors have ultimate responsibility for council policies and the delivery of council services. The mayors also select the members of the council cabinet, which can consist of representatives of various political parties.

The 1963 London Government Act did not affect the City of London, which remained unreformed by the legislation. The City of London Corporation (formerly the Corporation of London) is the local municipal authority of the City of London. Often, local government legislation makes special provision for the City to be treated as a London borough and for the Court of Common Council (the City of London Corporation's primary decision-making body) to act as a local authority. The City of London Corporation does not have authority over the two Inns of Court known as the Middle Temple and Inner Temple, as these are extraparochial areas, meaning that, historically, they have lain outside the corporation's boundaries. In reality, however, many of the City of London Corporation's statutory functions do extend to the two Inns. The City of London Corporation is headed by the apolitical Lord Mayor of London, who is supported by advisers known as sheriffs. The Lord Mayor represents the City of London's interests in local and national politics and also hosts visiting heads of state. The Lord Mayor, who serves a one-year term, also plays a major role in promoting the UK's financial and business services.

Subsequent amendments to the 1963 London Government Act have seen changes to the organization of London's upper tier of authority. For example, in 1986, the Greater London Council (GLC) was abolished. The GLC was formed in 1965 as part of the effort to improve living conditions in post–World War II London. The London of the 1950s was home to numerous derelict residential streets that resulted from wartime bombing, while houses that had survived the bombing were often overcrowded and provided poor living standards. London had also begun to exceed the boundaries of the London County Council (LCC), which had acted as the main local government authority for the County of London since its creation in 1889.

In the postwar era, there was a general feeling that London's governance needed to be refreshed. Consequently, in 1957, the UK government established a commission that recommended the abolition of the LCC and the creation of the Greater London Council. The commission also recommended establishing 52 local authorities as London Boroughs, though ultimately, 32 London Boroughs were approved. Each borough was allowed two representatives on the GLC.

The GLC was responsible for providing London's roads, housing, leisure services, and population-growth management while encouraging prosperity. Initially, the GLC ran into problems when in 1973, construction on a London highway network it proposed was canceled, though the proposed elevated section of the Westway (a 2.5-mile dual carriageway of the A40 trunk road in West London) between Paddington and Kensington was built. The GLC's record on housing was also mixed. When the LCC was abolished, the GLC became responsible for clearing London's slums. However, Inner Londoners protested vehemently when the GLC started to relocate them from their squalid inner-city homes to London's suburbs and satellite towns. At the same time, people in other parts of England, such as Barnstaple in Devon, southwestern England, rejected the idea of accepting relocated Londoners because they feared the presence of Londoners would spoil rural areas.

From the late 1960s, the GLC's role as a housing provider was reduced. When the Conservatives took control of the GLC in 1967, a program was implemented that allowed council house tenants to buy their homes at a discount. It was introduced because the Conservatives felt local authorities should not own property. The LCC had long been dominated by Labour because it was influenced by left-wing, Inner London politicians. In contrast, the new GLC was intended to be more politically balanced, as it encompassed many wealthy suburban areas of London. For this reason, throughout the 1960s and 1970s, control of the GLC switched between Labour and the Conservatives. In 1977, however, a hard-left division began to emerge within the London Labour Party, which actually denounced its own party's 1977 general election manifesto. The Labour Party lost the general election, and control of the GLC passed to a Conservative administration that reduced public spending. Ultimately, the GLC housing plan influenced UK prime minister Margaret Thatcher's housing philosophy and paved the way for the right-to-buy program that was introduced by the Thatcher government in the Housing Act 1980.

The GLC did change London's transport and housing, however. For instance, the GLC oversaw the development of new landmarks, including the Blackwall Tunnel (a pair of road tunnels beneath the River Thames in East London) and the creation of the Woolwich Ferry (a vehicle and pedestrian ferry across the River Thames in East London that connects Woolwich on the south bank with North Woolwich on the north bank). The GLC also increased funding for London's arts programs and antipollution initiatives. Political tensions prevented the GLC from making greater progress—the GLC was hampered by the friction that existed between central and local governments, and by that between rival Conservative and Labour representatives on the GLC itself.

During its 21 years of existence, control of the GLC switched from Labour to Conservative four times. To complicate matters further, the main party in charge of the GLC was almost always the opposite to that in power nationally. For this reason, GLC projects were often blocked by national government or at the borough level when boroughs refused to cooperate. An example of this occurred in 1973, when the Labour government refused to promote council house sales as promoted by the Conservatives, who were in charge of the GLC. Such political rivalries occurred throughout the 1960s and 1970s and were likely a contributing factor in the GLC's eventual downfall.

The most prominent politician associated with the GLC was undoubtedly Ken Livingstone (commonly referred to in the UK as "Red Ken" because of his socialist beliefs) who was first elected to the GLC in 1973, having been elected to Lambeth Borough Council in 1971. From 1977 to 1981, Livingstone led a left-wing faction within Labour's representatives in the GLC, which was, at that time, run by the Conservative Party. In the 1981 GLC elections, Labour won a majority, prompting Livingstone to stage a coup against the Labour Party's moderate GLC leader Andrew McIntosh, even though McIntosh had guided the Labour Party to victory in the election. Since Livingstone enjoyed support from the majority of Labour GLC councillors, he was able to assume control of the GLC. The British prime minister at this time, Margaret Thatcher, was horrified by the left-wing domination of London and took action when Livingstone intervened in national current affairs, including his inviting members of Sinn Féin (the political wing of the Irish Republic Army or IRA) to London, professing support for Fidel Castro against the U.S. economic embargo, and supporting Argentina's ownership of the Falkland Islands during the 1982 Falklands War in which the UK fought Argentina for control of the islands.

In 1986, Thatcher abolished the GLC along with other large metropolitan councils in England. The GLC was superseded by the Greater London Authority (GLA, known colloquially as City Hall after its seat on the River Thames's south bank near Tower Bridge), which was founded in 2000. The GLA was created by the government of Prime Minister Tony Blair following a 1998 referendum and uses a system of an elected mayor and assembly. The referendum was held because Blair's Labour Party had come to power the year before on a platform of devolving power to London and the English regions as well as Scotland, Wales, and Northern Ireland. Livingstone remained a thorn in the side of Blair's government, however, for in May 2000, he became the first elected mayor of London despite the fact that he had to run as an independent candidate because the Labour government refused to accept him as its mayoral candidate.

THE MAYORS OF LONDON

The position of the Lord Mayor of London is separate from the role of directly elected mayor of London. The role of Lord Mayor of London is one of the world's oldest continuously elected civic positions, with the first Lord Mayor, Henry Fitz-Ailwyn, holding office from 1192 until 1212. By far the most famous Lord Mayor of London is Richard "Dick" Whittington, who served three terms as lord mayor of London: 1397–1399, 1406–1407, and 1419–1420. By 1400, Dick Whittington had become so hugely wealthy that he was able to loan money to King Henry IV (r. 1399–1413) and King Henry V (r. 1413–1422). On his death, Whittington bequeathed his fortune to charitable causes. Whittington's success as Lord Mayor means he has become a British folk hero. The Lord Mayor of London has an official residence at Mansion House, located in the heart of the City of London. The Lord Mayor is elected every Michaelmas (September 29) and takes office on the Friday before the second Saturday in November during a swearing-in ceremony known as the Silent Ceremony, which is held at the Guildhall, a building in the Moorgate area of the City of London. The ceremony is so called because, save for a short speech made by the new Lord Mayor, no other speeches are heard. The Lord Mayor's "show" is the day after the new Lord Mayor takes office. During the show, the new Lord Mayor travels in procession to the Royal Courts of Justice on the Strand. At the Royal Courts of Justice, the Lord Mayor swears loyalty to the sovereign in front of the justices of the High Court. The Lord Mayor's main responsibility is to represent and support the City of London's businesses and residents.

In the modern era, among Ken Livingstone's early achievements as head of the GLC was the introduction of the Fares Fair policy, which cut London transport fares by 25 percent through raising funds via higher taxes. Like many of Livingstone's ideas, the Fares Fair plan inspired both enthusiasm and disbelief among Londoners. Indeed, the plan was subsequently judged illegal: it was challenged in the courts by the Conservative leader of the Bromley London Borough Council, who argued successfully that people living in the London borough of Bromley were having to pay higher taxes for the London Underground even though the Underground did not operate in the borough. Livingstone went on to actively promote a new form of left-wing politics that emphasized minority rights, most particularly those of women, ethnic minorities, and LGBTQ communities. Sympathetic commentators referred to this new politics as the "rainbow coalition," while detractors dubbed Livingstone and his politics "the loony left." While today, such causes seem fairly mainstream, at the time, they were considered controversial by many. Detractors also objected to the fact that Livingstone would give funding to minority groups and organizations that had not been properly vetted.[3] Consequently, in the 1983 Conservative general election manifesto, the party promised to abolish the GLC on the grounds that it was wasteful and unnecessary. In 1983, the Conservative Party suggested the abolition of the GLC in a government white paper (a policy document setting out proposals for future legislation) called *Streamlining the Cities: Government Proposals for Reorganising Local Government in Greater London and the Metropolitan Counties*, which ultimately led to the abolition of the GLC and England's metropolitan county councils (MCCs). The white paper came in response to Outer London Conservative groups wishing to be free of what they considered the GLC's tax high, spend high attitude as well as its left-wing ideology.

In May 2000, Livingstone became the first directly elected mayor of London. The highlight of Livingstone's first term in office was the traffic management plan known as the Congestion Charge, which, controversially, aimed to reduce London's congestion by charging a fee on most motor vehicles driven within the Congestion Charge Zone (CCZ). Critics of the plan denounced the Congestion Charge as a tax that prevented poorer Londoners from driving in the city. However, an increase in commercial traffic in London together with a booming London economy meant Livingstone's plan was praised by some business groups. Another notable achievement occurred in 2003, when Livingstone oversaw the introduction of TfL's Oyster card, an electronic fare-payment system. Since its introduction, the Oyster card has become an integral part of most Londoners' lives, as the card is accepted on various modes of transport across London, including the Tube, buses, the Docklands Light Railway (DLR), the London Overground rail service network, Tramlink (a tram system serving Croydon and surrounding areas of South London), some riverboat services, and most of the National Rail services that fall within the London fare zone.

In 2004, Livingstone was readmitted to the Labour Party and the same year was re-elected mayor of London. As mayor, Livingstone was part of a successful campaign that saw London awarded the honor of hosting the 2012 Olympic and Paralympic Games. The following year, Livingstone was also praised for his response to the 7/7 terror attacks. Livingstone's other achievements as mayor include the creation of the London Climate Change Agency (a municipal company owned by the London Development Agency that works with the private sector to create low-energy projects for London) and the creation of the international environmental organization called the Large Cities Climate Leadership Group (now called the C40 Cities Climate Leadership Group). Livingstone also introduced the London Partnerships Register, a voluntary system by which same-sex couples could register their partnership. This system paved the way for the UK government's introduction of civil partnerships and same-sex marriage. Livingstone did much to encourage sport in London, not just through the Olympics but also through the introduction of charity 10K running races and a successful campaign to bring the 2007 Tour de France cycle race to London.

While in office, Livingstone continued to attract controversy, and in 2006, he was suspended temporarily from the Labour Party after likening a Jewish journalist to a Nazi. At the next mayoral election in 2008, Livingstone was defeated by the Conservative candidate Boris Johnson, who went on to become British prime minister in 2019. In 2012, Johnson won a second term as London mayor, a post he held until 2016. As editor of the world's oldest weekly magazine, *Spectator*, and a host of the BBC television comedy quiz show *Have I Got News for You*, Johnson was already famous across the UK for his bumbling persona and use of flamboyant language. In 2001, Johnson became the Conservative MP for affluent Henley-on-Thames, a town in southeastern England that straddles the River Thames. Johnson was often viewed as more liberal than many Conservatives, for he argued against state interference in people's lives and voted in favor of same-sex civil partnerships.

During the mayoral election, Livingstone viewed Johnson as a formidable political opponent and tried to derail Johnson's election campaign by depicting Johnson as a racist, homophobic bigot, citing language Johnson used in his writing as evidence. Johnson countered the claims by saying the writing was satirical and by emphasizing his own Turkish heritage. To downplay accusations of racism further, Johnson later went against Conservative party policy to endorse amnesty for illegal immigrants. Nonetheless, claims that Johnson was racist were exacerbated when the fascist British National Party (BNP) urged its supporters to vote for Johnson as their second preference in the mayoral vote.

While Johnson was a divisive figure as mayor, he arguably oversaw some improvements to London life. For example, under Johnson, crime and homicides reduced dramatically: the homicide rate (covering murder, manslaughter, and infanticide) fell from 163 in 2007–2008 to 109 in 2015–2016, a decrease that began during Livingstone's second term as mayor. Johnson's tenure also saw 94,001 affordable homes constructed between April 2008 and March 2016, though critics have questioned whether many of these homes were truly affordable to Londoners on low incomes. During Johnson's time as mayor, use of the London Underground also increased to record levels, many Tube line experienced upgrades, and services became more frequent. Johnson also put in place plans for the creation of a night-time Tube service, despite opposition from transport unions (the night service began after Johnson left office, a year later than planned). In 2008, Johnson vowed to bring back a version of London's iconic Routemaster buses: the open-backed, double-decker buses that allowed passengers to jump on and off between bus stops. At the same time, Johnson scrapped the so-called "bendy buses," long, articulated buses that Johnson claimed were unsuitable for London roads and allowed people to avoid paying fares. The new Routemaster (dubbed the "Boris Bus") was a hybrid diesel-electric double-decker that retained the "hop-on, hop-off" rear open platform of the original Routemasters but with updated features that made it fully accessible. The new Routemasters entered service in 2012. While the new buses were environmentally friendly, they were also costly, and some passengers found them unbearably hot. Transport for London (TfL) ordered 1,000 of the costly new buses, and Johnson's critics noted that during his mayoralty, TfL bus fares rose by 47 percent.[4] Subsequently, Sadiq Khan dumped the Boris Buses because they were so expensive to produce. Johnson's most famous transport initiative was, however, the so-called Boris Bikes. Launched in 2010, this bicycle-hire program allowed both Londoners and visitors to rent bicycles to ride around the city, with 700 bicycle docking stations providing access to over 10,000 bikes. The bicycles could be rented for 24 hours, with the first 30 minutes free of charge and each 30 minutes thereafter charged at a rate of £2. Frequent users could buy an annual pass for £90, which worked out to 25 pence per day. Johnson promoted the bike-rental program by riding the Boris Bikes himself, and during Johnson's last year as mayor, the number of bicycle rentals reached over 10.3 million.[5] However, critics pointed to the £11million per year cost of keeping the bikes on the road. Others noted that plans for a bike-hire program had been announced while Livingstone was mayor. Less successfully, in 2012, Johnson opened the UK's first urban cable car, the Emirates Air Line service, which carried passengers from near the O2 arena in North Greenwich across the River Thames to the Royal Victoria Dock, part of East London's Docklands development. The cable car cost £60million to install but was used by comparatively few people and attracted very few regular users.[6]

As mayor, Johnson was involved with the organization of the 2012 Olympics, which were widely regarded as a great success both in terms of a sporting spectacle and as a boost to London's economy. A less successful feel-good project broached by Johnson was the Garden Bridge, the concept of a pedestrianized garden bridge over the River Thames. The bridge was intended to be financed using private and public money, but the project was scrapped in 2017 when it had already cost £53million, of which £43million came from public funds. Johnson also promoted the idea of a London island airport in the Thames estuary, but the idea was rejected on the grounds of cost and environmental impact. In 2015, Johnson decided to return to Parliament before his time as mayor ended and so took on the seat of Uxbridge and South Ruislip in North West London. Under Prime Minister Theresa May, Johnson was appointed foreign secretary and then pulled out of the race for Conservative Party leader. Johnson then went on to become a leading figure in the Vote Leave campaign during the 2016 referendum on whether the UK should leave the European Union (EU), despite highlighting the benefits of being in the EU single market while he was mayor.

Johnson was succeeded as London mayor by the Sadiq Khan, who as a British Pakistani Muslim was London's first mayor from an ethnic minority and first Muslim mayor. Previously, Khan had served as MP for Tooting in South London, a councillor for the London Borough of Wandsworth, and a shadow minister for London under Labour Leader Ed Milliband. As mayor, Khan remains a member of the Labour Party. As London Labour's candidate, in 2016 Khan defeated his Conservative rival, the wealthy environmentalist and writer Zac Goldsmith. Khan's win over Goldsmith represented the biggest vote for any London mayor to date; he won more than 1.3 millon votes or almost 57 percent of all votes cast in the election.[7] Weeks after Khan's victory, the EU referendum result went against the wishes of many Londoners, something that meant for many Londoners Khan had become a symbol of an inclusive London at odds with the rest of the UK (table 4.1).

The mayor of London, Sadiq Khan, opens the Festival of Diwali in London on October 16, 2016. Diwali is a major celebration for London's Hindu, Sikh, and Jain communities and sees the city's skies lit with fireworks over the course of many nights. (Lorna Roberts/Dreamstime.com)

While Khan has succeeded in increasing the

number of affordable homes in London by winning £4.8billion of government funding to create 116,000 affordable homes by 2022, violent crime in London has risen during his tenure.[8] Khan has also taken highly controversial steps to improve London's air quality with the introduction of measures such as the Ultra Low Emission Zone (ULEZ), which was expanded to cover more areas in 2021. At the same time, TfL has experienced serious financial problems: in 2018, TfL announced a record loss of almost £1billion due to falling passenger numbers on some services and to freezes on fares (one of Khan's manifesto pledges), which likely cost TfL £640 million at a time when TfL faced the phased withdrawal of government subsidies.[9] Additionally, Crossrail (a new £18 billion train line running west-east across London, the construction of which is Europe's largest building project) is both over budget and behind schedule. Khan's supporters counter criticism over lack of progress and delayed projects by arguing that a four-year term is too short for any leader to make a real impact. While Khan's anti-Brexit stance has allowed him to capture the general public mood of liberal and multicultural Londoners he has faced criticism from some quarters. For instance, many business leaders have voiced concerns about Khan's seeming lack of engagement with them; and some political commentators have criticized Khan for what they consider his showboating actions, such as entering into a spat with U.S. president Donald Trump: in 2019, Khan allowed a giant, inflatable balloon caricaturing Trump as a diaper-wearing baby to be flown over Parliament Square during the president's visit to London.

In June 2020, Khan took a 10 percent voluntary pay cut and froze the pay for senior officials at City Hall in order to ease the financial strain on London's public finances during the COVID-19 pandemic. In May 2021, Khan was reelected mayor of London.

LONDON'S OUTLIER POLITICS

During the 2016 EU referendum, London stood out, for the city bucked the English trend by voting 59.9 percent in favor of remaining part of the EU. This was in stark contrast to many areas of England outside of London, which voted by 55.4 percent to leave. For many commentators, this vote confirmed that, politically, London was set apart from the rest of England. The referendum even led to calls from some Londoners for the city to apply for its own EU membership,[10] while some political commentators have even talked of an emerging "London nationalism" among Londoners angry at the Brexit result.

In general, Londoners' political views often differ widely from those found in the rest of England. For instance, Londoners are more likely to hold left-wing attitudes, to dislike authoritarianism, and to support the

Labour Party rather than the Conservatives. Londoners also tend to be more pro-immigration than people elsewhere in England. Similarly, fewer Londoners identify as English than other people in England when asked about their national identity. This may be one of the reasons that the majority of London's residents supported holding a second EU referendum and maintaining the UK's access to the EU single market.[11] It may be that Londoners' political divergence from the rest of England reflects a general rural-urban division within the UK, for London was but one of the English cities to vote "Remain" in the Brexit referendum. However, research has shown than Londoners hold political opinions that are unique unto themselves, thereby suggesting that London's divergence does go beyond a rural-urban divide. The two main reasons for this are likely London's demographics—Londoners tend to be younger, more diverse, and better educated than city dwellers in other UK cities—and geography—Londoners tend to mix with people from diverse backgrounds and come into contact with more immigrants than in other cities. In short, Londoners tend to be more liberal, tolerant, and outward looking than other Brits. For this reason, there are growing calls in the light of Brexit for greater devolution of powers to London. At the heart of Londoners' calls for devolution is the fear that Brexit will likely prove detrimental to London in terms of the city's reputation as a global capital and financial center.

Some non-Londoners within the UK feel the UK's political and economic power is too centralized in London and that, as a result, London benefits unfairly. This attitude was evinced by a 2014 poll showing that around 67 percent of adults in the UK felt that London held too much sway over the way in which much of England was run, while over 70 percent felt that because of London's sway over the rest of the country, the city receives preferential treatment. Similarly, another poll found that most non-Londoners in the UK felt that the government was too London-centric.[12] The sense that London receives preferential governmental treatment has given rise to anti-London sentiments that run deeper than a north-south, rural-urban divide. Indeed, in 2014, commentators noted that many non-Londoners viewed London as a separate city-state that followed a way of life and culture at odds with the rest of the UK. The seeming separateness of London from the rest of the UK means that Londoners are sometimes referred to disparagingly as the "metropolitan elite" or as the "London bubble." To many political commentators, London's metropolitan elite is symbolized by the North London borough of Islington, which is home to the so-called Islington Set, left-leaning Londoners inspired initially by Prime Minister Tony Blair and his left-centrist New Labour movement that dominated British politics from the mid-1990s to the 2010s. Islington's place in London and, indeed, UK politics was cemented by the Blair-Brown deal (also known as the Granita Pact). This was a 1994 gentlemen's agreement struck between Tony Blair and his fellow Labour Party politician Gordon Brown while they were shadow home secretary and shadow chancellor of the exchequer, respectively. It is widely understood that the politicians met in the Islington restaurant Granita and that during the meeting, Brown agreed to not oppose Blair in the forthcoming Labour leadership election. Subsequently, Blair won the leadership race and then, in 1997, became prime minister. Islington's left-wing credentials were further enhanced when socialist politician Jeremy Corbyn served as Labour Party leader from 2015 to 2020, losing the 2019 UK general election to Boris Johnson's Conservatives. Since 1983, Corbyn has served as the MP for the parliamentary constituency of Islington North.

Social and political commentators have noted that many non-Londoners see London as symbolic of most of the UK's ills.[13] Many polls that seek to determine the political difference between Londoners and the rest of the UK pick up on differences in how Remain and Leave voters view London. For instance, polls tend to find that Leavers (people who voted in favor of the UK leaving the EU) have less pride in London as a capital city than those who voted Remain (i.e., for the UK to remain part of the EU). Nonetheless, the majority of both Leavers and Remainers (59 percent) still retained pride in London as a capital city, including 51 percent of people in northern England.[14] There are also differences between how Leavers and Remainers described London, for Leavers tended to hold more negative views of London, describing the capital as expensive, crowded, and dirty, while Remainers were more likely to describe London as diverse and dynamic.[15] However, around 75 percent of non-Londoners felt London contributed significantly to the UK's economy, though just 16 percent of those polled felt that London contributed to the economy where they lived.[16] This figure suggests that while the economic contribution of London to the UK is recognized in theory, non-Londoners do not believe that the contribution translates into tangible benefits for non-Londoners, something that leads to resentment of London holding political power over the UK.

In the 2019 UK general election, only four London constituencies changed hands politically: the Conservatives gained two seats but also lost two seats, and both the Labour party and the Liberal Democrats (the UK's third political party) gained and lost a seat. This means that London bucked the national trend of a swing to the Conservatives that occurred across the rest of the country. As in the 2017 general election, Labour held onto 49 of London's 73 constituencies, the Conservatives retained 21 seats, and the Liberal Democrats held 3 constituencies. Voters in the marginal constituency of Uxbridge and South Ruislip elected Boris Johnson, who increased his majority by over 2,000 votes to 7,210, despite widespread speculation before the election that he might lose his seat.[17]

The UK's post-Brexit future remains extremely unclear, though the government's economic forecasts suggest that whatever happens in terms of the UK's post-Brexit negotiations with the EU, Brexit will have a greater negative economic impact on areas of the UK outside of London. In contrast, London may experience the smallest negative economic impact of any part of the UK, something that may deepen anti-London sentiments outside of the capital. Brexit is both a symbol and a cause of London's otherness, for it highlights differences between the city and the rest of the UK, as well as the disjunct between the UK's urban and rural areas, the north and the south, and England and the rest of the UK (i.e., Scotland, Wales, and Northern Ireland). While the EU referendum threw light on the increasing political, economic, and cultural gap between London and the rest of the UK, at the same time, Brexit may also provide opportunities to

Table 4.1   Modern Elected London Mayors: Name, Party (if Any), Years in Office

Ken Livingstone	Independent Labour	2000–2004
		2004–2008
Boris Johnson	Conservative	2008–2012
		2012–2016
Sadiq Khan	Labour	2016–present

DID YOU KNOW?   CHIEF MOUSER TO THE CABINET OFFICE: THE DOWNING STREET CAT

"Chief Mouser to the Cabinet Office" is the title given to the official resident cat of the British prime minister, though the cats do not necessarily belong to the prime minister. It is thought a resident cat has been kept by the government since the 1500s, when Cardinal Thomas Wolsey sat with his cat while serving as Henry VIII's lord chancellor. While modern records of the government cat start in 1929, in 1909 Frilly was listed on the official payroll. Though other cats have served Downing Street as both a mouser and pet, the present incumbent, Larry, is the first to hold the official title. The longest-serving cat was Wilberforce, who served under four different prime ministers: Edward Heath, Harold Wilson, Jim Callaghan, and Margaret Thatcher. The first official cat to capture the British public's imagination was Wilberforce's successor, Humphrey, who is reputed to have been given a tin of sardines by Thatcher that she brought home from Moscow. Larry, who has held the position since 2011, was brought in to control a Downing Street rat problem. It is rumored that Larry failed to get along with the then chancellor George Osborne's cat, Freya, and had a fractious relationship with the Foreign Office's much younger cat, Palmerston. However, in August 2020, Palmerston "retired" to spend time in the countryside. You can follow Larry on Twitter: @Number10cat.

improve relations between the various parts of the UK and reconsider how the UK is governed. Indeed, Brexit may represent a chance to help those non-Londoners who feel disenfranchised from London-based politics to reconnect both with national and local politics. It may well be necessary for London-based politics to reengage with the rest of the UK if good relations are to be restored between London and the rest of the UK. Further, the Northern Powerhouse (a government program to boost northern England's economic growth through improving local economies while simultaneously devolving powers to elected representatives in the north) may help rebalance some of the power within the UK, repositioning the UK's political power and economy away from London.

NOTES

1. Tony Travers, *The Politics of London: Governing an Ungovernable City* (London: Palgrave Macmillan, 2003).

2. "Council Tax," London Councils, https://www.londoncouncils.gov.uk/our-key-themes/local-government-finance/local-taxation-council-tax-and-business-rates/council-tax.

3. Esther Webber, "The Rise and Fall of the GLC," *BBC News*, https://www.bbc.co.uk/news/uk-england-london-35716693.

4. Reuters Staff, "Factbox: Incoming PM Johnson's Record as London Mayor," Reuters, July 23, 2019, https://uk.reuters.com/article/uk-britain-eu-johnson-record-factbox/factbox-incoming-pm-johnsons-record-as-london-mayor-idUKKCN1UI1TV.

5. "Boris Johnson: What's His Track Record?" *BBC News*, July 23, 2019, https://www.bbc.co.uk/news/uk-politics-48663963.

6. Heather Saul, "Boris Johnson's £60m Cable Cars Used Regularly by Just Four Commuters," *The Independent*, November 21, 2013, https://www.independent.co.uk/news/uk/politics/boris-johnsons-60m-cable-cars-used-regularly-by-just-four-commuters-8954646.html.

7. Susana Mendonça, "Sadiq Khan's First 12 Months as London's Mayor," *BBC News*, May 8, 2017, https://www.bbc.co.uk/news/uk-england-london-39815592.

8. Joe Murphy and Jonathan Prynn, "The Sadiq Khan Audit: Evening Standard Investigation Reveals Mayor Is Way behind Target on New Homes, and Violent Crime and Robberies Rise," *Evening Standard*, September 3, 2018, https://www.standard.co.uk/news/mayor/the-sadiq-khan-audit-standard-investigation-reveals-mayor-is-way-behind-target-on-new-homes-and-a3926246.html.

9. Ibid.

10. Chujan Sivathasan, "How Does London's Politics Differ from the Rest of England? Let's Look at the Data," City Metric, November 11, 2019, https://www.citymetric.com/politics/how-does-london-s-politics-differ-rest-england-s-let-s-look-data-4845.

11. Ibid.

12. Roch Dunin-Wasowicz, "London Calling Brexit: How the Rest of the UK Views the Capital," *LSE Blog*, November 13, 2018, https://blogs.lse.ac.uk/brexit/2018/11/13/london-calling-brexit-how-the-rest-of-the-uk-views-the-capital.

13. Ibid.

14. Ibid.

15. Ibid.

16. Ibid.

17. Ross Lydall, "London Election Results Map 2019: How Did the Capital Vote in the UK General Election?" *Evening Standard*, December 13, 2019, https://www.standard.co.uk/news/politics/london-election-results-map-2019-uk-general-election-vote-a4312801.html.

5

Economy

Over recent years, London has proven itself to be a thriving capital city with a strong economy. At present, London's economy has many specializations, including professional, scientific, and technical services; finance; and information services and communications. Other key areas of the London economy include the hospitality, retail, arts, and tourism sectors.

London is arguably more important internationally than any other UK city and, moreover, one of only a few truly global cities along with the likes of New York, Tokyo, and Paris. London's position on the world stage means the city attracts direct foreign investment that results, ultimately, in jobs and investment elsewhere in the UK. London contributes a disproportionately large amount to the UK's economy, for while Londoners make up only 13 percent of the UK's population, London is responsible for 23 percent of the national economy.[1] Indeed in 2019, the UK's Office for National Statistics (ONS) highlighted London's disproportionate economic might by revealing that during the period from 2012 to 2019, London's economic growth outshone the growth in all other regions of England by 19 percent. In contrast, northeastern England saw economic growth of just 5.9 percent. However, the ONS also revealed that quarterly data for 2018 showed London's economy had experienced zero growth in the last three months of 2018, largely because London's financial services sector had flagged due to uncertainty over whether the UK would opt for

Brexit, that is, leave the European Union (EU).[2] Brexit also caused London's building industry to stall as projects were suspended over financial concerns over whether London will retain its position as a global city once the UK leaves the EU.

London is located in an area that is sometimes referred to as the Wider South East, an economic megaregion that comprises Greater London plus southeastern and eastern England. The Wider South East is the only part of the UK that contributes more in taxation than it receives in public expenditure, an economic situation that is known as a fiscal surplus. Furthermore, of all the areas of the Wider South East megaregion, London's fiscal surplus is especially high, as seen in the 2016–2017 period, when London contributed £32.6 billion more to the national purse than the city received in public spending. The money London contributes to the fiscal surplus is redistributed around the UK, financing infrastructure such as hospitals, schools, and transport. Indeed, if London declared itself independent of the rest of the UK, the rest of the country would quickly become bankrupt.[3]

London receives many benefits in return for its contribution to the nation's finances. For example, in 2016–2017, Greater London received the most public spending per person of anywhere in England. Much of London's public spending comes in the form of capital investment, usually in the form of infrastructure projects, such as the Crossrail train line, that overwhelmingly benefit London and surrounding areas. The benefits that London receives breed resentment among some non-Londoners. However, many economists argue that the resentment felt toward London on account of the benefits the capital receives is misplaced, for Londoners suffer from high living and housing costs that mean the average Londoner is actually worse off financially than people living elsewhere in the UK. That Londoners are often worse off than people living outside London is especially true for households that earn a lower-than-average income, for while London is home to some of the UK's wealthiest areas, the city is also home to some of the UK's most deprived communities. Additionally, London's child poverty rates are the highest of anywhere in the UK, and between 2009–2010 and 2017–2018, London suffered a disproportionate 30 percent of all local authority spending cuts in Britain.[4] Some commentators suggest this situation may worsen in the future as the result of factors that include Brexit and any COVID-19-induced recession.

LONDON EMPLOYMENT

The makeup of London's economy has changed significantly over the last 40 years, for there has been a significant decrease in manufacturing in

London alongside a large increase in the professional and business services industries. Overall, the total number of jobs in London has risen from 4.6 million in 1971 to 5.5 million in 2015. Over this period, employment has more than trebled in professional services, real estate, scientific positions, and technical industries, rising from an estimated 279,000 jobs in 1971 to 877,000 jobs in 2015. In contrast, jobs in London's manufacturing sector declined rapidly, from 872,000 in 1971 to 128,000 jobs in 2015.[5] Between 1971 and 2015, the number of Londoners employed in the arts, entertainment, and recreation sectors increased from 121,000 to 201,000, while jobs in the administrative and support services rose from 327,000 to 550,000. Meanwhile, since 1996, London has seen a great increase in information and communication roles (up 180,000 to 426,000 jobs), education (up 195,000 to 423,000), and health care and social work (up 191,000 to 545,000). In 2015, roughly 90 percent of all London jobs were in the service sector.[6]

While Outer London is home to 60 percent of Londoners, 62 percent of jobs are located in Inner London, a pattern that has remained largely unchanged since 1971. However, between 1971 and 2014, Greater London's population increased by almost 950,000 residents, while during the same period the number of jobs increased by 400,000 jobs.[7] Following a rise in unemployment across London from the early 1980s to mid-1990s, employment growth has been fastest in Inner London, while employment rates in Outer London have remained fairly stable. Today, 39 percent of Inner London employment occurs in four highly specialized sectors: information and communication, finance and insurance, real estate, and professional, scientific, and technical services. However, these sectors account for less than 17 percent of Outer London employment. Instead, in Outer London, 23 percent of jobs are in education, health care, and social work, while 25 percent of jobs are in retail, the transport sector, and storage businesses.[8] Recently, there has been significant employment growth in areas around Heathrow Airport as well as around London City Airport, in East London, and Stratford, also in East London, where the growth is related to the Queen Elizabeth Olympic Park and Westfield shopping center.

Indeed, employment in London has long seen certain types of employment concentrated in specific areas. For instance, Hatton Garden, in Holborn, has long been associated with jewelers and the diamond trade, Harley Street, in Marylebone, is synonymous with medical services, and Fleet Street, which is mostly located within the City of London, is the home of the British press. Employment in London's professional, scientific, and technical services, finance, and information services and communications industries is concentrated in inner-city areas. This is apparent in figures from 2014 showing that over 70 percent of jobs in the City of London,

50 percent of jobs in Tower Hamlets, and 33 percent of jobs in Camden, Islington, Southwark, and Westminster were associated with these specialities.[9] Richmond upon Thames and Kingston upon Thames, in South West London, also have pockets of workers employed in these industries, as do areas bordering central London. Central London also draws in visitors and tourists who, in turn, support jobs in hospitality, accommodation, food and drink, the arts and entertainment, and retail services. However, in 2014, the retail, accommodation, and food and drink sectors accounted for around one in three jobs in the West London Borough of Kensington and Chelsea, one in four jobs in the London Borough of Newham, in East London, and one in five jobs in the London Borough of Haringey, in North London.[10]

Employment in much of Outer London, as well as in the Inner London Boroughs of Wandsworth and Lewisham, tends to revolve around serving the local population in the health-care and education sectors, business administration and support services, and retail. In some parts of Outer East and Outer West London, employment is focused on industrial sectors that require greater land use, such as transport, storage, and manufacturing. For example, Waltham Forest in Outer East London is home to the Temple Mills Depot that maintains the Eurostar international rail network, while in the Outer West London areas of Hillingdon and Hounslow, many people work in jobs connected to nearby Heathrow Airport. These areas of Outer West London are unusual, for the jobs associated with Heathrow exist alongside a relatively high rate of employment in information and communication roles, as well as in the professional, scientific, and technical industries.

Different areas of London are associated with different industries. On the whole, central London is associated with high-status employment in business, industry, public services, and scientific and technical activities. A workforce of 1.8 million people exists in the areas of Camden, the City of London and Westminster in Inner West London.[11] The information and communication services, accommodation and food and drink services, and administrative and support services are also major employment sectors in central London. In Kensington and Chelsea, 23,000 people work in retail while 19,000 are employed in accommodation and food and drink services. The reliance on these sectors for employment is likely because this area of London is popular with visitors. In suburban Wandsworth, the main areas of employment are health care and social work and retail and education. Meanwhile, in the West London Borough of Ealing, the retail sector is the largest employer. However, Ealing is unusual: it is the London borough with the largest manufacturing sector, with products made in the borough including ready-prepared foods, clothes, and bicycles.

LONDON'S EMPLOYMENT SECTORS

Information and Communications Sector

London's information and communications sector divides into two main areas: publishing and communications and information technology. Jobs in publishing and communications are concentrated in central Inner London as well as in London's southwest. In particular, Inner West London is associated with the publishing of books and periodicals, for many major publishers have offices in the area; they include Penguin Random House, in Westminster, and Bloomsbury Publishing, in Camden. Indeed, 15 percent of workers in the West London borough of Hammersmith and Fulham are employed in the information and communications sector, making the sector the borough's largest employment sector.[12] Employment in information technology is concentrated mainly in the Inner London Boroughs of Westminster, Tower Hamlets, Islington, and Camden, as well as the City of London. Computer programming and highly specialized technology jobs are also major employers in the Outer London areas of Greenford, Feltham, and Hounslow, which are home to technology companies such as IBM, Sega Europe, and Cisco.

Film, television, and music production are concentrated in Outer West London, however. For example, the London Borough of Ealing and surrounding areas are notable for being home to many people employed in the film and television industry. Until recently, the BBC had offices in nearby White City, and many BBC employees continue to live in the area. Sky UK has offices and studios in Isleworth, just across the Ealing–Hounslow boundary. A number of television and cinema businesses are located in nearby Chiswick, while Ealing itself is home to Ealing Studios, which is world famous for its film and television productions.

Finance and Insurance Sector

London's financial and insurance sector is highly concentrated in the City of London and the Inner London borough of Tower Hamlets, which borders the City of London to the east. The City of London is one of the world's most important financial centers, home to the headquarters of numerous international finance and insurance companies, including Aviva, Standard Chartered, and the Lloyd Banking Group. The London Stock Exchange, the Lloyd's of London insurance and reinsurance market, and the Bank of England are also based in the area. In the South Outer London Boroughs of Bromley and Croydon, many people are employed in supporting roles in the financial and insurance services, with around 1 in 20 people in Bromley and 1 in 23 people in Croydon employed in such roles.[13]

Professional, Scientific, and Technical Industries

The professional services sector (i.e., services that provide customized, knowledge-based services to clients) is London's largest employment sector. Jobs in this sector are particularly concentrated in central Inner London, especially in the boroughs of Camden, Islington, Southwark, Tower Hamlets, and Westminster as well as the City of London. Indeed, two out of three jobs in London within the legal, accounting, advertising, and market research services are located in these boroughs. The Outer boroughs of Richmond upon Thames, in South West London, and Harrow, in North West London, are also home to many people who work in this sector. Richmond upon Thames is particularly related to scientific research and development, for the area includes several scientific parks and research centers associated with Royal Botanic Gardens, Kew, and the National Physical Laboratory (the UK's national measurement laboratory). Pockets of employment in the professional services are located elsewhere in Outer London, with the likes of GlaxoSmithKline (GSK) based in Brentford, Fujitsu Laboratories of Europe in Hillingdon, and Ipsos Mori in Harrow. Richmond upon Thames, Wimbledon, and Hammersmith are also the location of the head offices of many international companies. For example, Richmond upon Thames is home to eBay and Paypal Europe, Wimbledon is the UK base for the beauty company Coty UK and Lidl supermarkets, and Hammersmith is home to Sony Mobile, Walt Disney, and L'Oréal, among others. Hillingdon is also home to the business parks Stockley Park, Uxbridge Business Park, and Hayes Park, which are the location of the head offices for companies that include Canon, Toshiba, and Heinz, while the Bedfont Lakes office park in Hounslow contains the base for the Swiss confectionery company Lindt & Sprüngli UK. Other multinational companies with their head offices located in Outer London include McDonald's (in East Finchley), Diageo (in Brent), Danone (in Chiswick), and Unilever (in Kingston upon Thames). Employment in administrative and support services is located across Outer London, especially in West London around the River Thames and Heathrow, as well as in boroughs of South, North, and North East London. For example, in Lambeth, South London, 24,100 people are employed in this sector.[14]

Retail

The retail sector is a major employer across the UK but especially in London, where the sector accounts for around 400,000 jobs or 9 percent of all employment. London's retail industry contributes significantly to the city's economy, for the sector accounts for 40 percent of all money spent in London.

Clothes shops are the most common specialist retail shops in London and account for roughly 78,000 jobs. The next most common type of specialty shop is food shops, of which there are 22,000, including bakers and butchers. Bookshops, chemists (pharmacies), electrical goods, furniture shops, and hardware shops constitute the third most common type of shops in London, providing approximately 10,000 jobs each. In London, the market share of nonspecialist big retailers has been increasing recently. Many of the major chain stores have outlets in central London, while Oxford Street, Regent Street, and New Bond Street are home to flagship stores. London is also famous for its numerous street markets, which include markets exclusively devoted to food and drink, markets at which crafters and artisans sell, and vintage fairs that feature, antique, pre-loved and retro items.[15]

Retail is an especially important employment sector in the borough of Kensington and Chelsea, where one in five jobs falls under the retail sector.[16] Major local employers include the Harrods, Peter Jones, and Harvey Nichols department stores as well as the Whole Foods megastore. Outer London's large shopping malls and retail parks, such as the Brent Cross Shopping Centre and Wembley Retail Park, in Brent; Ealing Broadway Shopping Centre, in Ealing; Westfield Stratford City, in Newham; the Bentall Centre in Kingston upon Thames; and the Whitgift Centre in Croydon also provide many employment opportunities. Additionally, the UK's two biggest shopping malls, Bluewater, in Kent, and Lakeside, in Essex, are situated just outside London. As well as established shops belonging to chains and major retailers, London is also home to numerous independent shops that give local communities their individuality while also providing residents with essential services. Pitshanger Lane, in Ealing, is a prime example of a "high street" or main street comprising independent retailers; it won the title of London's best high street in the 2016 Great British High Street competition.

Hospitality

London attracts huge numbers of visitors, both tourists and business travelers. Consequently, London is home to numerous hotels, guesthouses, and other forms of accommodation as well as a thriving restaurant scene and food and drink sector. Visitors to London are not confined to just central areas, for Outer London also contains many famous sites, including Greenwich and Kew. The location of transport hubs such as Heathrow Airport and some travelers' preference to stay near such hubs combine to prompt many hotels to be located close to London airports and train stations.

As is the case with retail, the borough of Kensington and Chelsea sees many residents work in the accommodation industry; in 2014, 6,000 of the residents worked in accommodation, while 12,900 worked in jobs related to food and drink services. One of the reasons for this is that the borough is home to large hotels, including the Mandarin Oriental.[17] Jobs in the London arts, entertainment, and recreation scene are strongly concentrated in Lambeth (3,300 jobs), Westminster (11,200 jobs), and Camden (4,100 jobs). The sector is also an important employer in Hammersmith and Fulham (5,500 jobs), Richmond upon Thames (4,900 jobs), and Kingston upon Thames (3,500 jobs).[18] This is because Hammersmith is home to sites including the Apollo entertainment venue and the Lyric theater, Richmond upon Thames contains Twickenham Stadium and Hampton Court Place which both serve as venues for events, and Kingston upon Thames is home to Chessington World of Adventures theme park. Besides Twickenham Stadium (the home of English rugby), other London sporting venues that employ local people include numerous soccer and cricket grounds and the All England Lawn Tennis and Croquet Club (the location of the Wimbledon tennis championship), though employment at such venues is often seasonal or only during events.

Public Sector

Most London jobs in public administration are concentrated in Westminster, where 58,200 people work in the sector. As well as local authority jobs, Westminster is also the home of the UK parliament, with government offices located around Whitehall. Consequently, this sector accounts for 9 percent of all jobs in the borough.[19] Across London, universities and hospitals are also major employers in their locales. Tertiary education is a particularly big employer in the Bloomsbury area of Camden, which is home to numerous faculties and universities. Similarly, many people working in roles associated with hospitals can be found in Lambeth, which is home to King's College Hospital and St. Thomas' Hospital.

London Business

London is home to numerous businesses and workplaces. This is true particularly of the subregion of London referred to in the mayor of London's London Plan spatial development blueprint as the Central Activities Zone (CAZ). The CAZ comprises the City of London, much of Westminster, and the inner areas of the boroughs of Camden, Islington, Hackney, Tower Hamlets, Southwark, Lambeth, Kensington and Chelsea, and Wandsworth. The zone is uniquely important to London as it is the location not just of government offices, headquarters, and embassies but also the largest concentration of London's financial and business services and the offices of trade, professional institutions, and businesses associated with communications, publishing, advertising, and the media. Significant concentrations of workplaces also occur elsewhere in London, however. This is especially true of West London, and the various Strategic Industrial Locations (SILs, part of the London Plan's spatial development framework), such as the River Road employment area in the East London borough of Barking and Dagenham.

Across London, however, 86 percent of all workplaces are part of very small businesses that typically employ fewer than 10 employees, with the figure rising to 90 percent in the boroughs of Barnet, Haringey, Hounslow, Islington, and Richmond. In contrast, in the City of London, only 76 percent of workplaces employ fewer than 10 people.[20] Throughout London, small and medium-sized businesses (SMEs) that have fewer than 249 employees constitute 99 percent of all businesses, but they account for just over half of all London employment and just less than half of London's income. Therefore, while companies that employ 250 or more employees are less widespread in London, they employ almost half of all of London's workforce and account for over half of London's turnover.[21] These workplaces form a belt that runs from West London through central London and out to pockets of South London and North London.

Due to the competitive nature of business in London, start-up rates are much higher than those elsewhere in the UK. The net start-up rates are highest in East Inner London and East and North Outer London. Although the start-up rates for London were negative during the 2009 recession, they have increased since and continue to rise. The highest number of start-ups can be found in the CAZ and the area dubbed the NIOD (northern Isle of Dogs, an area of East London). Start-up businesses across London provide jobs for the city's workers. Theoretically, the relatively high potential earnings on offer from start-ups should increase the size of an area's workforce by attracting both local workers and talent from afar. Moreover, as wages rise, other workers will enter an industry, while people who are unemployed (including those in education) will join the industry in search of higher rewards; thus earnings reflect the demand for workers, especially those with specialist skills.

In 2015, average hourly pay for workers throughout London was £15.80 as opposed to the UK average of £11.80. The figure was even in higher in Inner London, for the average hourly pay in Inner London was £17.50, reflecting that Inner London is the location for numerous specialized, high-value industries. Indeed, in the City of London, the average hourly pay is £24.20 per hour, whereas in neighboring Hackney, it is £13.65. The Hackney rate is still higher than the average hourly rate for workers living in Outer London, however, for Outer London workers receive an average hourly pay rate of £13.15. Examples of below-average hourly pay exist in the Outer London Boroughs of Bexley (£11.70), Enfield (£11.60), Harrow (£10.90), and Waltham Forest (£11.00). West Outer London tends to have higher rates of average pay, however, as they are home to specialized industries. Consequently, relatively higher average earnings can be found in Hounslow (£15.90), Hillingdon (£14.40), and Richmond upon Thames (£14.35).[22]

The lower average hourly pay received by workers in Outer London is offset partly by the fact that living costs in Outer London are usually lower than those in Inner London. In order to help London workers and their families afford the cost of living and save for the future, some London employers have signed up for the London Living Wage (LLW), an hourly pay rate currently set at £10.75. As of 2019, 60,000 Londoners working for 1,758 employers received the LLW. The pay rate is calculated independently to reflect the high cost of living in London, and so the LWW is set at a higher rate than the UK's National Living Wage (the UK's minimum hourly wage rate), which is set at £9.30.[23] Workers in and around London are also helped by the London weighting, an allowance paid to people in certain jobs (civil servants, teachers, airline employees, police and security officers) as well as doctoral students. The London weighting is designed to help workers with their living costs, thereby encouraging essential workers to remain in Greater London. The concept of the London weighting was introduced in 1920 to help civil servants, and since 1974, the program has operated as a partnership run by the UK government and the Greater London Council (and subsequently the mayor of London). In some professions, such as teaching, a different level of weighting is applied, depending on whether an employer exists in Inner London or Outer London. Additionally, many employers implement different pay grades rather than a fixed rate, while some employees, such as the police, receive both a London weighting and an extra allowance.

According to the 2011 UK census, 795,100 non-Londoners over 16 years of age work in the city. This figure is offset to a degree by the 273,700 Londoners who work elsewhere in the UK. This means that every working day, London has a net inflow of 521,400 commuters. Westminster and the City of London (824,500 people) and Camden (164,100 people) see the largest net inflow of commuters, while Wandsworth experiences the biggest net outflow, at 60,700 commuters.[24] Typically, only 27 percent of Londoners live in the borough in which they work. Contrastingly, 55 percent of London workers travel to work in a different borough to the one in which they live, while 18 percent commute into London from outside the city.[25]

LONDON UNEMPLOYMENT

In the first quarter of 2020, London's unemployment rate rose from 4.3 percent to 4.7 percent, as the economy shut down due to the COVID-19 pandemic.[26] Official research showed that in April 2020, unemployment increased by 1.2 million across Great Britain. In London, this was an increase of 145,000 over the previous month, an increase of 33 percent. At the same time, the number of people claiming universal credit (a state benefit paid by the UK government to help people who are unemployed or earn low wages) rose by 80 percent, which was 10 percent more than the number for Great Britain in general.[27]

It is likely that the Coronavirus Business Retention Scheme (the UK government's initiative to help businesses retain furloughed staff during the COVID-19 pandemic, thereby preventing mass layoffs) kept unemployment at a lower level than if the program had not been implemented. While the unemployment figures for London were lower than during the 1980s, a period notorious in Britain for its high unemployment rates, the figures reveal that unemployment in London has risen significantly since the start of 2020. Across the UK, the lowest earners before the COVID-19 pandemic have become unemployed at a rate four times quicker than the highest earners (8 percent rather than 2 percent), while 18- to 24-year-olds are twice as likely to have been furloughed or lost their job as those ages 40 to 49 years.[28] People in atypical employment, such as temporary and agency workers, were far more likely to have become unemployed than were the self-employed and workers in more usual jobs.

LONDON POVERTY

According to official figures, around 2.5 million Londoners live in relative poverty,[29] meaning they live in households whose income is less than 60 percent of the national average. Over the last six years, the number of Londoners living in poverty has fallen from 29 percent to 27 percent. However, this figure is still higher than the figure for the rest of England (21 percent). While the rate of poverty has decreased, the depth of the poverty has increased, for the proportion of London households whose income is less than half the average UK income has risen by 1.5 percent over the last five years. This increase reflects the fact that in London, wealth inequality is a significant issue. Indeed, according to the poverty charity Trust for London, 50 percent of London's poorest households own just over 5 percent of London's wealth, while the wealthiest 10 percent of households own over half of the city's wealth.[30]

Following the EU referendum, the sterling-euro exchange rate fell by 11 percent before falling a further 4 percent in July 2019, when a no-deal Brexit became more likely. Exchange-rate devaluations result in higher import prices and inflation and thus make people worse off. Consequently, the Bank of England has warned that, in the long term post-Brexit, sterling may depreciate by 5 percent, leading to higher prices for food and drink.[31] A no-deal Brexit may also lead to additional tariffs and lower wages, both of which may increase prices. According to UK government research, food, fuel, and medicine might also be in short supply if a no-deal Brexit were to happen. Such changes would impact low-income households the most, and the impact would be felt most keenly in London, which has higher poverty levels than the rest of the UK. London's low-income households have already suffered disproportionately under the government's austerity measures and welfare reform, and these households are the most likely of any London households to lose work if a recession were to occur. On a more positive note, increases in London house prices and rental rates have eased, though this may be because households are unwilling to commit to buying or renting new properties due to uncertainties surrounding Brexit.

At 32 percent, the poverty level for Inner London is considerably higher than that of Outer London (26 percent). However, in recent years, the poverty rate in Outer London has increased slightly. Around 1.5 million Londoners of working age, or one in four London workers, are shown to live in poverty once their housing costs are taken into account. Of this figure, around 60 percent of working-age Londoners live in what is classified as persistent poverty.[32] At the same time, however, the average London income, before housing costs are taken into account, is £589 per week, which is higher than in any other UK region, for elsewhere the average comparable income is £517. London's higher income results not only from higher wages but also from the fact that Londoners receive higher levels of housing benefit: more London households live in private, rented accommodation, so their costs are higher. Consequently, the amount paid to Londoners in state housing benefit and universal credit contribute to higher levels of income in London before housing costs are taken into account. In London, private housing rents are more than double that of the average cost for England in general, so, for example, renting the cheapest possible two-bedroom home in London will cost around £1,250 per month while elsewhere in England, a comparable home would cost £500 per month. Since the cost of London housing is significantly more expensive than elsewhere, the average figure for incomes after housing costs are accounted for is only slightly higher than for the whole of the UK (£454 per week in London vs. £448 for the UK).[33] Indeed, the high cost of housing in London is the main reason for London's high level of relative poverty. Over the past five years, the growth in private home rentals has also grown fastest in London, at a rate of 20 percent compared to a rate of 8 percent across England.[34] Therefore, Londoners are more likely to live in private, rented accommodations than other people in England.

Children in London are more likely to live in poverty than are adults, for 39 percent of London's children live in poverty. This percentage represents around 800,000 children and means that more children currently live in low-income households than at any time since data was first collected in 1994–1995. After housing costs are taken into account, the percentage of Inner London children who live in poverty rises to 45 percent, while 35 percent of children in Outer London live in poverty.[35] Most children in London who live in poverty are part of a working household. However, London children who live in households in which adults are unemployed are more likely to be in poverty than those who live in working households. Material deprivation, as opposed to poverty, affects many London children. In the UK, the term *material deprivation* is usually taken to mean that a household is unable to afford items considered essential to life, such as children's winter coats, daily fresh fruit and vegetables, and an annual holiday. In London, 45 percent of children are

JONAS HANWAY (1712–1786): LONDON'S UMBRELLA PIONEER

DID YOU KNOW?

Following his father's death, Hanway's family moved to London from Portsmouth. In 1729, Hanway was apprenticed to a merchant in Portugal, and then in 1743, after several years in business in London, Hanway entered into a business partnership with a Russian merchant. Subsequently, Hanway traveled throughout Russia and Persia. During his travels, Hanway experienced attacks by pirates and the confiscation of his possessions. Having survived these experiences, Hanway traveled back to England via Germany and the Netherlands. Hanway spent most of the remainder of his life in London, where his travel memoirs made him famous.

Over time, Hanway gained a reputation as a philanthropist. In 1756, Hanway was the chief founder of the Marine Society, the world's oldest public maritime charity. Through the Marine Society, Hanway enabled destitute boys to acquire naval training. The training allowed the boys to develop a career when few other opportunities were available to them. In 1758, Hanway became a governor of London's Foundling Hospital, a children's home that cared for abandoned children. Hanway was also instrumental in the establishment of the Magdalen Hospital, a refuge for prostitutes that allowed the women to rehabilitate back into society. In 1761, Hanway instigated an improved system of birth registration in London. A memorial to Hanway stands in the Westminster Abbey. However, despite his many achievements, Hanway is best known for being the first man in London to carry an umbrella and for helping to popularize the use of umbrellas in England.

classified as materially deprived, compared to 38 percent across the rest of England.[36]

Recently, poverty among London pensioners has risen rapidly to a rate of almost 1 in 4 (or 24 percent) after housing costs. This is in contrast to the rest of the UK, where pensioners are more likely to be classified as living in poverty before their housing costs are taken into account. The difference between London and the rest of the UK is that while many of London's pensioners own their homes and so do not have to pay high housing costs, more London pensioners rent their homes than pensioners elsewhere in the UK. Around 1 in 10 London pensioners are classified as living in persistent poverty, which means they have lived in poverty for at least three out of the last four years. Material deprivation among Londoner pensioners is far higher than elsewhere in the UK, for 13 percent of London pensioners are unable to afford or access such essentials as a dampness-free home or a telephone. The number of materially deprived pensioners in London has fallen recently, though at present, 19 percent of pensioners in Inner London are classified as suffering material deprivation.[37]

LONDON'S FUTURE: BREXIT AND BEYOND

In 2016, the UK voted narrowly in favor of leaving the EU. Originally, Brexit was expected to occur in March 2019, but an extension was agreed to that extended the UK's EU membership until the end of January 2020. The future level of the UK's involvement with the EU is unresolved currently, though, and many potential outcomes have been suggested, all of which will affect London differently. By October 2018, businesses' uncertainty over Brexit meant the UK's economy lost an estimated 2 to 2.5 percent of its GDP, while by October 2019, the loss in GDP was closer to 3 percent.[38] In the short term, a general global economic slowdown coupled with the adverse effects of leaving the EU and economic damage caused by the COVID-19 pandemic may slow London's economy. By February 2021, the number of Londoners receiving government furlough payments stood at 710,800, a figure 2 percent above the UK average. While those on furlough were not classed as unemployed, as the job retention scheme winds down progressively more of these workers may become jobless. Indeed, as of May 2021, the COVID-19 pandemic had increased London's unemployment rate by 8.2 percent.[39] The Organisation for Economic Co-operation and Development (OECD) predicts that the UK's post-pandemic unemployment will peak at the end of 2021 as the Coronavirus Job Retention Scheme is withdrawn.

While many business leaders feel London will be able to recover from COVID-19, it is unknown how exactly the impact of the pandemic will intertwine with the ramifications of Brexit. The arrival of COVID-19 masked somewhat the impact of new post-Brexit strictures on immigration and trading so it is hard to distinguish Brexit's most recent impact on London's economy. In the longer term, it is likely that leaving the EU will reduce London's position as a welcoming, global hub, for it will cease to enjoy the free movement of goods, people, services, and capital across international borders that it enjoyed when the UK was part of the EU. The introduction of tariffs, customs, and nontariff barriers (NTBs, trade barriers that restrict the import and exports of goods and services through mechanisms other than tariffs) will increase costs for businesses and will probably make some businesses unviable. While some economists have theorized that a no-deal Brexit will cause London less economic damage than elsewhere in the UK, it remains the case that a no-deal Brexit will most likely cause London economic harm.

Some economists believe the finance, information, communications, and professional services industries that dominate London's economy will experience decreased productivity associated with an economic shift in terms of economic activity and employment. This fall in productivity will likely be caused by uncertainty surrounding the UK's future trading relationship with the EU. London has already seen the number of business closures rise while the number of business start-ups has fallen from 6.1 percent in 2016 to 1.0 percent in 2017.[40]

London is the world's leading recipient of foreign direct investment (FDI) and is the location for numerous companies' European or global headquarters. It is possible that Brexit will make London seem insular, while the possible introduction of immigration controls will make London less attractive to international companies looking for bases for their headquarters. Immigration controls may also reduce the number of high-skilled workers able to come to London. Foreign migrants contribute disproportionately to London's economy, with 14 percent of jobs in London held by workers from the European Economic Area (the EU member states plus Iceland, Liechtenstein, and Norway). Only 6 percent of London jobs are held by workers from elsewhere in the UK.[41] However, in the year ending March 2019, work-related migration from EU member states to the UK fell from 190,000, in the year ending June 2016, to 92,000.[42] This reduction suggests that Brexit may already be deterring workers from within the EU from settling in London and elsewhere in the UK. At the same time, however, the number of students from outside the EU who are going to the UK has risen, because a lower exchange rate makes the UK more financially attractive. This rise benefits London's universities while potentially providing London with a more skilled workforce in the future.

However, while the UK government has suggested that it will implement a skills-based immigration system post-Brexit, 60 percent of jobs held by EEA workers in London will not fall under the proposed skills criteria. Additionally, 33 percent of jobs in London are considered lower-skilled occupations under the new proposals, meaning the EEA workers in these roles would not meet the proposed qualification threshold.[43]

Up to September 2019, consumer confidence in London remained positive, unlike in the rest of the UK. This situation was likely fueled by London's fairly healthy labor market and increases in real wages. However, despite consumer confidence, 60 percent of Londoners feared London's economy would either change little or worsen slightly in the near future, while 50 percent of Londoners thought Brexit would have a detrimental effect on the economy.[44]

The COVID-19 pandemic is another issue with the potential to affect London's long-term economic future. Initially, the OECD warned that the UK's economy was likely to be the hardest hit of all global economies and forecast that during 2020, the UK's economy would shrink by 11.5 percent, which would be slightly more than that of such comparable countries as Germany and France. Further, the OECD warned that a second wave of the virus would cause the UK's economy to contract by 14 percent. The reason the UK might fare worse than other, similar countries is that the UK has a mainly service-based economy, which has suffered especially badly under government-imposed lockdown restrictions. Moreover, in June 2020, the ONS revealed that the UK economy shrank by 2.2 percent between January and March 2020, which was the biggest decrease since 1979, as all sectors of the country's economic suffered at the onset of the pandemic. In 2021, however, the OECD projected the UK would experience strong GDP growth of 7.2 percent in 2021 and 5.5 percent in 2022 because a large proportion of the UK population was vaccinated and restrictions on the UK's economic activity were relaxed gradually allowing the rebound of consumption, particularly services. Ultimately the OECD predicts that the UK's GDP would return to its pre-pandemic level by early 2022.[45]

Following the UK's lockdown in March 2020, the coronavirus pandemic saw all main sectors of the economy continue to shrink significantly. While a sharp fall in consumer spending in March resulted in a significant increase in households' savings, at the same time, the UK's GDP contracted by 6.9 percent. The services sector (i.e., the financial services industry, hospitality, and tourism), which accounts for about 75 percent of the UK's GDP, shrank by a record 2.3 percent, while production output decreased by 1.5 percent as factories shut down production.[46] Meanwhile, London's position as an international travel hub suffered under the quarantine imposed by the UK's government and the travel bans implemented by other nations. As a consequence of a reduction in flights to the UK, London airports experienced a steep decline in passenger numbers. For example, Heathrow experienced a 97 percent fall in passengers,[47] leading to the airport starting a program of voluntary layoffs for its frontline workers and management. London's tourism sector and creative industries were also badly affected by the coronavirus crisis. Estimates suggest that 119,000 permanent workers in the creative industries will be laid off by the end of 2020, while 287,000 creative freelancers will be unemployed by 2021. Moreover, research by the Society of London Theatre and UK Theatre suggested that 70 percent of theaters could be bankrupt by the end of the year,[48]

An empty Covent Garden street during a COVID-19 lockdown, 2020. Londoners were ordered to stay home to combat the virus, leaving usually busy areas bereft of visitors. (VVShots/Dreamstime.com)

leading to job losses. The closure of London theaters would affect not only theater staff but also restaurants located nearby that rely on theatergoers for their clientele.

The hit taken by the UK's economy was exacerbated by the UK government opting to pay tens of billions of pounds to furloughed workers as part of the government's highly lauded decision to keep millions of furloughed workers on payrolls. The ONS's Business Impact of Coronavirus Survey (BICS) found that during the period May 18, 2020, to May 31, 2020, 30 percent of workers in the UK had been placed on furlough, with 5 percent of furloughed workers returning to work by June 14, 2020.[49] As of the end of June 2020, anecdotal reports suggest many people who worked in central London before lockdown continued to work from home even when able to return to their offices. Consequently, cafes and shops in and around London offices suffered a loss of trade. Additionally, the lockdown forced many London businesses to adapt to a working-from-home structure that may affect office demand in the city in the long-term future, as companies ponder whether they wish to pay high office-rental rates and even whether they need to have offices or headquarters in the capital. However, despite so many UK workers being furloughed, the Office for Budget Responsibility has revised down its estimated cost of the furlough program to £60 billion (a reduction of £24 billion).[50] The reduction in the estimate came about because the average wages of those being furloughed were far lower than expected.

Analysis of the furlough rates for London show great variation across the city. For example, the area of London with the highest number of furloughed workers was Hounslow, where 32 percent of workers were furloughed. This high rate may have been due to the fact that many people in Hounslow work in positions connected to Heathrow. Hounslow's rate was double that of the local authority with the lowest number of workers on furlough: Camden, where 16 percent of workers were furloughed.[51] Data from June 2020 reveals that claims for jobseeker's allowance (an unemployment benefit people can claim while looking for work) and universal credit among Londoners rose by 167 percent (around 310,000 people) between March 2020 and June, a percentage increase that was above the UK increase (126 percent). London also accounted for 20 percent of the increase in UK benefit claims over this period. The highest increase in claimants among London workers occurred among London workers between 25 and 29 years of age (an increase of 238 percent), possibly because this age group is more likely to work in pubs, restaurants, shops, and so on that were closed during lockdown. Meanwhile, Newham was the borough that experienced the largest increase in the benefit claims (16,505 extra claimants), while West Ham, Tottenham, and East Ham were the parliamentary constituencies that experienced the largest increases in claims.[52] The OECD has warned that the impact of the coronavirus pandemic will be compounded by the possibility of a no-deal Brexit, for the lack of a deal would lead to new trade barriers and, in turn, would hinder trade with the EU.

Londoners aged 25 to 64 years were most likely to struggle financially because of lockdown (13 percent), while only 4 percent of Londoners over 65 years of age claimed they were struggling financially. This is likely because Londoners in the older age group are more likely to own their own home,[53] while young Londoners are more likely to rent their accommodation and could not reduce the proportion of their income they spent on essential items, including rent and food. A typical London household spends 58 percent of its weekly budget on such essentials, the highest of any part of the UK.[54]

At the end of June 2020, the Bank of England's chief economist Andy Haldane suggested the UK's economy may experience a "V-shaped" economic recovery whereby the economy snaps back to strength quickly after a steep decline. Haldane also warned, however, that unemployment across the UK may remain in a downward spiral.[55] Whatever the future holds, it is undoubtedly true that London's economy has suffered a shock from which it will need time to recover. A great deal of uncertainty surrounds the recovery because the course of the coronavirus pandemic is unknown, and so is the final outcome of Brexit.

WORKING IN A WEST LONDON PUB DURING THE COVID-19 PANDEMIC

LIFE IN THE CITY

The place was becoming quieter after the prime minister recommended that the public should stay away from pubs. We had a lot of cancellations for Mothering Sunday lunches, usually one of our busiest days of the year, and spent one afternoon phoning the remaining guests to see if they were intending to keep their bookings. We had already canceled our weekly events, such as quiz night, and we could see that temporary closure was imminent.

Once the pub had closed, workers were placed on the furlough scheme. The scheme gave us much appreciated financial security, because we were paid our full monthly salaries for the next three months while not having to do any work. Personally, I can't see how I could complain about that. We were assured the pub would reopen, so I felt fairly relaxed about the situation. When pubs reopened on July 4, new guidelines had to be introduced for both the staff and the customers. All customers had to be seated at tables (both inside the pub and in the garden). All the tables were now spaced over a meter apart, which meant losing quite a few tables inside our tiny pub. There could only be a maximum of six guests per table, and tables had to be sanitized after every use. Menus had to be laminated for easy cleaning or, if paper, discarded after each use. The staff also had to ensure that one person from each party had signed our "Track and Trace" form. No one could now sit or linger at the bar, and we provided full table service. We also shortened our opening hours.

Customers have been divided in terms of behavior. Most were very unsure how they were supposed to act: Do you approach the bar? Can you order at the bar? Do I need a mask? and so forth. Plenty had to be told repeatedly and forcefully on how to behave in light of the guidelines, as they just reverted straight back into their usual behavior of sitting in large groups from multiple households, no distancing, table hopping, crowding the bar—the "lockdown" memory had completely disappeared. Others have been zealously cautious, refusing to use pens provided for the "Track and Trace" form and complaining that people were too noisy. The most fearful often sat in the garden, as they felt too nervous to remain indoors. To entice the public back into pubs and restaurants, the government introduced the Eat Out to Help Out scheme. For the establishments that signed up with the scheme, the government covered 50 percent of the customers' food and soft drink bill. This was, to start with, an excellent idea to help the hospitality industry across the country. The scheme ran Monday through Wednesday throughout August 2020. By the second week, the scheme had turned into an excuse for customer greed. They would buy the most expensive meals on the menu, sometimes adult portions for little children, who would never be able to eat it all. The majority of the food was then thrown away, and the demand for food outstripped supply. Wednesday nights had turned into Saturday nights. Customers were queuing onto the streets to get in, becoming verbally abusive to staff, demanding they have food, and bemoaning the fact they had to wait to be served. Sometimes we had to close the pub's kitchen early due to the sheer number of orders. The sense of "entitlement" from people had become unsavory. When the scheme ended, all the staff breathed a huge sigh of relief.

—Alexandra Williams

NOTES

1. Jack Brown, "London Is Still the UK's Golden Goose—and That Needs to Change," *The Guardian*, May 20, 2019, https://www.theguardian.com/comment isfree/2019/may/20/london-uk-economy-decentralisation.

2. Phillip Inman, "London's 19% Economic Surge Underlines Divide with Rest of England," *The Guardian*, September 5, 2019, https://www.theguardian.com /business/2019/sep/05/londons-19-economic-surge-underlines-divide-with -rest-of-england.

3. Brown, "London Is Still the UK's Golden Goose."

4. Ibid.

5. Ibid., 4.

6. Ibid., 7.

7. Ibid., 8.

8. Ibid., 10.

9. Aaron Girardi and Joel Marsden, *A Description of London's Economy*, GLA Economics Working Paper 85, March 2017, https://www.london.gov.uk/sites /default/files/description-londons-economy-working-paper-85.pdf.

10. Ibid., 2.

11. Ibid., 14.

12. Ibid., 14.

13. Ibid., 23.

14. Ibid., 26.

15. London's Economic Plan. "London's Retail Industry," UNCSBRP, http://www .uncsbrp.org/retail.htm.

16. Girardi and Marsden, *A Description of London's Economy*, 27.

17. Ibid., 28.

18. Ibid., 29.

19. Ibid., 30.

20. Ibid., 35–36.

21. Ibid., 36.

22. Ibid., 41.

23. Will Noble, "London Living Wage Has Just Risen to £10.75 an Hour," Londonist, November 11, 2019, https://londonist.com/london/news/london-living-wage -rise-10-75-2019.

24. Girardi and Marsden, *A Description of London's Economy*, 42.

25. Ibid., 43.

26. Mike Hope and Eduardo Orellana, "Return to Work Starts amid Economic Gloom," *London's Economy Today*, issue 213, May 2020, https://www.london.gov .uk/sites/default/files/londons_economy_today_no213_280520.pdf, 9.

27. Ibid., 6.

28. Nye Cominetti, Laura Gardiner, and Hannah Slaughter, *The Full Monty: Facing Up to the Challenge of the Coronavirus Labour Market Crisis*, June 2020, https://www.resolutionfoundation.org/app/uploads/2020/06/The-Full-Monty.pdf.

29. Rachel Leeser, "Poverty in London 2018/19," Greater London Authority, March 27, 2020, https://data.london.gov.uk/blog/poverty-in-london-2018-19.

30. "27% of Londoners in Poverty," 2020, https://www.trustforlondon.org.uk /news/27-londoners-poverty (site discontinued).

31. Mike Hope, *The Economic Impact of Brexit on London*, Greater London Authority, October 2019, https://www.london.gov.uk/sites/default/files/brexit -analysis-final.pdf, 2.

32. Leeser, "Poverty in London."

33. Ibid.

34. "27% of Londoners in Poverty 2018/19."

35. Leeser, "Poverty in London."

36. "Material Deprivation of Children," Trust for London, 2020, https://www .trustforlondon.org.uk/data/children-and-material-deprivation.

37. Ibid.

38. Ibid., 2.

39. William Wallis, "Can London Reinvent Itself After the Pandemic?," Financial Times, May 5, 2021, https://www.ft.com/content/952df035-d857-4c65-a91f -c33157eb0c14.

40. Ibid., 3.

41. Ibid., 2.

42. Ibid., 4.

43. *Potential Impacts of Immigration Policies Based on Skills and Salary Thresholds in London*, Greater London Authority, July 2019, https://www.london .gov.uk/sites/default/files/executive-summary-cin58-59.pdf, 7.

44. Hope, *Economic Impact of Brexit on London*, 4.

45. "United Kingdom Economic Snapshot," OECD, May 2021, https://www.oecd .org/economy/united-kingdom-economic-snapshot/.

46. "Coronavirus: UK Economy Hit by Worst Contraction in 41 Years," *BBC*, June 30, 2020, https://www.bbc.co.uk/news/business-53231851.

47. Gordon Douglass and Eduardo Orellana, "Outlook for London's Economy Remains Gloomy as Lockdown Is Eased." *London's Economy Today*, issue 214, June 2020. https://www.london.gov.uk/sites/default/files/londons_economy_today _no214_250620.pdf, 6.

48. Ibid., 6.

49. Ibid., 5.

50. Ibid.

51. Ibid.

52. Ibid., 3.

53. Douglass and Orellana, "Outlook for London's Economy," 4.

54. Ibid., 4.

55. Philip Aldrick, "UK Recovery Is Coming Sooner and Faster than Predicted, Says Bank of England's Andy Haldane," *The Times*, June 30, 2020, https://www .thetimes.co.uk/article/uk-recovery-is-coming-sooner-and-faster-than-predicted -says-bank-of-england-s-andy-haldane-08r66vstt.

FURTHER READING

Brown, Jack. "London Is Still the UK's Golden Goose—and That Needs to Change." *The Guardian*, May 20, 2019, https://www.theguardian.com/commentisfree /2019/may/20/london-uk-economy-decentralisation.

Cominetti, Nye, Laura Gardiner, and Hannah Slaughter. *The Full Monty: Facing Up to the Challenge of the Coronavirus Labour Market Crisis.* June 2020. https://www.resolutionfoundation.org/app/uploads/2020/06/The-Full -Monty.pdf.

Douglass, Gordon, and Eduardo Orellana. "Outlook for London's Economy Remains Gloomy as Lockdown Is Eased." *London's Economy Today*, issue 214, June 2020. https://www.london.gov.uk/sites/default/files/londons_economy_today _no214_250620.pdf.

Girardi, Aaron, and Joel Marsden. *A Description of London's Economy.* GLA Economics Working Paper 85, March 2017. https://www.london.gov.uk/sites /default/files/description-londons-economy-working-paper-85.pdf.

Hope, Mike. *The Economic Impact of Brexit on London.* Greater London Authority, October 2019. https://www.london.gov.uk/sites/default/files/brexit-analysis -final.pdf.

Inman, Phillip. "London's 19% Economic Surge Underlines Divide with Rest of England." *The Guardian*, September 5, 2019. https://www.theguardian .com/business/2019/sep/05/londons-19-economic-surge-underlines -divide-with-rest-of-england.

Leeser, Rachel. "Poverty in London 2018/19." Greater London Authority, March 27, 2020. https://data.london.gov.uk/blog/poverty-in-london-2018-19.

Noble, Will. "London Living Wage Has Just Risen to £10.75 an Hour." Londonist, November 11, 2019. https://londonist.com/london/news/london-living -wage-rise-10-75-2019.

Potential Impacts of Immigration Policies Based on Skills and Salary Thresholds in London. Greater London Authority, July 2019. https://www.london.gov.uk /sites/default/files/executive-summary-cin58-59.pdf.

"27% of Londoners in Poverty." Trust for London, 2020. https://www.trustforlondon .org.uk/news/27-londoners-poverty/ (site discontinued).

6

Environment and Sustainability

In 2018, London was named the world's most sustainable city. London achieved this ranking based on its status as a global economic powerhouse whose citizens enjoyed an excellent quality of life (in terms of access to health care, education, and culture) combined with environmental sustainability: London is one of the world's greenest capital cities, for it contains over 3,000 green spaces.[1]

However, London has not always fared so well in terms of the environment, especially water and air pollution.

LONDON'S WATER

Approximately 373 miles of rivers and streams flow through Greater London into the tidal Thames. This figure includes 39 rivers, of which only one is classified as having "good ecological potential" under the Water Framework Directive[2] that obliges the UK government to protect the country's water environment. The Carshalton arm of the River Wandle in South London was recently classified as having good ecological potential but subsequently saw its water quality downgraded to moderate. Work by both volunteers and the South East Rivers Trust, which manages the river, means the Wandle is likely to see the river's water quality upgraded to good again in the near future, as the river is now sufficiently clean for trout to live in its waters.[3]

London's authorities have long struggled to keep the city's waterways clean. For many hundreds of years, the River Thames has served as a dumping ground for Londoners, for the flowing river has been used as a repository for all forms of waste, including sewage, corpses, household trash, and industrial waste. Under the northern side of Tower Bridge is a waterside alcove that in the nineteenth century served as a virtual mortuary. Corpses floating in the Thames would wash up regularly on this section of the river, so on the eastern side of the bridge, steps were created that led to the water and allowed authorities to retrieve the bodies.

Historically, it was sewage entering London's rivers that proved the biggest problem. In the seventeenth century, the Rivers Fleet and Walbrook, like the Thames, were also used as sewers. Consequently, in times past, London's rivers stank in hot weather and were a source of disease. This was especially true of the Thames. Although metropolitan sewers were introduced to London in the eighteenth century, many of these sewers resulted in the formation of cesspits and cesspools that were prone to explosions caused by the accumulation of methane gas contained in the human excrement.

By the start of the nineteenth century, London had become a bustling commercial hub. As such, the city underwent a population explosion: at the start of the century, the city was home to fewer than 1 million people, but by the 1850s this population had doubled. Indeed, by the end of the nineteenth century, 1 in 5 of the UK's citizens lived in London, with 6.5 million people inhabiting Greater London.[4] The population increase left London overcrowded and placed London's public services under huge strain, especially the city's supply of fresh water and its ability to dispose of sewage and other forms of waste. Associated with these problems was how to keep London's densely packed population healthy—particularly, how to prevent outbreaks of such diseases as cholera, typhoid, tuberculosis, and smallpox. In 1832, however, 6,536 Londoners died as a result of the city's first cholera outbreak. A major cholera epidemic in 1848 and 1849 killed twice this number of Londoners, while 10,738 Londoners died in a third outbreak from 1853 to 1854.[5] The cholera outbreaks resulted from a combination of London's increasingly crowded living conditions, poor water supply system, and the failure of the city's authorities to deal with London's growing amounts of sewage and trash. One of the major problems facing London at this time was that the city's wooden water pipes dated largely from medieval times. The issue of the aging water infrastructure was exacerbated by the fact that by the mid-1800s, London was the world's richest and most powerful city, meaning many Londoners enjoyed access not only to clean drinking water but to flushing lavatories that had become standard in most houses. The human waste captured by the newfangled lavatories was flushed into the River Thames with disastrous results.

London's summer of 1858 was exceptionally hot and dry, conditions that left the city smelling noxious. The Thames became especially unpleasant in the hot weather, for, starved of rain, the river became stagnant and overflowing with human excrement, animal corpses, rotten food, and poisonous raw materials emitted by riverside factories. That year, the high temperatures combined with the Thames's severe pollution caused the event known as the Great Stink, which resulted in London's authorities finally tackling the problem of the river's water pollution. During the Great Stink, the smell from the Thames become unbearable, much to the horror of politicians sitting in the House of Commons located next to the river. In order to alleviate this problem, the politicians rushed through Parliament a bill giving the go-ahead for the construction of a new London sewer system as well as the building of the Thames Embankment, which would improve the flow of London's water and traffic. The new sewer system was masterminded by the chief engineer of the Metropolitan Board of Works, Sir Joseph Bazalgette. The sewer construction was enormously expensive, equating to between £240 million and £1 billion ($290,488,800 to $1,210,370,000).[6] Bazalgette designed an extensive underground sewer system that united London's existing patchwork of public drains. The new sewers funneled waste downstream through London before dumping the waste into the Thames Estuary during high tide. To make the sewer system functional, 1,100 miles of new drains were constructed under London. In turn, the drains fed into 82 miles[7] of newly built, brick-lined sewers that transported waste to six so-called intercepting sewers. Many of the intercepting sewers were once open streams, while some of London's rivers, including the Fleet, were lined in bricks and covered over so that they could serve as giant hidden channels of waste.

Together with John Snow's discovery that cholera originated in contaminated water, the new sewer system greatly reduced the incidence of waterborne diseases in London. This is evinced by the fact that from 1850 to 1860, in Whitechapel, East London, the death rate from typhoid (caused by ingesting contaminated water or food) stood at 116 per 100,000 but by 1890 to 1900, this rate had fallen to 13 per 100,000.[8]

The bombing London suffered during World Wars I and II destroyed sections of Bazalgette's sewer system, making it difficult for the city's authorities to keep the river clean. Postwar, London lacked the resources to repair the sewers, and some politicians doubted the need to keep the Thames clean. As a result of waste entering the river through the broken sewer system, in the late 1950s, London's Natural History Museum stated the Thames was dead biologically, while news reports from around that time describe the river as being akin to a foul-smelling open sewer that contained no oxygen for miles around London Bridge. The lack of oxygen was caused by bacteria in the water, for while bacteria help rivers break down sewage, they do this by using up oxygen, leaving no oxygen for other life-forms. From the late 1960s, however, London's sewage system was repaired gradually as part of the UK's wider postwar recovery. The repairs meant that the Thames was able to breathe once more. That said, London still has some problems in relation to sewage. Today, heavy rainfall tends to overload London's sewers. Often when the rainwater enters the sewer system it mixes with sewage before being discharged into the Thames. In order to reduce the frequency with which the rain-sewage mix enters the Thames, the Thames Tideway Tunnel that is currently being constructed will stretch from Acton in West London to Beckton in East London, going under the river's tidal section and through the center of the city. In doing so, the tunnel will capture, store, and carry virtually all the sewage and rainwater that currently flows into the Thames. The amount of sewage and rainwater needs to be reduced in order to comply with the EU's Waste Water Treatment Directive (UWWTD) as well as to improve the ecology of the river. The 16-mile-long tunnel is due for completion in 2024. Similarly, Tideway (the consortium behind the tunnel plan) is creating new areas of public open spaces to connect Londoners more closely with the river. The creation of the tunnel will also see the establishing of three acres of new public spaces along the Thames at seven locations, including the Thames Embankment and King Edward Memorial Park in East London, which will flood at high tide and allow Londoners to paddle in the Thames's clean waters.

Another major threat to London's river quality is the problem of misconnected pipes that transport pollution into London's rivers via the city's surface water drainage system. When domestic appliances are misconnected (i.e., installed incorrectly) to London's surface water drains, wastewater flows into London's rivers, damaging them by adding to their phosphate and ammonia levels. The Environment Agency has cited misconnected appliances as one of the reasons London's rivers do not achieve "good" ecological ratings.

In the 1970s and 1980s, growing environmental awareness in the UK led people to question the use of pesticides and fertilizers that were subsequently washed into Britain's rivers, leading to the creation of tighter regulations to improve the health of London's waterways. Then, at the start of the 2000s, pollution from toxic metals in the Thames lessened. This reduction was due in part to stricter industry regulations and also because of technological changes. For example, silver is a common pollutant from the photographic industry, but less silver entered the Thames in the 2000s as people started to use digital cameras. The closure of factories also led to an improvement in London's water quality. Consequently, salmon, sea trout,

A gray seal in the River Thames. Seals can be found in South West and South East London. In 2014, a survey recorded around 2,000 seals in the river. (Chrismrabe /Dreamstime.com)

roach, and flounder returned to live in the tidal Thames, and seahorses have been found in the river at Greenwich in South East London. Dolphins, seals, and porpoises can be seen at Teddington Lock, with large pods living close to Kew Gardens, in South West London, and Deptford, in South East London. Shrimps, prawns, and eels have all also been found in London's waters. Two species of shark, the tope and the smooth hound, are also thought to breed in the waters found at the outer edges of the Thames. London's waterways continued to improve throughout the 2000s. Consequently, a 2014 survey by the Zoological Society of London recorded around 2,000 seals in the Thames[9] as well as hundreds of porpoises and dolphins, 125 species of fish, and a whale.[10] The fish returned naturally to the clean river and now serve as a food source for the marine mammals. Sea lampreys (parasitic, eel-like creatures) have also returned to the Thames; they have been found in Fulham, South West London. This is a hugely encouraging sign for the Thames, as sea lampreys only live in very clean water and are extremely sensitive to pollution. Birdlife along London's waterways includes herons, cormorants, gannets, grebes, kingfishers, shelducks, pochards, and terns.

Wildlife living along the Thames faces some issues despite the river's improved ecology. For example, in central London, the Thames is surrounded by high walls, and the water is used as a thoroughfare for passenger boats that render the river too noisy, busy, and fast flowing for many porpoises or dolphins to swim upstream. Seals are better able to cope with some of these problems, as they do not rely on sound for hunting. Plastic pollution is another major threat to the Thames's aquatic wildlife. In 2015, a study discovered that around 75 percent of some fish species living in the Thames had plastic in their stomachs,[11] while albatrosses were feeding their chicks plastic.[12] Additionally, predatory animals were becoming ill after eating smaller creatures that had fed on plastic. The Cleaner Thames Campaign was launched by the Port of London Authority in 2015. The authority, which recovers around 300 tons of trash from the Thames annually—especially plastic bottles, as well as cotton buds and microbeads contained in facial scrubs and toothpaste—aims to combat plastic pollution in the Thames. It is difficult to stop plastic pollution from entering the Thames, however, as tiny pieces of plastic are often flushed down lavatories or bathroom sinks before passing through sewage treatment plant filters. The plastic can take many decades to decompose. Plastic shopping bags and thin plastic packaging also enter London drains if they blow out of public trash cans. Thames Water (the utility company in charge of London's water supply and wastewater) has to remove over 25,000 tons of such garbage from London's sewage system each year.[13]

LONDON'S AIR

In the past, Londoners could be distinguished by both their sallow skin and their distinctive accent, which was affected by their need to breathe through their mouths because their nasal passages were congested. Londoners' skin and nostrils were filled with an airborne compound of powdered granite, soot, and other substances. The pollution was detrimental to Londoners' health to the extent that during the Anglo-Boer War (1899–1902), only two in nine working-class male Londoners were fit enough to fight.[14]

In the Victorian era, landscaped urban parks were created to alleviate some of London's issues of overcrowding and poor living conditions, with such green spaces as Victoria Park in East London providing breathing space for slum-dwelling Londoners. For this reason, today, London's parks are still referred to sometimes as the "Lungs of London." By 1880, the parks provided Londoners not only with fresh air but also with fresh water through a network of park drinking fountains and troughs. Despite the creation of the parks, nothing could remove the fumes produced by London's homes and industry. By the 1830s, most London homes used coal fires that produced noxious fumes. Therefore, as London's population grew, so did the number of domestic coal fires that polluted the city's air. As the twentieth century progressed, motor vehicle emissions were added to this toxic mix.

Over time, London's dirty air gave rise to some of history's most notorious episodes of air pollution, the infamous London fogs known as "peasoupers." London gained a reputation for its smog, a term invented at the start of the twentieth century to describe the city's characteristic blend of smoke and fog. The term "peasouper" was invented to describe the densest London smog, which was caused by the smoke and sulfur dioxide pollution emitted by London's coal fires and suspended in the city's air. As early as the medieval period, London's dirty air was exacerbated by domestic fires that burned wood and bituminous coal known as sea-coal. Queen Elizabeth I (1533–1603) proclaimed that she disliked "the taste and smoke of sea-coales,"[15] while in 1661, the writer and gardener John Evelyn (1620–1706) wrote a report for King Charles II of England called *Fumifugium or the Inconveniencie of the Aer and Smoak of London Dissipated*. In the report, Evelyn decried the damaging effects of air pollution caused by processes such as burning sea-coal, which Evelyn felt had turned London into a hellish place so choked by smoke and sulfur that it was full "of Stink and Darknesse."[16] By the start of the nineteenth century, some fogs lasted a week and were so dense that people could not read by daylight. The health issues the fog created among Londoners included smarting eyes and breathing difficulties.

The peasouper originated in the 1840s when London's rapid growth resulted in a rise in the number of coal fires. The smoke from the fires mixed with the factory pollution of the Industrial Revolution, an era when new technologies allowed the UK to transition from being a largely agrarian society to an industrial one. The peasoupers were at their worst in the winters of the 1880s, when there were on average some 60 fogs a year, as the smoke and emissions combined with the dampness and mist that are

---

THE PEASOUPER IN LITERATURE

DID YOU KNOW?

In 1849, American author Herman Melville became the first person to compare London's fog to pea soup. However, it was Charles Dickens who first used London's fog as a literary motif; the opening lines of *Bleak House* (1853) describe the "soft black drizzle" of soot falling on the city. Dickens also invented the phrase "London ivy" to refer to the sooty residue left behind by the fog. The term "London particular" used to describe the fog in *Bleak House* was in common usage as early as the 1790s. Dickens saw London's fog as a symbol of death, confusion, and illusion. Other novelists considered the fog a metaphor for the sickness of urban society or the apocalypse. For example, British author William Delisle Hay, in *The Doom of the Great City* (1880), portrays London as overwhelmed by a suffocating fog.

habitually hemmed in by the low hills surrounding London.[17] After the 1890s, the number of peasoupers and fogs in London began to decrease as gas fires and stoves became popular, electric motors replaced steam engines, and London's industry started to relocate to outer boroughs.

Prior to this change, the area of London worst affected by the smog was the residential and industrial belt of Inner London, especially London's East End, which had the highest density of factory and domestic chimneys coupled with London's lowest-lying land, factors that hindered the smog's dispersal. London's fog problems persisted well into the twentieth century. One of the worst twentieth-century fogs developed in December 1952, as a cold front descended on London and caused the air to become very still and smoke to hang in the air. The suspended smoke then developed into a thick yellow fog that smothered the city, lasting for one week and extending 20 miles from London's center. The smog was so invasive that it crept under doors to enter people's homes and was so thick that it obscured the stage in London theaters; audiences could not see the stages, sporting events were canceled, public transport was restricted, and flights were suspended. More seriously, the fog was dubbed the Great Killer Fog because as many as 12,000 deaths were attributed to it,[18] particularly among Londoners who suffered from preexisting lung conditions, while over 100,000 Londoners suffered ill health related to the smog.[19] Initially, the UK government refused to link the smog to the premature death of Londoners but rather blamed the deaths on an outbreak of influenza. Other commentators shrugged off the deaths as one of the consequences of living in a city where coal was used, or blamed the weather for creating an unusual atmospheric condition that had trapped London's smoke while, at the same time, an easterly wind was transporting polluted air from continental Europe into the city. Proponents of the latter theory pointed out that the bitterly cold weather had forced Londoners to retreat into their homes, where they burned extra coal to heat their homes and thereby created more smoke and, ultimately, the smog hanging over London. At this time, London householders burned a low-grade, high-sulfur variety of coal, because higher-grade coals were sold abroad. One of the worst side effects of this pollution becoming suspended in the air was that the burnt coal gave off sulfur dioxide (SO_2). In turn, the sulfur dioxide was converted into a haze of concentrated sulfuric acid suspended in London's damp air. The Met Office estimated that during the Great Smog, 1,000 tons of smoke particles, 140 tons of hydrochloric acid, 14 tons of fluorine compounds, and 370 tons of sulfur dioxide were emitted daily, leading to the creation of 800 tons of sulfuric acid. For this reason, the Great Smog has been described as "the worst air pollution event in UK history."[20] The last great London peasouper occurred in 1962, though well into the 1960s, smokier parts of East London experienced a reduction in winter sunshine caused by occasional smog.

The problem of London's smog was improved by parliamentary legislation known as the Clean Air Acts of 1956 and 1968, which banned the burning of coal. The Clean Air Act stopped the worst of the London smog and, together with the reduction of London's manufacturing sector, London's air has improved significantly. London's weather is so variable that photochemical smog (smog caused when sunlight interacts with high levels of ozone and nitrogen oxides) experienced by cities with more stable weather conditions, cannot develop in London. However, fumes from London's traffic can become trapped by both the hills surrounding the city and the city's urban heat island.

In recent years, London's air quality has continued to improve through the introduction of further environmental regulations that include the Ultra Low Emission Zone (ULEZ), which charges drivers of the most polluting vehicles extra to enter the central London congestion zone area, and the Low Emission Bus Zones where only buses that meet the cleanest emission standards are allowed to operate. Some of these buses are electric or hydrogen powered. In June 2021, Sadiq Khan unveiled England's first double-decker hydrogen buses that run from East Acton in west London to Oxford Circus. The new buses produce zero exhaust pollution and can be charged once per day within five minutes. The buses's only direct by-product is water. TfL has over 500 electric buses in its fleet and hopes to be zero emission by 2030.[21]

Despite these innovations, some estimates suggest that London's air pollution results in 9,000 people dying every year,[22] for air pollution has been linked to asthma, strokes, heart disease, and dementia. It has also been blamed for some London children having stunted lungs. However, it is important to note that most pollutants found in London's air are not present at levels that affect human health. While many pollutants are contained in London's air, including sulfur dioxide, lead, benzene, and ozone, the two most significant pollutants in London are nitrogen dioxide (NO_2), which at high concentrations can affect lung function and breathing, worsen asthma, and inflame people's airways, and particulate matter (PM), which can be inhaled deep into the lungs, thereby harming people's hearts and lungs.

Most of London's air pollution derives from road transport and domestic and commercial heating systems. The UK Air Quality Standards Regulations 2010 provides standards for pollutants that are injurious to both human health and the environment. The standards are based on European Union (EU) limits. Around half of London's nitrogen oxide (NOx) pollution comes from road transport, with the rest caused by construction work or emitted by buildings, aviation, and industry. While London's total NOx emissions reduced by 25 percent from 2008 to 2013, thereby indicating that the city's air quality was improving, the amount of NO_2 in some locations of London's air exceeded the EU annual mean limit value of 40 micrograms per cubic meter.[23] Further, in 2013, around 1.9 million Londoners lived in areas, particularly in central and Inner London, where average nitrogen dioxide (NO_2) concentrations breached EU limits.[24]

The COVID-19 pandemic led to an incidental decrease in the amount of NO_2 in London's air. Before measures to curb people's movements were introduced during London's pandemic lockdown, levels of NO_2 had already fallen by 35 percent in central London compared to the same period in 2017. Beginning on March 16, 2020, when the UK government advised people to work from home, road traffic in London halved and levels of NO_2 decreased by an additional 26 percent, as Londoners stayed home and only used public transport for essential journeys.[25] Since March 16, 2020, London has experienced several spikes in the level of particulate pollution, which proves the city's air pollution is not caused exclusively by road transport but also by factors such as agricultural emissions. One of the challenges facing London's authorities is that much of the pollution affecting the city originates outside of London. Recent analysis reveals that around half of London's fine particulate matter ($PM_{2.5}$) air pollution comes from outside London and includes industrial, agricultural, and transport emissions from abroad. The $PM_{2.5}$ pollution is believed to contribute to almost 75 percent of London's cardiovascular hospital admissions.[26] Much of the NO_2 effecting London also derives from outside the capital. The pollution in London's air not only causes ill health but also has an economic cost, for the health impact of the air pollution is thought to cost around £3.7bn annually. For these reasons, London's authorities work closely with European countries to reduce emissions across continental Europe and address the issue of transboundary, international pollution.[27]

While London's greenhouse gas emissions are lessening, most of the energy used to heat London's homes comes from gas-fired boilers. At the same time, 1 in 10 of London's electricity substations are close to full capacity,[28] meaning there is a need to redevelop the city's power infrastructure if Londoners' increasing demand for energy is to be met.

GREEN LONDON: BIODIVERSITY AND SUSTAINABILITY

London parks cover almost 18 percent of the city (more than the combined amount of London land given over to railways and roads).[29] Of London's 3,000 parks, 8 are classified as "royal" parks: Hyde Park, Kensington Gardens, Richmond Park, Bushy Park, St. James's Park, Green Park, Greenwich Park, and the Regent's Parks and Primrose Hill. The royal parks were once owned by the monarch, but today they are the responsibility of the UK government and managed by a charity.

THE ST. JAMES'S PARK PELICANS

DID YOU KNOW?

In 1664, the Russian ambassador gave King Charles II a pair of pelicans as a gift. The pair were placed in St. James's Park, near Buckingham Palace, and their descendants have lived there ever since. Today, there are six St. James's Park pelicans—Gargi, Tiffany, Isla, Sun, Moon, and Star—that live on an island of rocks in the park's lake. The present-day pelicans consist of five Eastern White pelicans and one South American White pelican. In 2013, three of the Eastern White pelicans arrived from Prague as a gift to London from the Czech capital. The pelicans are especially viewable between 2:30 p.m. and 3:00 p.m., when they are fed fish by the park rangers. The pelicans are also known to steal fish from London Zoo. Extremely sociable creatures, the pelicans are used to company and have been known to sit on the parks' benches alongside bemused humans. During the 2020 lockdown, photographs of the pelicans walking along London's deserted streets went viral on social media, with many people believing the pictures to be fake as they did not know pelicans lived in St. James's.

Green space is very important in London for it is beneficial to Londoners' physical and mental health and also enhances London's reputation as a place that is good to live in and visit. London mayor Sadiq Khan is committed to protecting both London's green spaces and the Green Belt, as doing so will not only enhance Londoners' quality of life but also reduce the city's emissions and help London respond to climate change. London is home to over 8 million trees, and 21 percent of London's land contains trees that help offset some of London's air pollution.[30] Indeed, London has the lowest carbon emissions per person of any English region.[31] This is partly because London lacks heavy industry and has a high population density and an extensive public transport network but also because some of London's carbon emissions are offset by the city's many trees.

As climate change intensifies, so London's rainfall may become heavier, resulting in increased incidents of flooding. London's water supply is already under pressure, with London expected to have a water deficit of over 400 million liters (87,987,699 gallons) per day by 2040.[32] This means that there won't be enough water to meet London's needs. London already gets a large proportion of its water from groundwater and surrounding rivers, which damages the health of rivers and threatens the city's future water supply. At the same time, climate change may lead to more frequent heat waves, which, coupled with the city's urban heat island effect (when human activity causes an urban area to be significantly warmer than surrounding rural areas), will make central London significantly warmer than areas around the city. Increased heat could make London's buildings and

---

DID YOU KNOW?

OCTAVIA HILL (1823–1912)

A philanthropist and reformer, Hill believed passionately that the environment influenced people's well-being; thus she campaigned for both better housing and to allow people access to the countryside. Consequently, Hill was the leader of the British open-space movement, which resulted in the foundation in 1895 of the National Trust for Places of Historic Interest or Natural Beauty (now the conservation organization the National Trust). Through her family, Hill met prominent thinkers, including the intellectual John Ruskin, who instilled in Hill the belief that everyone needed access to art and nature. In 1864, Ruskin gave Hill money, which she used to establish a housing project in the slums of London's St. Marylebone area. The following year, Hill oversaw other London housing projects, while in 1884, she was placed in charge of a property in Southwark, where she trained and paid a group of women to manage mass housing. Today, Hill's Octavia Housing organization continues to provide social housing for thousands of inner-city Londoners. Meanwhile, the National Trust has evolved to preserve the UK's countryside and noteworthy buildings. Before her death, Hill's belief that private enterprise was preferable to government intervention came to sit at odds with the advent of the welfare state. Recently, however, Hill's legacy has been reevaluated: her conviction that everyone should have access to art and nature and her role in empowering other women have gained her widespread admiration.

---

public transport uncomfortable and, potentially, dangerously hot, while increased demand for cooling systems may place greater stress on London's power supplies, threatening London's sustainability through greater emissions.

Waste can have a big impact on London's environment. Most of London's municipal waste comes from recyclable materials such as paper, card, plastics, glass, and metals (54 percent), followed by food and garden waste (23 percent), and materials such as textiles, waste electrical goods, wood, furniture, and household cleaning chemicals (23 percent). London produces 1.5 million to 1.75 million tons of food waste each year. Some London Boroughs run curbside collections of food waste, but most of the city's food waste ends up in landfills or is incinerated, thereby producing 250,000 tons of carbon dioxide equivalent (CO_2e) emissions[33] (the standard unit for measuring carbon footprints). However, some of the emissions caused by food waste are offset, for they are captured as heat and used to produce electricity. At present, 41 percent of the 7 million tons of waste generated by London's homes and businesses annually are recycled, with landfill capacity expected to run out by 2026.[34] Sadiq Khan has set a target of seeing 65 percent of London's garbage recycled by 2030, with no biodegradable or recyclable items dumped in landfill sites by 2026.[35] However, potential hindrances to achieving this rate of recycling are that each London borough runs its own recycling program while the mayor has no statutory responsibility for London's waste management. Food packaging (including single-use coffee cups and plastic bottles) contributes to plastic pollution and littering in London. A 2016 report suggested that 125,000 tons of plastic bottles were produced in London each year. The report also suggested that Londoners bought around 1.2 billion single-use plastic bottles annually, with only a third of the bottles recycled in the home.[36] More recently, a certain social stigma has become attached to the use of single-use plastic bottles in London, with many London cafes asking customers to bring their own refillable cups with them if they wish to purchase beverages.

In July 2019, London became the first city in the world to be designated a National Park City, as the mayor of London, organizations, and individuals signed a London National Park City Charter to demonstrate their support for making London greener and wilder. The National Park City plan was masterminded by the geographer Daniel Raven-Ellison. One of the main aims of the plan was to increase London's total area of greenery by creating more living roofs and walls as well as "rain gardens" that prevent flooding while providing habitats for wildlife. While the National Park City plan may not transform London radically, it may bring about incremental increases in London's green land, sparking interest in biodiversity among Londoners through events such as the National Park City Festival, which ran from July 20 to 28, 2019 and featured environmentally friendly activities that included beekeeping, open-water swimming, and wildlife photography.

The title National Park City reflects London's status as the UK's most biodiverse area. The city is home to almost 15,000 species, including hundreds of species of birds, eight bat species, and England's largest population of stag beetles. Foxes are a common sight on London's streets, and rats, bats, badgers, deer, and rabbits are plentiful. London is also home to many types of birds, including pigeons, parakeets, owls, birds of prey, and various finches and tits.

However, while some wildlife is thriving, London's hedgehog population has fallen by nearly a third since 2000. That said, some areas of London are home to noteworthy hedgehog populations: Regent's Park, in North West Inner London; Hampstead Heath, in North London; and Roehampton Golf Course; Barnes Common; Putney Lower Common; and the WWT Wetland Centre, in South West London. Adding to London's biodiversity is the fact that the city is home to almost as many trees as people: around 8.4 million trees—among them, birch, apple, sycamore, oak, holly, and hawthorn—can be found in London.[37] The commonest tree in London is the London plane (*Platanus x hispanica*), which is a hybrid of

---

DID YOU KNOW?

THE LONDON PARAKEETS

Ring-necked parakeets are a familiar sight across Greater London, where they roost in large flocks. The parakeet population has been increasing steadily, with estimates suggesting there are more than 8,500 breeding pairs, concentrated in southeastern England. The ring-necked parakeets are native to arid tropical areas of West Africa and lowland India south of the Himalayas. Despite their tropical origins, parakeets have adapted to cope with British winters, inhabiting suburban parks, gardens, and orchards, where they can find reliable supplies of fruit, berries, nuts, seeds, grain, and household scraps. Parakeets are also frequent visitors to London bird tables and garden feeders, particularly in winter. Quite how the parakeets came to England is unknown. One theory suggests they were introduced deliberately by rock star Jimi Hendrix, while another suggests that a pair escaped from Shepperton Film Studios during the making of the film *The African Queen* (1951). A more mundane suggestion is that the parakeets are descended from pet birds that either escaped or, unwanted, were released into the wild.

---

the American sycamore and the Oriental plane. The London plane was discovered during the seventeenth century, and then in the eighteenth and nineteenth centuries, it was planted throughout London. The tree can grow to 115 feet tall and live for hundreds of years. The tree is a popular choice for city planting projects because it tends not to shed its branches and can withstand compacted soil and urban pollution levels. Many of London's trees have been mapped, and Londoners can embark on personalized "tree walks" using the Tree Talk website.

Currently, many London borough councils run programs to try to conserve the population of beneficial insects. This is in response to the rapidly dwindling number of pollinating insects in the UK, which is caused in part by the fact that since World War II, 97 percent of the country's wildflower meadows have disappeared.[38] For example, Brent Council in North London has sown a seven-mile-long "bee corridor" of wildflowers to try to increase London's population of bees and other pollinating insects. The bee corridor consists of 22 wildflower meadows that total 50,000 square meters (roughly 12 acres) spread across the borough's open spaces.[39] The meadows consist of ragged robins, cowslips, and common poppies, which are known to encourage bees, butterflies, moths, and dragonflies. Such insects are essential for maintaining a healthy ecosystem and contribute to global food security.[40] Similarly, in 2019, the West London borough of Ealing, which borders Brent, created 200,000 square meters (slightly less than 50 acres) of wildflower areas in local parks, at road shoulders, and along pavements in order to boost local wildlife, including bees and butterflies.[41]

LONDON'S GREEN FUTURE

London's authorities are investing heavily in public transport while trying to increase levels of walking and cycling among Londoners. The phasing out of buses with polluting diesel engines is also ongoing, as the more-polluting buses are replaced by new lower- and zero-emission buses. Under the Climate Change Act 2008 (intended to ensure that the UK reduce its greenhouse gas emissions by 80 percent relative to 1990 levels by 2050), London's local authorities were already committed to 80 percent emissions reduction by 2050.[42] In 2019, the UK government amended the Climate Change Act, aiming for zero carbon by 2050. In order to achieve this reduction, the UK government established the 2017 Clean Growth Strategy that sets out various policies intended to enable the country to meet the carbon budget. In 2018, the mayor of London published the main Climate Change Act policies for London, including the improvement of energy efficiency in buildings and the provision of more environmentally friendly transport. London Boroughs such as Richmond upon Thames have published local plans that reveal their policies for how their borough can become more sustainable, minimizing emissions and energy consumption while promoting renewable energy. For example, in order to produce zero carbon by 2050, Richmond upon Thames's council actively promotes sustainable transport (public transport use, cycling, and walking), encourages people to work from home in order to reduce commuter journeys within the borough, and has installed building energy management systems (BEMS) in all council buildings. BEMS control heating and air-conditioning to make buildings more energy efficient.

Also encouraging energy efficiency is the mayor of London's Energy for Londoners program for both individual Londoners and London businesses. Elements of the Energy for Londoners program include helping London's buildings use cleaner power—such as through solar power–production initiatives—rolling out a system of smart power meters that use less energy, and helping London businesses to use less packaging and do more recycling.

Since March 2020, the COVID-19 pandemic has caused immeasurable changes in London's transport. For instance, social distancing rules that have required people to stay two meters apart from one another have dramatically reduced the capacity of the London Underground, trains, and buses. According to Transport for London (TfL), during the pandemic the Underground's capacity fell from 325,000 people boarding the Tube every 15 minutes to 50,000 travelers every 15 minutes, and the buses that have typically carried 85 passengers are only allowed to hold 15 people.[43] In May 2020, the UK government announced that in order to prevent overcrowding on public transport in the light of the coronavirus pandemic, more people would be expected to cycle and walk in London rather than use buses, trains, and private cars. To this end, the UK's transport minister Grant Shapps unveiled a £2 billion financial package that placed cycling and walking at the heart of the government's transport policy. Among the measures proposed by the government were temporary cycle lanes, wider sidewalks, and streets to be used exclusively by bicycles and buses. The use of e-scooters would also be encouraged through e-scooter rental programs. Meanwhile, electric-vehicle ownership would be encouraged through the creation of additional on-street charging points. Other changes to London's transport that were brought about by the COVID-19 outbreak included staggering the start of work and school in London to help transport entities reduce volumes at peak times. Subsequently, the mayor of London together with TfL announced the controversial, fast-tracked London Streetspace plan. This plan will see London adapted to accommodate 10 times as many cyclists and 5 times as many pedestrians once London's lockdown restrictions are eased.[44] TfL will work with all London Boroughs to focus on three main issues:

- The rapid implementation of a cycling network aimed at reducing the number of people using the Tube, rail, and buses. By mid-May 2020, some temporary cycle lanes had already been installed on major roads such as central London's Euston Road and Park Lane.

- The transformation of the local town center to encourage walking and cycling. The pavements in shopping areas will be widened to allow greater foot traffic, thus encouraging people to shop locally and queue outside shops while having enough space to pass each other when necessary and at a safe social distance. By mid-May 2020, pavements were doubled in width along Camden High Street and Stoke Newington High Street in North West London. Meanwhile, in South West London, the pavements were widened and a one-way system for pedestrians implemented along the main shopping street in Richmond upon Thames.

- The reduction of motor traffic on residential streets to make walking and cycling easier.

TfL says that in time it will review these temporary measures. However, TfL has also said the changes may become permanent. While it is likely that such measures will have beneficial effects on London's environment, the measures have proven controversial, as people living outside the capital or in Outer London Boroughs have questioned how they are expected to reach Inner London, while disability rights campaigners and senior citizen groups have lamented the focus on walking and cycling. Small businesses have also voiced concerns that they will be unable to make deliveries or transport heavy equipment around the capital. The mayor of London and TfL have also announced that areas of central London will be transformed to form the largest car-free zone of any capital city in order to both enable social distancing on public transport and improve London's air quality. In mid-May 2020, the mayor and TfL asserted that for the foreseeable future, public transport must only be used for essential journeys, people should work from home where possible, and Londoners must spend their leisure time close to home in order to avoid unnecessary travel. To ensure these lifestyle changes are followed, some major London streets will be open only to pedestrians and cyclists, while some will be accessible only by pedestrians, cyclists, and buses. The changes will affect the busy streets between London Bridge and Shoreditch, Euston and Waterloo, and Old Street and Holborn, as well as Waterloo Bridge and London Bridge. In these areas, access for emergency services and disabled people is permitted, but deliveries have to occur outside of Congestion Charge operating hours, which on June 22, 2020, were extended from 7:00 a.m. to 6:00 p.m., Monday through Friday, to 7:00 a.m. to 10:00 p.m., every day. The Congestion Charge also increased from £11.50 per day to £15 per day. According to the mayor, the price rise will reduce car journeys within the Congestion Charge zone by a third,[45] thereby discouraging Londoners from driving in London. In turn, the mayor hopes the reduction in car journeys will reduce air pollution in central London. However, when the Congestion Charge increase was announced, many Londoners took to social media to argue that the price rise was unfair, given that many people had little choice but to drive to work since they were also expected to avoid public transport.

NOTES

1. "London Beats Competitors to Be Ranked as the Most Sustainable City in the World, according to Research by Leading Global Consultancy Arcadis," Design & Build UK, December 17, 2018, https://designandbilduk.net/london-beats-competitors-to-be-ranked-as-the-most-sustainable-city-in-the-world-according-to-research-by-leading-global-consultancy-arcadis.

2. *Tackling Pollution in London's Rivers*, Zoological Society of London, November 2017, https://www.zsl.org/sites/default/files/media/2017-12/1710_CP_Outfall Report_Final.pdf.

3. Twitter conversation between the author and London Waterkeeper (@LDNWaterkeeper), May 17, 2020, https://twitter.com/LDNWaterkeeper/status /1262084533635158017.

4. Beverley Cook and Alex Werner, "Breathing in London's History: From the Great Stink to the Great Smog," Museum of London, August 24, 2017, https:// www.museumoflondon.org.uk/discover/londons-past-air.

5. Miriam Bibby, "London's Great Stink," Historic UK, https://www.historic-uk .com/HistoryUK/HistoryofBritain/Londons-Great-Stink.

6. Alwyn Collinson, "How Bazalgette Built London's First Super-Sewer," Museum of London, March 26, 2019, https://www.museumoflondon.org.uk/discover /how-bazalgette-built-londons-first-super-sewer.

7. Ibid.

8. Bibby, "London's Great Stink."

9. Zoological Society of London, "ZSL's Seal Survey 2014," Thames Marine Mammal Survey, https://sites.zsl.org/inthethames/main/#ZSL's%20surveys (2014 site discontinued).

10. Sophie Hardach, "How the River Thames Was Brought Back from the Dead," *BBC*, November 12, 2015, http://www.bbc.co.uk/earth/story/20151111-how-the-river -thames-was-brought-back-from-the-dead.

11. "Cleaner Thames Campaign," Port of London Authority, https://www.pla.co .uk/cleaner-thames.

12. Hardach, "How the River Thames Was Brought Back from the Dead."

13. Ibid.

14. Cook and Werner, "Breathing in London's History."

15. Christine L. Corton, *London Fog: The Biography* (Cambridge, MA: Belknap Press of Harvard University Press, 2015), 2.

16. Ibid.

17. P. D. Smith, "London Fog by Christine Corton: The History of the Pea-Souper," *The Guardian*, November 27, 2015, https://www.theguardian.com/books /2015/nov/27/london-smog-christine-corton-review.

18. Corton, *London Fog*, 284.

19. Madsen Pirie, "When a Killer Smog Hit London," Adam Smith Institute, December 4, 2019, https://www.adamsmith.org/blog/when-a-killer-smog-hit -london.

20. Ibid.

21. Dimitris Kouimtsidis, "England's First Double-Decker Hydrogen Buses Unveiled in Ealing," Ealing Nub News, June 23, 2021, https://ealing.nub.news/n /england39s-first-double-decker-hydrogen-buses-unveiled-in-ealing.

22. Cook and Werner, "Breathing in London's History."

23. *London Environment Strategy* (London: Greater London Authority, May 2018), https://www.london.gov.uk/sites/default/files/london_environment_strategy _0.pdf, 47.

24. Ibid., 51.

25. *Estimation of Changes in Air Pollution in London during the COVID-19 Outbreak. Response to the UK Government's Air Quality Expert Group Call for Evidence*, Greater London Authority, April 2020, https://www.london.gov.uk/ sites/default/files/london_response_to_aqeg_call_for_evidence_april_2020. pdf, 4.

26. *London Environment Strategy*, 53.

27. Ibid.

28. Ibid., 15.

29. "Parks and Green Spaces," Greater London Authority, https://www.london .gov.uk/what-we-do/environment/parks-green-spaces-and-biodiversity/parks-and -green-spaces.

30. Tom Edwards, "Climate Change: The Challenges Facing London," *BBC News*, January 20, 2020, https://www.bbc.co.uk/news/uk-england-london-51151983.

31. Ibid.

32. *London Environment Strategy*, 14.

33. Ibid., 279.

34. Ibid., 277.

35. Edwards, "Climate Change."

36. Ibid., 279.

37. Emma Marris, "One Man's Plan to Transform a Major City into a National Park," *National Geographic*, April 20, 2017, https://www.nationalgeographic.com/news/2017/04/london-national-park-greenspace-urban-conservation.

38. Harry Cockburn, "London to Build Seven-Mile 'Bee Corridor' to Boost Dwindling Numbers of Pollinators," *The Independent*, May 7, 2019, https://www.independent.co.uk/environment/london-bee-corridor-wildflower-meadows-brent-council-climate-change-a8903456.html.

39. Ibid.

40. Ibid.

41. Facebook conversation between author and Richard Strange, on the Ealing Wildlife Group, May 20, 2020, https://www.facebook.com/groups/ealingwildlife/1142059499498011/?comment_id=1142119642825330&reply_comment_id=1142705286100099&notif_id=1590040557796859&notif_t=group_comment_mention.

42. London Borough of Richmond. *Climate Change and Sustainability Strategy 2019–2024*, https://www.richmond.gov.uk/media/17738/climate_change_and_sustainability_strategy_2019_2024.pdf p18.

43. Tom Edwards, "Coronavirus: What Will London Transport Look Like after the Lockdown?," *BBC*, May 8, 2020, https://www.bbc.co.uk/news/uk-england-london-52579871.

44. "Mayor's Bold New Streetspace Plan Will Overhaul London's Streets," Greater London Authority, May 6, 2020, https://www.london.gov.uk/press-releases/mayoral/mayors-bold-plan-will-overhaul-capitals-streets.

45. "Car-Free Zones in London as Congestion Charge and ULEZ Reinstated," Greater London Authority, May 15, 2020. https://www.london.gov.uk/press-releases/mayoral/car-free-zones-in-london-as-cc-and-ulez-reinstated.

FURTHER READING

Bibby, Miriam. "London's Great Stink." Historic UK. https://www.historic-uk.com/HistoryUK/HistoryofBritain/Londons-Great-Stink.

"Cleaner Thames Campaign." Port of London Authority. https://www.pla.co.uk/cleaner-thames.

Cockburn, Harry. "London to Build Seven-Mile 'Bee Corridor' to Boost Dwindling Numbers of Pollinators." *The Independent*, May 7, 2019. https://www.independent.co.uk/environment/london-bee-corridor-wildflower-meadows-brent-council-climate-change-a8903456.html.

Collinson, Alwyn. "How Bazalgette Built London's First Super-Sewer." Museum of London, March 26, 2019. https://www.museumoflondon.org.uk/discover/how-bazalgette-built-londons-first-super-sewer.

Cook, Beverley, and Alex Werner. "Breathing in London's History: From the Great Stink to the Great Smog." Museum of London, August 24, 2017. https://www.museumoflondon.org.uk/discover/londons-past-air.

Corton, Christine L. London Fog: The Biography. Cambridge, MA: Belknap Press of Harvard University Press. 2015.

Edwards, Tom. "Climate Change: The Challenges Facing London." BBC News, January 20, 2020. https://www.bbc.co.uk/news/uk-england-london-51151983.

Edwards, Tom. "Coronavirus: What Will London Transport Look Like after the Lockdown?" BBC News, May 8, 2020. https://www.bbc.co.uk/news/uk-england-london-52579871.

Estimation of Changes in Air Pollution in London during the COVID-19 Outbreak. Response to the UK Government's Air Quality Expert Group Call for Evidence. Greater London Authority, April 2020. https://www.london.gov.uk/sites/default/files/london_response_to_aqeg_call_for_evidence_april_2020.pdf.

Hardach, Sophie. "How the River Thames was Brought Back from the Dead." BBC, November 12, 2015. http://www.bbc.co.uk/earth/story/20151111-how-the-river-thames-was-brought-back-from-the-dead.

"Health and Exposure to Pollution." Greater London Authority, 2020. https://www.london.gov.uk/what-we-do/environment/pollution-and-air-quality/health-and-exposure-pollution.

Leahy, Stephen. "London Becomes World's First 'National Park City.' What Does That Mean?" National Geographic, July 21, 2019. https://www.nationalgeographic.co.uk/environment-and-conservation/2019/07/london-becomes-worlds-first-national-park-city-what-does-mean.

"London Beats Competitors to Be Ranked as the Most Sustainable City in the World, according to Research by Leading Global Consultancy Arcadis." Design & Build UK, December 17, 2018. https://designandbuilduk.net/london-beats-competitors-to-be-ranked-as-the-most-sustainable-city-in-the-world-according-to-research-by-leading-global-consultancy-arcadis.

London Borough of Richmond. Climate Change and Sustainability Strategy 2019–2024. https://www.richmond.gov.uk/media/17738/climate_change_and_sustainability_strategy_2019_2024.pdf.

London Environment Strategy. London: Greater London Authority, May 2018. https://www.london.gov.uk/sites/default/files/london_environment_strategy_0.pdf.

Marris, Emma. "One Man's Plan to Transform a Major City into a National Park." National Geographic, April 20, 2017. https://www.nationalgeographic.com/news/2017/04/london-national-park-greenspace-urban-conservation.

Pirie, Madsen. "When a Killer Smog Hit London." Adam Smith Institute, December 4, 2019. https://www.adamsmith.org/blog/when-a-killer-smog-hit-london.

Smith, P. D. "London Fog by Christine Corton: The History of the Pea-Souper." The Guardian, November 27, 2015. https://www.theguardian.com/books/2015/nov/27/london-smog-christine-corton-review.

Walawalkar, Aaron. "Back to Work: 'Capacity of Transport Network Will Be Down by 90 Percent.'" *The Guardian*, May 9, 2020. https://www.theguardian.com/world/2020/may/09/back-to-work-capacity-of-transport-network-will-be-down-by-90.

Zoological Society of London. "Thames Conservation: Thames Marine Mammal Conservation." https://www.zsl.org/conservation/regions/uk-europe/thames-marine-mammal-conservation.

7

Local Crime and Violence

Throughout its long history, London life has often been brutal, for Londoners have experienced invasions, riots, murders, serial killings, theft, gang violence, assassinations, terrorism, and more. The first violence recorded in London was the Roman invasion of 43 CE. Subsequent bloody unrest came in the form of tribal rebellions as well as the ninth-century Viking invasion. Another bloody event in London's early history was the anti-Jewish violence connected to the coronation of King Richard I on September 3, 1189. Prominent English Jews were invited to the coronation at Westminster Abbey, but many English Christians held superstitions about Jews being present at a sacred Christian occasion. Consequently, the Jewish attendees were flogged after the coronation, and Christians attacked the predominantly Jewish neighborhood of Old Jewry (a Jewish ghetto in London's financial district), setting the Jews' houses on fire and killing those Jews who tried to flee. The king was outraged when he heard about the killings, but only some of the attackers were punished. Other notable London riots include the anti-Catholic Gordon Riots (1780) that involved widespread violence and looting—including attacks on Newgate Prison, in the City of London, and the Bank of England—and the Poll Tax riots of March 31, 1990. The Poll Tax riots were a demonstration against the new Community Charge (commonly called the "poll tax") and resulted in London's Trafalgar Square becoming a battleground between police and protesters. During the riots, several thousand demonstrators attacked the police with bricks, bottles, and scaffolding, resulting in over 100 people being injured, numerous police officers among them. The riots also saw the arrest of hundreds of protesters.

Over time, the famous London landmark the Tower of London has acquired a reputation as a site of torture and death. For example, it became known as the Bloody Tower and is strongly associated with the alleged murder of the 12-year-old king Edward V and his younger brother, Richard, Duke of York, in 1483. In the sixteenth century, King Henry VIII's second wife, Anne Boleyn, and fifth wife, Catherine Howard, were executed at the Tower of London (in 1536 and 1542, respectively), while in 1554, Queen Mary I (nicknamed Bloody Mary) authorized the execution of 17-year-old Lady Jane Grey (known as the Nine-Day Queen, great-granddaughter of Henry VII) at the Tower of London.

Ordinary Londoners have faced the prospect of attack by their peers frequently and in far more mundane settings than the Tower of London. For instance, in Victorian times, crime generally declined, though there was occasional public outcry caused by crime waves. For example, in the 1850s and 1860s, there were panics about a type of London street robbery called garroting. This crime saw the attacker stalk a victim, place an arm, cord, or wire tight around the victim's neck, and then rob the victim. While "garotte" robberies were not very numerous, they were subject of

---

DID YOU KNOW?

THOMAS BLOOD (1618–1680): THE MAN WHO STOLE THE CROWN JEWELS

In 1671, Irishman Thomas Blood decided on a bold scheme to steal the Crown Jewels from a basement in the Tower of London. Disguised as a clergyman, Blood went to see the Crown Jewels and over several days befriended the basement's keeper. On May 9, 1671, Blood and his accomplices knocked the keeper unconscious, stabbing the man with a sword. He then removed a grille from in front of the jewels and snatched the crown, orb, and scepter, bashing the crown with a mallet and stuffing it into his bag, and placing the orb down his breeches. The scepter was too long to fit in a bag, so Blood's accomplice tried to saw it in half. However, the keeper regained consciousness, prompting Blood to drop the scepter. Blood was then arrested as he tried to leave the Tower. In custody, Blood refused to answer to anyone but the king, so he was questioned by King Charles, Prince Rupert, the Duke of York and other royals. King Charles admired Blood's audacity, and Blood not only received a pardon but was given land in Ireland. Subsequently, Blood became a London celebrity and made frequent appearances at Court. The tower keeper recovered from his wounds and was also rewarded by the king.

lurid media headlines, and Parliament responded by enacting legislation that saw garroters flogged and imprisoned. But generally, violence in the form of street robberies or murder did not figure significantly in London crime statistics or in court proceedings of the time. Rather, most offenses involved petty theft, and most offenders were young men. The most common offenses committed by women included prostitution, soliciting, drunkenness, and vagrancy. Cases of domestic violence seldom came before the courts, for domestic violence was usually committed in the home either among the working classes, who tended to tolerate such behavior, or among members of higher social classes, who did not wish to go to court because the ensuing publicity would damage their family's reputation.

Victorian London's press reveled in sensationalist stories involving violence, especially if the violence was combined with a sexual element. For this reason, from August 7 to September 10, 1888, the public imagination and press headlines alike were captured by the story of the serial killer Jack the Ripper, who operated in a small area of East London's notoriously squalid Whitechapel district. Jack the Ripper killed and mutilated at least five women in a way that suggested the killer possessed knowledge of human anatomy (disemboweling some of the victims and removing internal organs). At that time, prostitution in London was illegal only if it caused a public disturbance, so thousands of brothels and similar establishments managed to exist in London. At the same time, however, the murder of prostitutes was rarely mentioned in the press. Jack the Ripper's crimes displayed such savagery though that they were grimly remarkable and became a media sensation. Various theories about the

An 1888 illustration of London's most notorious serial killer, Jack the Ripper, who murdered at least five women. The killer has become the focus of numerous films and television programs as well as a macabre London tourist industry. (*Illustrated London News*, October 13, 1888)

killer's identity have been suggested, including claims that he was the famous painter Walter Sickert or Prince Albert Victor, Duke of Clarence (grandson of Queen Victoria). However, despite numerous investigations, the killer's identity remains unknown. Jack the Ripper continues to be a figure of fascination, and London is home to a ghoulish Jack the Ripper industry that includes guided tours of the murder locations. The case has also spawned countless books, films, and television productions. Other infamous London serial killers include John Haigh (nicknamed the Acid Bath Murderer), who operated in Kensington during the 1940s; John Christie, who killed at least eight women at his home, 10 Rillington Place, Notting Hill, during the 1940s and 1950s; Dennis Nilsen, who in the late 1970s and early 1980s murdered many young men in North London; and Levi Bellfield, who killed several young women in South West London during the early 2000s. Bellfield is Britain's only serial killer to be sentenced to two whole life sentences. This means Bellfield will spend the rest of his life in prison.

In addition to crime perpetrated by individuals, London also has a history of organized crime. Traditionally, London's organized crime centered

---

DID YOU KNOW?

RUTH ELLIS (1926–1955): THE LAST WOMAN TO BE HANGED IN THE UK

Ruth Ellis was a London bar hostess and prostitute who became the last woman to be hanged in the UK after she murdered her lover, David Blakely, an alcoholic racing driver. Ellis and Blakely had an extremely tumultuous relationship, during which Blakely caused Ellis to miscarry a baby after punching her in the stomach. In 1955, Ellis shot Blakely dead outside a Hampstead pub and was arrested immediately.

Ellis had met Blakely through Mike Hawthorn, who went on to become the first British Formula One world champion. During her trial, Ellis maintained a glamorous appearance, which her defending counsel felt counted against her. More importantly, Ellis stated on oath that she had intended to kill her lover, thereby guaranteeing a guilty verdict and mandatory death sentence. Indeed, the jury took only 20 minutes to convict Ellis, who remained at London's Holloway Prison while awaiting execution. Ellis was hanged by the famous hangman, Albert Pierrepoint. She was then buried in an unmarked grave within the walls of the prison, though in the 1970s, her remains were reburied elsewhere. Ellis's case caused widespread controversy, evoking intense media coverage and public interest to the point that 50,000 people signed an unsuccessful petition asking the Home Office to show Ellis clemency. The Ellis case helped strengthen support for the abolition of the death penalty. In 2003, Ellis's case was referred back to the Court of Appeal by the Criminal Cases Review Commission. Though the appeal was rejected, it was on the grounds that the conviction was based on the law as it stood in 1955.

around families living in the city's East End. The most notorious figures of London's organized crime scene were the Kray twins Ronald "Ronnie" Kray (1933–1995) and Reginald "Reggie" Kray (1933–2000). During the 1950s and 1960s, the Krays ran organized crime in the East End, heading up a gang known as "the Firm," which was responsible for murders, armed robberies, arson attacks, protection rackets, and assaults. The Krays also ran nightclubs in London's West End, something that allowed them to attain a level of seedy glamor and become celebrities who mixed with famous politicians and entertainers. In 1969, however, the Krays were jailed, and both brothers were sentenced to life imprisonment, In 1995, Ronnie Kray died in the high-security, psychiatric Broadmoor Hospital, while Reggie was released shortly before his death in 2000. Some of London's working-class neighborhoods are still thought to be home to family-run organized crime groups. These organized crime families tend to be territorial, committing crimes close to home while also being involved in international crimes such as money laundering and trafficking.

Despite London's violent past and infamous crimes, today it is one of the world's safest cities in terms of crime and violence. In 2017, London's

---

ALBERT PIERREPOINT (1905–1992): BRITAIN'S MOST FAMOUS HANGMAN

DID YOU KNOW?

Pierrepoint came from a family of hangmen and became famous for executing high-profile prisoners. Pierrepoint trained at Pentonville Prison in London and went on to work at some of the UK's most famous institutions, including London's Wandsworth and Holloway prisons. During his career, Pierrepoint hanged 200 individuals, including Ruth Ellis; Derek Bentley, who received a posthumous pardon after being wrongly convicted of murdering a London policeman; the London serial killer John Christie; and also Timothy Evans, the man originally convicted of some of Christie's murders. The Evans case is acknowledged as a miscarriage of justice, and, along with the cases of Ellis and Bentley, played a major part in the abolition of capital punishment in the UK. Pierrepoint also executed Gordon Cummins (dubbed the Blackout Ripper), who in a six-day period in 1942, killed four London women and attempted to murder two others; and John Haigh (a.k.a. London's Acid Bath Murderer). Pierrepoint's executions for high treason include William Joyce (nicknamed Lord Haw-Haw) who broadcast anti-British propaganda on behalf of Nazi Germany. Pierrepoint also hanged Theodore Schurch, a British soldier who in 1946 became the last person in the UK to be executed for treachery. During World War II, Pierrepoint hanged German spies and U.S. servicemen found guilty by court martial of committing capital crimes in England. After the war, Pierrepoint was sent to Germany, where he executed war criminals for acts committed at Bergen-Belsen and Auschwitz concentration camps.

rate of suspected murders was 150 percent lower than that of New York, and during the period 2016–2017, the city had only the ninth-highest murder rate in the UK.[1] For official purposes, London's authorities employ the World Health Organization (WHO) definition of violence: "The intentional use of physical force or power, threatened or actual, against oneself, another person, or against a group or community that either results in or has a high likelihood of resulting in injury, death, psychological harm, maldevelopment, or deprivation." Reports focused on violence in London tend to look at interpersonal violence—that is, between family members, partners, friends, and acquaintances, as well as between strangers. These reports examine youth violence, partner violence, and sexual violence and include all violence against the person (murder, violence with injury, and violence without injury), all forms of sexual assault, and robbery. Although domestic abuse, gang violence, and knife crime are specific forms of violence that are documented in London, these are not classed as specific offense types and so are not defined in offense data.

London is one of the world's biggest cities, covering 32 boroughs of varying size, with some boroughs as large as medium-sized cities. London is home to around 9 million people, and the characteristics of London's neighborhoods and communities vary greatly. One important variable is population density. For example, in Tower Hamlets, South East London, the population is much more densely packed, with 160 people per hectare, than in Bromley, South London, where there are 22 people per hectare. Levels of wealth vary greatly across the capital too. Given such variations across the city, it is unwise to generalize about changes in levels of violence London-wide, as doing so can mask major differences across the city. Disparities in London crime are evident when crime is looked at from a borough level, for "combined rates of violence against the person, sexual offenses and robbery range from just under 2,000 per 100,000 people in Richmond-upon-Thames," in South West London, to almost 4,000 in Hammersmith and Fulham, in West London.[2]

Violence in London is proportional to London's share of the UK's population, though the city's robbery rate is disproportionately high. Violence against the person is the most prevalent form of violence in London. However, London's rate of violence is fairly proportional to the city's population, for London accounts for 15 percent of the UK's population and for 15 percent of all violent offenses in England and Wales.[3] Nonetheless, London's robbery rate is four times higher than that of the rest of England and of Wales, with London accounting for 40 percent of all robberies in the two countries. One of the key reasons for London's high street-robbery rate is that around 2 million people travel into London every day, which makes for a larger supply of potential victims.[4]

Several factors indicate a real rise in both the frequency and severity of violence in London. For instance, there was an over 20 percent increase between 2013–2014 and 2017–2018 in ambulance calls to violent incidents in London and a 32 percent increase in the number of hospital admissions due to assaults with sharp objects, confirming an increase in knife use during the same period.[5] At the same time, the number of murders, which are reliably recorded by the police because they are such a severe crime, rose by 4 percent.[6]

Since 2014, there has been a 73 percent rise in the rate of sexual assaults recorded in London, while in 2018 there was an increase in the number of rapes reported, with the figure rising to 7,613 from 6,392 the previous year.[7] According to official statistics, 15 percent of all recorded sexual offenses in the UK occur in London, though analysis suggests that the increase in sexual offenses in London is probably due mainly to improved recording of such offenses. Despite the rise in the number of sexual crimes in London, only 6 percent of government funding is spent on helping victims of sexual assault.[8]

It is hard to tell the extent of domestic abuse in London, because domestic abuse is often underreported; victims do not want to come forward, resulting in many instances of domestic abuse not being captured by the police. Additionally, domestic abuse is not a specific offense. Rather, incidents are identified as domestic when recorded that way by the police. However, it is believed that rates of domestic violence in London have risen dramatically in recent years with a report released by the Mayor's Office for Policing and Crime revealing that between 2011 and 2018, there was a 63 percent increase in domestic abuse offenses in London, with 246,700 adults 16 to 59 years of age having experienced such abuse during this period. The report found that 5.9 percent of London women had experienced domestic violence compared to 2.9 percent of London men.[9] Consequently, Mayor Khan announced an extra £15 million in funding for domestic violence victim support services.

Increases in knife crimes have, arguably, captured Londoners' attention more than any other crime issue. From June 2018 to June 2019, record highs of 15,023 knife crime offenses occurred. This total, which does not include knife possession offenses, included 79 attempted murders, 63 murders (according to the UK's Office for National Statistics, ONS, this number represents a decrease of a third in fatal stabbings in London), 4,855 assaults involving a blade, 164 knife-point rapes or sexual assaults, and 812 threats to kill using a blade.[10] A possible reason for the most recent increase in knife crime could be increased police enforcement, resulting in more offenders being apprehended. Since 2014, London has also witnessed a small rise in the proportion of robberies and attempted murders that involve knives, though the use of knives in other offenses has remained roughly the same. The rise is the use of knives in crime has resulted in a general belief among Londoners that knife crime is a problem in the area in which they live. According to research by the Public Attitudes Survey (PAS, an annual survey in which 12,800 Londoners are interviewed about their experiences and attitudes toward policing and crime), since 2014 the number of Londoners that felt knife crime was a problem in their locale grew by approximately 5 percent across London, to 28.6 percent in 2018–2019.[11] However, this average percentage masks local variation in Londoners' fears over knife crime. For instance, in Barking and Dagenham, in East London, there was a 9 percent increase in such worries, as 33 percent of residents feared knife crime in 2018–2019, whereas in Ealing, West London, the percentage of residents who considered knife crime a problem in their area remained stable during this period, at around 25 percent. Meanwhile in Lambeth, South East London, people's concerns over knife crime fell from 52 percent in 2014–2015 to 26 percent the following year but then rose to 42 percent in 2018–2019.[12]

Since 2010, the detection rates for knife crime in London have fallen, to 13 percent in March 2019. At the same time, charge rates for violence decreased to 8 percent.[13] As a result of these decreases, Londoners' perception of the police's ability to deal with both violence and crime in general, as well as their ability to protect the public, also worsened. Consequently, there is a perceived rise in violence in London. This has become something of a self-fulfilling prophecy: the lack of faith in the police can result in victims of crime perpetrating violence themselves as they react in kind, carry weapons, or seek protection from groups other than the police. There is evidence that during the same period, the street drug trade saw increases in the supply and purity of cocaine, a change that made the drug scene more lucrative, while the drug trade also became more competitive owing to greater competition from drug suppliers online. The rise of the dark web (secret, encrypted online networks) as a place to trade drugs may have increased the competition between drug gangs in London as the street drug market becomes smaller and less lucrative. A more lucrative yet smaller street drug market may be behind an increase in London violence, for the reduction in the size of the street drug market means there is increasing competition between organized criminal drug-peddling groups. The competition between criminal gangs may also be a factor in the rise of "county lines," that is, drug gangs from big cities that have expanded their operations to smaller towns. Violence is a primary component of these drug networks. But typically, county lines rely not only on violence to drive out local community leaders but also the exploitation of vulnerable individuals as drug couriers.

Increased competition in the illegal drug trade may also have driven increases in London violence. There is no data to explore changes in drug supply and demand in London. However, the Home Office Serious Violence Strategy (which establishes the UK government's response to serious violence, including increases in murder and knife and gun crime) suggests that a surge in the cultivation of coca (from which cocaine is derived) in Colombia since 2013 has greatly influenced rising rates of violence in England and Wales. The increase in coca cultivation has caused crack cocaine to have greater purity; between 2013 and 2016, crack cocaine purity in England rose from 36 percent to 71 percent.[14] The increased purity may make the drug more addictive, thereby increasing demand. This may be the case in the UK, for the Home Office Serious Violence Strategy has reported a recent increase in the number of people asking for treatment for crack cocaine problems. In general, in recent years the UK has seen an increase in drug use among people ages 16 to 24, with a particularly sharp rise in the number of 16- to 24-year-olds using powder cocaine.

London's crime and violence have tragic human consequences. Both also cost London financially, for there are costs incurred in anticipating and responding to crime as well as in the direct results of violent crime— not just the loss of victims' time and quality of life but also their economic output. In 2019, violence in London cost £3 billion.[15] Violence in London has increased significantly in recent years, following almost a decade during which rates of violence declined. For instance, police data shows there has been an increase of more than 60 percent since 2014 in violent crimes, including murder and violence with and without injury.[16] Much of the violent incidents recorded in London are driven by an increase in knife use.

In London, violence is highly concentrated geographically with significant variations according to location. Therefore, it is difficult to a degree, to give a London-wide picture of violence. Some parts of London have low or decreasing rates of violence while other areas of the city may be experiencing high or increasing levels of violence. Recent data confirms that many violent crimes are particularly grouped in a very small, localized geographical area. For this reason, London's authorities believe it is necessary to take a highly localized approach to anticipating and responding to violence in London. From 2013 to 2017, most parts of London did not experience a rise in violence but rather experienced a decrease in such crimes. This was true even for parts of London situated close to parts of the city that saw a high increase in violence. In fact, between 2013 and 2017, only 1 percent of London neighborhoods had a significant or increasing violent crime rate.[17] London's geographic clustering of violence suggests an interaction between specific locations that share demographic and social characteristics. For instance, areas of London that experience high levels of crime and violence are also more likely to have higher levels of deprivation and particularly low income levels than areas of London with lower rates of crime and violence. Deprivation and a lack of a sense of community between neighbors allow gangs to flourish. According to the London School of Economics (LSE), gangs tend to evolve in parts of London that are more deprived, with higher number of migrant residents, lower house prices, and lower levels of education attainment. The deprivation experienced in the parts of London most vulnerable to gang violence is deep seated: over half the poorest London neighborhoods were also the poorest London neighborhoods over a century ago, while the gang territories identifiable today correspond to poor areas identified in 1900.[18] Levels of social cohesion help to protect parts of London against violence. While low income is the greatest factor in whether or not a London neighborhood is vulnerable to violence, the relationship between income deprivation and violence is not consistent, for neighborhoods that have low levels of violence can exist in highly deprived areas, while a smaller number of high-violence neighborhoods are located in areas of the city that are not deprived. It is impossible to say why this is the case, but community cohesion and the level of trust people have in their neighbors seem to be major factors. Evidence suggests that when people know and trust each other and also share common beliefs in how their neighborhood should be, they are more likely to take collective responsibility for public safety in their locale, for instance, by confronting people who disturb the public peace. Additionally, such areas are more likely to work with the police and other bodies to prevent violence in their neighborhood. A reduction in government spending resulting from the 2008 global recession is thought to have led to increased violence in some parts of London. While it is impossible to conclude that there is a causal link between the recession and rates of violence in the city, both past research and current data indicate that when the most deprived parts of London experience reduced economic opportunities, falling wages, and reductions in public spending, the neighborhoods become more vulnerable to crime and violence. Recessions are linked to increased crime rates, because during recessions, people find it harder to find or stay in employment; they suffer greater mental stress resulting from financial stress and more spare time. It is probable that reductions in state expenditure on public services since 2010 have made it harder for London's authorities to identify, anticipate, and, therefore, prevent violence. For instance, between 2011 and 2019, around half of all funding for London's youth services ended. Research by the LSE suggests a link between these cuts and increases in the rates of knife crime. Cuts to the UK's police and criminal justice service also affect authorities' ability to stop violence in London. For instance, since 2010, London's Metropolitan Police Service (MPS) has experienced a 10 percent fall in the number of frontline police, while the number of police civil support staff has decreased by 37 percent.[19] At the same time, cuts in public sector finances in general resulted in an increase in noncrime demand on the police (i.e., public safety and concern for welfare incidents), meaning that the police's time was stretched further. The rise in noncrime demand made it harder for the MPS to concentrate on building relationships with the communities they served and to perform crime prevention work within neighborhoods that were prone to violent incidents.

Various proposals to counteract the number of violent incidents in London have been proposed. For example, street- and neighborhood-level crime analysis is carried out to identify areas' vulnerability to crime and violence, as this also allows resources to be targeted for maximum impact. In the short term, it has been discovered that the most effective way to target this funding is to focus on the most violent neighborhoods and to explore patterns of violence in these neighborhoods, such as identifying the times when most violence occurs. Once particularly violent neighborhoods are identified, London's authorities work to develop strategies that are tailored to an individual locale in order to prevent violence and help people feel safe. These strategies can include deploying police officers to certain locations (i.e., schools or bus stops) or implementing changes to

Police officers on the beat in London. The city's centralized police force (the Metropolitan Police) was established in 1829 by Sir Robert Peel. For this reason, London's police are sometimes referred to as "bobbies." (Mark Sepple/Dreamstime.com)

the physical landscape, such as improved street lighting. London's authorities consider it necessary to improve their understanding of the nature of violence—to see how frequently violence occurs, why it occurs, and who are the victims of violence. For this reason, research has been commissioned on neighborhoods and what drives violence in London. The key questions being asked by the research are these: Why are some deprived neighborhoods more vulnerable to violence than others, what proportion of violent incidents are premeditated, and which violent incidents are impulsive? The risk of violence in individual neighborhoods is assessed, as are the causes of or motives for violence, the contexts in which violence occurs, and the behaviors that result in violence. However, authorities realize that even the best antiviolence initiatives will fail if the people who need them most do not want to participate in the initiatives or cannot access them. For this reason, the relevant authorities try to identify and remove the barriers that people face. Barriers to access can be structural, such as a lack of time or money that prevent people from using a service, or behavioral/psychological—for example, when people feel let down by services, they may not engage with them in the future. At the moment, there are hundreds of violence-prevention initiatives being implemented across London. Many of these initiatives involve multiple agencies and aim to break down cultural differences and increase cohesion across social boundaries. Analysis for the College of Policing reveals that many forms of violent crime are heavily concentrated in a very small proportion of neighborhoods and that since 2014, most of London's neighborhoods have not experienced increases in violence. Between 2013 and 2017, violence in general increased in a handful of neighborhoods but decreased in many others, sometimes even when in close proximity to areas that have experienced a high increase. Between 2013 and 2017, only 0.12 percent of London neighborhoods saw a large and increasingly violent crime rate: three of these neighborhoods were in Lambeth, one was in Wandsworth, one was located in Haringey, and another was in Barking and Dagenham.[20]

Recent data analysis reveals that young Black men are more likely to be affected by violence in London, both as victims and offenders. This analysis has not considered whether the men were also more likely to reside in areas characterized by high rates of violence. Across London, violence is most common in areas that experience high rates of entrenched deprivation. Historical data reveals a strong correlation between poverty and violence, and in London there does seem to be a link between area-level deprivation and violence: three-quarters of the London Boroughs that experience the highest levels of violence appear in the top ten most deprived boroughs and have higher proportions of children living in poverty than the London average. Additionally, analysis by the Greater London Authority (GLA) shows rates of youth violence highest in boroughs that have high rates of long-term unemployment, low educational attainment rates, high numbers of residents who receive universal credit (a UK state benefit for people who are unemployed or on a low income), a high rate of mortgage nonpayment, more people earning less than the minimum wage, and higher rates of homelessness. London's high-violence neighborhoods also suffer greater barriers to accommodation and services, more health problems, and worse living conditions, including poorer quality housing and more air pollution.

The presence of gangs in some parts of London may explain the levels of violence in some neighborhoods, for in London, gangs exist in areas with the highest levels of poverty, higher numbers of migrants, lowest house prices, and lowest average education attainment levels. Poverty and a lack of community cohesion have led to gangs operating in these London neighborhoods and attract organized criminal activity from outside. Researchers have discovered that in London, knife crime may be especially associated with gangs and that the more gangs operate in an area, the higher the rate of knife crime, increasing the prevalence of knife crime between 15 percent and 35 percent.[21] The deprivation of some parts of London and their vulnerability to the presence of gangs run deep, for around half of London's poorest areas were also the poorest neighborhoods over a century ago. Similarly, the areas of London in which gangs operate today were identified as poor in 1898 and 1900. According to a commissioned government report titled "Violence in London," in 2020, it is not possible to explain the seemingly established relationship between neighborhood poverty, weak social cohesion, and individuals' vulnerability to involvement in gang activity. The report also could not explain concretely why some neighborhoods have a continued gang presence despite their populations changing significantly over time.[22] Possible explanations for a relationship between local poverty, weak community cohesion, and a location's vulnerability to gangs include poor planning of the built environment, a lack of access to transport, long-term underinvestment in services, and the availability of cheap accommodation that attracts people who might be vulnerable to gang involvement.

The availability of alcohol and the nighttime economy are also important factors in the violence seen in some areas of London. The availability of alcohol increases the likelihood of violence because alcohol influences people's reasoning and can make people act more aggressively. By impeding people's mental and physical functioning, alcohol can also cause people to become victims of violence. Research has shown that at a neighborhood level, the availability of alcohol (in terms of outlet density) is strongly associated with violence within a neighborhood. In particular, public violence is driven by alcohol, as evinced by the fact that most violent incidents involving alcohol in England and Wales happen on weekends and at night.

In England and Wales, 39 percent of victims of violence claim the perpetrator was under the influence of alcohol, and research has also shown a link between heavy drinking and domestic abuse.[23] In 2016, research by the GLA found a link between London's nighttime economy, crime, and alcohol. GLA analysis also reveals that much serious youth violence that occurs in the London borough of Westminster involves victims and perpetrators who do not live in the borough, thereby suggesting that London's nighttime economy is an important factor in Westminster's serious violence.

The 2008 recession and related reductions in public spending may have increased the vulnerability of some London neighborhoods to violence. Research suggests a strong link between reduced opportunities, lower wages, and reductions in public spending, and some parts of London's increased vulnerability to violence. Reductions in public spending may have made it more difficult to protect young people at risk of violence and identify those who may be in danger of becoming either a victim or perpetrator of violence. Between 2011 and 2019, roughly half of the funding for London's council youth services was axed, leaving young people at risk of involvement with violence without support networks and safe spaces. For instance, between June 2018 and 2019, 568 young Londoners were referred to London's Rescue and Response (R&R) project, which works with young people involved in county lines. Of the 568 young people, 72 percent had been reported missing at least once before they were referred, 58 percent were under social care at the time they were referred, 36 percent were recorded as being linked to a gang, and 50 percent had experienced child sexual abuse or sexual violence at the time of their referral. Researchers believe these figures suggest that London's authorities had missed earlier opportunities to intervene in the lives of these young people.[24]

Reductions in police numbers and the wider criminal justice service have also likely made it harder to deter violence in London. It is possible that a reduced presence of the police on the streets of London impedes the police's ability to prevent violent incidents. For example, research reveals that the surge in the number of police patrolling central London in the aftermath of the July 2005 bombings resulted in a small but significant drop in crime, including violent crime. This decrease in crime suggests that an increased police presence on the streets prevents crimes from occurring, particularly the crimes of common assaults, aggravated bodily harm, and harassment because perpetrators fear they have more chance of being apprehended by the law. Between 2010 and 2019, the number of frontline police in the MPS fell by 10 percent, meaning there were 8,000 fewer police officers and police community-support officers. At the same time, the number of civil support staff fell by 37 percent, from 14,330 to 8,968, while reductions in spending on the wider public sector resulted in an increase in noncrime demand to the police. Consequently, since 2010, the police and criminal justice system have seen their ability to apprehend and punish violent offenders reduced. Detection rates for knife crime have halved, from 27 percent in 2014 to 13 percent in 2019, and charge rates for violent crimes have fallen from roughly 15 percent in 2014–2015 to 8 percent in 2018–2019.[25]

Since 2011–2012, there has also been a significant fall in the rates of "stop and search." Stop and search is a controversial power that allows a police officer to stop and then search a person, vehicle, and anything being carried by an individual. Critics of stop and search claim Black people are targeted disproportionately by the police, which leads to damaged community relations. In recent years, the number of stop and search incidents has increased as London police attempt to tackle violent crime in the city. For instance, the number of searches rose from 1,836 in 2017–2018 to 9,599 in 2018–2019. Similarly, during the same period, the number of authorized section 60 orders, which allow the police to search anyone in an area if they believe serious violence may occur, rose by 219 percent.[26] The impact of stop and search on violent crime is unclear. One study looking at ten years of stop and search data recorded in London from 2004 to 2014 discovered that a 10 percent increase in the number of stop and search incidents led to just a 0.01 percent fall in nondomestic violent offenses. However, recent analysis by the LSE suggests that a reduction in stop and search, together with declines in enforcement activity, such as arrests, may have led to an increase in the prevalence of people carrying knives.[27] The research does not, however, capture the potential negative effects of a loss of trust in the police that has been caused by stop and search, so it is difficult to tell if there are public protection benefits to that particular police power. At the same time as these changes to policing occurred, a reduction in police numbers became central to the public discourse on violent crime in London, especially the public's perception of the police's ability to apprehend violent offenders. The lack of faith that Londoners have in the police's ability to curtail violent crime may have resulted in increases in violence. Indeed, while the public's perceptions that the police are unable to protect them has grown, the public increasingly fears violence. There is some evidence that a lack of trust in the police and criminal justice system can result in victims of crime becoming perpetrators themselves as they seek revenge, carry weapons, or seek protection from an unofficial source instead of asking for police help. This is true particularly when people believe that the risk of violence is rising while the ability of authorities to address violence is decreasing. Between 2014–2015 and 2018–2019, the proportion of Londoners who believed knife crime was an issue in their neighborhood increased from 23 percent to 28.6 percent, though some boroughs saw greater increases.[28]

Some areas of London that do not follow such patterns for some highly deprived neighborhoods do not have levels of high violence, while a smaller number of high-violence areas of London are not deprived. Researchers do not know why some parts of London are resistant to violence, though community cohesion is likely an important protective factor. Community cohesion can help protect neighborhoods from violence, because when society members know each other, they share common goals for their neighborhoods and take greater collective responsibility for public safety.

Founded in 2018, London's Violence Reduction Unit (VRU) brings together specialists from the police, health services, local government, the probation service, and community organizations to reduce violence across London while also tackling the causes of violent crime. The VRU reports that violence in London is concentrated in a small number of lower layer super output areas (LSOAs, geospatial statistical units used in England and Wales to allow the reporting of area statistics) and that from 2013 to 2017, fewer than 1 percent of these LSOAs experienced a large and increasing crime rate.[29] Since borough-level comparisons can mask variations in violence levels within boroughs, it is necessary to look at variations in violence rates within smaller geographical areas in order to identify areas that should be targeted for violence prevention initiatives. Once neighborhoods that are vulnerable to violence are identified, London's authorities try to understand why violence is high there so that they can develop strategies to tackle the issues. For example, research had found that around half of all victims and perpetrators of youth violence in Westminster are from outside the borough. This suggests that the nighttime economy of the Soho area of Westminster is probably an important factor in the area's violence.

The reduction in police numbers has become central to Londoners' discourse on their city's violent crime. Consequently, Londoners' worries over knife crime have increased. To prevent levels of violence rising as a result of a lack of trust in the authorities, as well as to combat Londoners' increasing concerns about violence, local bodies work with London's police to focus on places particularly associated with violence such as schools and other places where violence tends to occur at certain times, such as bus stops at the end of the school day or before soccer matches. Other place-based interventions include changing street layouts, reducing the availability of alcohol, and better street lighting.

Simply noting the number of violent incidents recorded by the police obscures differences in damage caused by various types of violence. This, in turn, can lead to resources being allocated incorrectly. Therefore, researchers have developed a "crime harm index" that assesses violent offenses based on offenses' severity, and severity is evaluated through the use of existing sentencing guidelines.

NOTES

1. Haroon Siddique, "How Does London's Spate of Killings Compare with Other Cities?" *The Guardian*, April 5, 2018, https://www.theguardian.com/uk-news/2018/apr/05/how-does-londons-spate-of-killings-compare-with-other-cities.

2. Handan Wieshmann et al., *Violence in London: what we know and how to respond*, Mayor of London's Violence Reduction Unit, January 28, 2020, https://www.london.gov.uk/sites/default/files/bit_london_violence_reduction_final_28_january_2020.pdf, 20.

3. Ibid., 13.

4. Ibid.

5. Ibid., 5.

6. Ibid., 16.

7. Lizzie Dearden, "London Sees 20 Percent Rise in Rape Reports in a Year, but Police Admit They 'Don't Understand' Reason," *The Independent*, February 23, 2018, https://www.independent.co.uk/news/uk/crime/rape-london-reports-met-police-rise-crime-sexual-assault-a8225821.html.

8. Sarah Marsh, "Domestic Abuse Offences in London Rise 63 Percent in Seven Years," *The Guardian*, February 27, 2019, https://www.theguardian.com/society/2019/feb/27/domestic-violence-london-rise.

9. Ibid.

10. Martin Bentham, "London Knife Crime at Record High with 15,023 Offences in a Year," *Evening Standard*, October 17, 2019, https://www.standard.co.uk/news/crime/london-knife-crime-at-record-high-with-15023-offences-in-a-year-a4264066.html.

11. Wieshmann et al., 19.

12. Ibid., 19.

13. Ibid., 6.

14. Ibid., 29.

15. Ibid., 5.

16. Ibid.

17. Ibid.

18. Ibid.

19. Ibid., 31.

20. Ibid., 21.

21. Ibid., 24.

22. Ibid.

23. Ibid., 25.

24. Ibid., 30.

25. Ibid., 31.

26. Simon Murphy, "Stop and Searches in London Up Fivefold under Controversial Powers," *The Guardian*, June 4, 2019, https://www.theguardian.com/law/2019/jun/04/stop-and-searches-in-london-soar-after-police-powers-widened.

27. Ibid., 31.

28. Ibid., 19.

29. Ibid., 5.

FURTHER READING

Arnold, Catharine. *Underworld London: Crime and Punishment in the Capital City*. London: Simon & Schuster, 2012.

Bentham, Martin. "London Knife Crime at Record High with 15,023 Offences in a Year." *Evening Standard*, October 17, 2019. https://www.standard.co.uk/news/crime/london-knife-crime-at-record-high-with-15023-offences-in-a-year-a4264066.html.

Dearden, Lizzie. "London Sees 20 Percent Rise in Rape Reports in a Year, but Police Admit They 'Don't Understand' Reason." *The Independent*, February 23, 2018. https://www.independent.co.uk/news/uk/crime/rape-london-reports-met-police-rise-crime-sexual-assault-a8225821.html.

Linnane, Fergus. *London's Underworld: Three Centuries of Vice and Crime*. London: Robson Books, 2004.

Marsh, Sarah. "Domestic Abuse Offences in London Rise 63 Percent in Seven Years." *The Guardian*, February 27, 2019. https://www.theguardian.com/society/2019/feb/27/domestic-violence-london-rise.

McFarlane, Andrew, and Alexis Akwagyiram. "Poll Tax Riots: 20 Years after Violence Shook London." *BBC News Magazine*, March 31, 2010. http://news.bbc.co.uk/1/hi/magazine/8593158.stm.

Murphy, Simon. "Stop and Searches in London Up Fivefold under Controversial Powers." *The Guardian*, June 4, 2019. https://www.theguardian.com/law/2019/jun/04/stop-and-searches-in-london-soar-after-police-powers-widened.

Siddique, Haroon. "How Does London's Spate of Killings Compare with Other Cities?" *The Guardian*, April 5, 2018. https://www.theguardian.com/uk-news/2018/apr/05/how-does-londons-spate-of-killings-compare-with-other-cities.

"What Londoners Tell Us around Knife Crime and Violence." Mayor of London, January 2019. https://www.london.gov.uk/moderngovmb/documents/s63353/Appendix%20B%20-%20MOPAC%20Surveys%20presentation.pdf.

Wieshmann, Handan, Matthew Davies, Ollie Sugg, Sophie Davis, and Simon Ruda. *Violence in London: What We Know and How to Respond*. Mayor of London's Violence Reduction Unit, January 28, 2020. https://www.london.gov.uk/sites/default/files/bit_london_violence_reduction_final_28_january_2020.pdf.

Wright, John D. *Bloody History of London: Crime, Corruption and Murder*. London: Amber Books, 2017.

8

Security Issues

In the UK, terrorism is defined legally under the Terrorism Act 2006 as "an action or threat designed to influence the Government or intimidate the public. Its purpose is to advance a political, religious or ideological cause."[1] London has a long history of terrorist incidents, ranging from the work of anarchist groups such as the far-left Angry Brigade, individual neo-Nazi extremists, Scottish nationalists, and, more recently, organizations linked to domestic and international politics.

It is hard to say which was the first act of terrorism in London. The most famous incident in London's early modern history is the 1605 Gunpowder Plot that saw Guy Fawkes and his coconspirators try to blow up the House of Lords on November 5. The Gunpowder Plot aimed to blow up the Palace at Westminster while King James I and his ministers attended the state opening of Parliament there, to avenge the king's increasing oppression of Roman Catholics in England. Today, the Gunpowder Plot is commemorated by England's Bonfire Night (or Guy Fawkes Night) tradition that sees bonfires and fireworks lit both at public displays and in private gardens every November 5. Traditionally, an effigy of Guy Fawkes known as a "guy" is burned atop the bonfires. Such is the cultural significance of the Gunpowder Plot in England that Bonfire Night is remembered via the popular rhyme "Remember, remember, the fifth of November, Gunpowder, Treason and Plot."

While the majority of recent terrorist incidents that have occurred in London have been linked to Irish or Middle East politics, London has also suffered terrorist attacks by others. For instance, in the 1999 London nail bombings, a series of homemade nail bombs exploded across London in attacks against London's Black, Bengali, and LGBTQ communities. Over three successive weekends (starting on April 17), homemade bombs containing long nails were detonated from carryalls left in public places. The first bomb exploded in Brixton, South London, which is home to a large African population and is a focal point of the UK's Caribbean community. The Brixton bomb injured 47 people.[2] The second blast, which injured six people, occurred on Brick Lane in Spitalfields in London's East End, which is famous for its preponderance of restaurants serving curry and its role in the development of Anglo-Indian cuisine. Brick Lane lies at the heart of London's Bengali (from Bangladesh and India) community and is sometimes called Banglatown. The third, and most infamous, explosion occurred at the Admiral Duncan, a pub located on Old Compton Street in Soho's West End that is popular with London's LGBTQ community. The Admiral Duncan blast killed 3 people, including a pregnant woman, and injured 140 others, with 4 people losing limbs. On May 2, 1999, the Met Police's Anti-Terrorist Branch charged a neo-Nazi paranoid schizophrenic, David Copeland, with murder. In 2000, Copeland was convicted of murder and given six life sentences to be served concurrently at the high-security Broadmoor Hospital.

LONDON AND THE TROUBLES

Before the 2000s, most terrorist attacks in London were linked to conflict in Northern Ireland that was often referred to as "the Troubles." On December 13, 1867, for example, in the attack known as the "Clerkenwell Outrage," a bomb planted by Fenians (organizations bent on the establishment of an independent Irish Republic during the nineteenth and early twentieth centuries) at New Prison in Clerkenwell exploded, killing twelve people. The Fenians also launched attacks in London over subsequent years at locations that included Underground stations, Nelson's Column, and police headquarters. The majority of terrorist attacks connected to the conflict in Northern Ireland involved the Irish Republican Army (IRA).

In 1939, the IRA launched a terrorist campaign against Britain called the S-Plan (or Sabotage Campaign). During this campaign, the IRA perpetrated numerous attacks, including multiple bombings of London's transport infrastructure, mailboxes, trash receptacles, and banks. Subsequently, the IRA and other republican groups committed hundreds more attacks in England, most of which occurred in London. For instance, during the period 1973 to 1982, the IRA committed 252 bombings and 19 shootings. As a result, 56 people were killed and 800 were wounded, many of them permanently injured.[3] The victims of the IRA attacks included politicians, soldiers, police officers, off-duty service personnel, shoppers, tourists, and children.

June 17, 1974. At 8:28 a.m., the IRA detonated a 20-pound bomb in a corner of Westminster Hall, causing a gas main to fracture. An ensuing fire spread rapidly through the building and took eight hours to extinguish. At least 25 percent of the basement and ground floor of the 900-year-old Westminster Hall was destroyed, and 11 people were injured, though the majority of the injuries were minor.[4] Just minutes before the explosion, a warning about the bomb was telephoned to the Press Association using a recognized IRA code word. The early morning detonation of the bomb meant that most people that worked in the Hall had not yet arrived. Had the bomb exploded later in the day, the number of injured would likely have been much higher. Nevertheless, the bombing was the worst terrorist attack on Parliament since 1604.[5] IRA leaders in Ireland blamed the bombing on a breakaway active service unit (ASU) operating in London and denied any direct role in the bombing. Despite the denial, UK authorities held the IRA responsible for the bombing, which led to some politicians demanding the death penalty for the terrorists.

The bombing led to a review of security around Parliament, as it was a widely held view that the bombing had been enabled by lax security: many of the builders who had access to Parliament were Irish workers who were passing through and had not undergone any kind of security checks. Authorities announced that an immediate review of security would occur and stressed that the bombing would not disrupt Parliament. A month later, on July 27, 1974, a bomb exploded in the Tower of London's basement exhibition space known as the Mortar Room, following a warning. At the time of the explosion, the small space was filled with tourists. The explosion killed 1 person and injured 41 others, including 8 children, with injuries including severe facial injuries and amputations.[6] The Tower of London reopened two days later, but the Mortar Room remained closed. No group claimed responsibility for the bombing, but the UK's authorities blamed the IRA or an IRA splinter group for the blast.

July 20, 1982. The IRA exploded two bombs in London's Hyde Park and Regent's Park during British military displays. The bombs killed 11 military personnel (4 soldiers at Hyde Park, and 7 bandsmen at Regent's Park). Seven horses also died in the attack. One of the worst injured surviving horses, Sefton, suffered 38 wounds, including the severing of a major artery in his neck.[7] Sefton was later awarded the title of the UK's "Horse of the Year."

December 17, 1983. A bomb exploded outside London department store Harrods during Christmas shopping hours. The Provisional IRA planted a time bomb and sent a warning shortly before the bomb exploded. Along with the real bomb warning, the terrorists also warned that other bombs had been planted in order to confuse the situation. As it was, the true bomb warning gave insufficient time for the police to clear the area, and the location was not evacuated in time. Consequently, 3 civilians and 3 police officers died in the explosion, while 90 others were injured.[8] Of the injured, 77 were civilians, while 13 were police officers; one policeman lost both legs and a hand in the blast.[9] The bomb also showered splinters of glass on Christmas shoppers and damaged all five floors of Harrods, though the shop reopened three days later despite the destruction. After the Harrods bombing, hundreds of extra police officers and bomb squads were mobilized in London to protect the public from further bombings.

At the time of the Harrods bombing, Sinn Féin, the political wing of the IRA, had begun to attract an increasing amount of electoral support as well as international backing. The attack on Christmas shoppers proved a public relations disaster for Sinn Féin, however. Consequently, Martin McGuinness (a former IRA leader turned Sinn Féin politician, later deputy first minister for Northern Ireland) issued a statement that declared IRA units were aware that they should avoid civilian casualties. McGuinness also declared that the Harrods bombing had not been endorsed by the IRA's High Command and that the coded warning proved there had been no intention to kill or injure the public. Despite this declaration, the Harrods bombing (as well as the 1984 attack on the Conservative Party's annual conference in Brighton) greatly harmed Sinn Féin's growing links between the party and British socialist groups who sympathized with some of the IRA's objectives. The Harrods bombing was also widely condemned in the United States, where the IRA earned much financial support through the Northern Irish Aid Committee (NORAID). The loss of finances from the United States hit the IRA hard and meant the organization had to rely increasingly on the Middle East (especially Libya) and Europe for both finances and weapons. The IRA attacked Harrods again in January 1993, when one pound of Semtex exploded in a litter bin in front of the shop. The blast injured four people and broke many windows.[10]

April 10, 1992. A massive bomb comprising military-grade Semtex wrapped in 300 pounds of ammonium nitrate exploded outside the Baltic Exchange (for shipping freight) in St. Mary Axe on the east side of the City of London. The explosion took place the day after the UK's general election, during which Gerry Adams of Sinn Féin lost his seat and the Conservative Party retained power. Although a man using a recognized IRA code word telephoned a warning to London's Waterloo Station to warn that a bomb would explode near the Baltic Exchange, the warning gave only 20 minutes' notice of the bomb.[11] The bomb killed 3 people and injured 91 others.[12] The number of deaths would likely have been much higher had the bomb exploded during traditional office hours. The bomb also caused an estimated £800 million (roughly $1.2 billion) of damage, a figure four times the amount of damage caused by over 10,000 explosions that had occurred during the IRA's activities in Northern Ireland up to that point.[13] Although the Baltic Exchange's trading floor reopened days after the explosion, authorities were unable to use the building in a manner that was consistent with the requirements of English Heritage (a charity that manages many English historic sites). In 1995, the Baltic Exchange site was sold in the hope that the building's interior could be saved and incorporated into some future development. Subsequently, however, it was found that the building was too damaged to restore. Today, the bomb site is part of the London skyscraper commonly called the "Gherkin."

April 24, 1993. A bomb composed of roughly 1,000 tons of fertilizer and planted in a stolen truck exploded outside 99 Bishopsgate (a commercial skyscraper in the financial heartland of the City of London). Several coded warnings were telephoned to the police that a huge bomb was set to explode and that the Bishopsgate area should be evacuated straightaway. However, the bomb, which detonated at 10:25 a.m., exploded while the police were still clearing the area of people. Fortunately, the fact that the bomb occurred on a Saturday morning meant Bishopsgate was largely empty of office workers, but office security guards, builders, and maintenance staff were injured by the blast. In total, the bomb killed 1 person (a young press photographer who had rushed to the area to record events) and injured 44 others while also damaging buildings up to 546 yards away, with 1.5 million square feet of office space damaged, and creating over 500 tons of broken glass.[14] The destruction caused approximately £350 million of damage.[15]

The Provisional IRA intended the explosion to cause the UK major economic damage and to prompt the UK government to enter into negotiations with Irish republicans. The most important aspect of the Bishopsgate bombing was that it served as a turning point in how antiterrorism security operated in London, for many new measures were implemented to detect and deter terrorism within the city. These measures included the so-called Ring of Steel that was established by City of London Police in July 1993. The Ring of Steel saw most roads into the City of London closed or made exit-only, while the police watched the remaining roads 24 hours per day. Additionally, armed police were stationed along roads that remained open, and closed-circuit television cameras were installed to monitor all vehicles moving around London, including two at each of the city's entry and departure points: one of the cameras read a vehicle's license plate while the other monitored the driver and any passengers. Another security measure introduced after the Bishopsgate bombing was the removal of 2,000 public trash cans from the streets of the City of London. The bins were reintroduced 20 years later.[16] The economic cost of the Bishopsgate bombing in the form of insurance payouts also triggered a financial crisis in the global insurance industry. As a consequence of the Bishopsgate bombing, the Pool Re program was initiated, whereby the UK government served as the reinsurer for losses over £75 million.[17] Pool Re influenced the development of the United States' Terrorism Risk Insurance Act (TRIA), established following the 9/11 attacks.

March 9, 11, and 13, 1994. On March 9, the IRA fired mortar shells at Heathrow Airport's northern runway, following a coded warning. It was the first of three such mortar attacks on the airport in the space of five days. None of the shells involved exploded, but the attacks caused serious travel disruption. Attacking Heathrow also served as a symbolic act because of the airport's importance to the UK's economy.

February 9, 1996. From February to September 1996, the Provisional IRA perpetrated a series of bombings and attempted attacks across London. Although the bombings did not cause mass casualties, they did cause significant economic damage while also threatening the burgeoning peace process between Irish groups and the UK government. The first, and most serious, attack occurred on February 9, when a 500-pound truck bomb explode in South Quay Station on the Docklands Light Railway. The explosion aimed to damage nearby Canary Wharf, one of London's biggest office and apartment complexes. Although the IRA sent warnings before the bomb exploded, the area was not fully evacuated in time to prevent the 2 deaths and injuries to 106 others. The bomb also caused an estimated £85 million worth of damage across a wide area.[18] The bombing marked the end of the IRA's 17-month-long cease-fire and came in reaction to the UK government's contention that the IRA must disarm before Sinn Féin could take part in peace talks with the government.

February 18, 1996. The Aldwych bus bombing involved an improvised bomb transported by a republican terrorist and detonated prematurely on a bus in Aldwych, near Trafalgar Square. The bomber died instantly, people both inside and outside the bus were injured, and the bus driver was left permanently deaf. The Aldwych explosion occurred three days after a failed bombing in London's Leicester Square entertainment area. The Leicester Square device had been hidden in a public telephone box and was primed to explode at lunchtime. However, the coded warning that the IRA telephoned revealed to police the location of the device, which was soon deactivated. Nobody was ever charged in connection with this failed bombing.

A third bombing occurred on March 9, 1996, when an improvised device exploded in a recycling bin outside Brompton Cemetery, in West

London. While the IRA group responsible for the bomb did not issue a prior warning of the bomb, nobody was injured by the blast, though the explosion did damage several homes around Earl's Court and South Kensington. Then, on April 17, 1996, a bomb exploded in the upscale Boltons residential area in the Royal Borough of Kensington and Chelsea, in West London. The IRA issued a warning a half hour before the bomb exploded, resulting in the bomb causing no casualties and limiting damage to houses in the immediate area. Six days later, two more bombs that had been planted beneath Hammersmith Bridge in West London malfunctioned and failed to explode. Consequently, the bomb caused no injuries or damage.

On July 15, 1996, the Metropolitan Police discovered bomb-making equipment at addresses in Tooting and Peckham, in South London. The authorities believed the equipment was intended to make bombs to attack utility installations in London and across southeastern England. Then, in September 1996, antiterrorist raids occurred on IRA hideouts in West London. During the raids, 10 tons of Semtex and other explosives were discovered along with trucks, assault rifles, and handguns, while an IRA gunman was killed during an exchange of fire. In response to the raids, then British prime minister John Major threatened to call off all contact with Sinn Féin, having previously agreed to include the party in peace talks surrounding the conflict in Northern Ireland. Major also insisted that the IRA reinstate its cease-fire. The IRA complied with this request in July 1997.

On April 10, 1998, the Good Friday Agreement (or Belfast Agreement), a peace agreement between the British and Irish governments, was signed. The Agreement ended most of the violence of the Troubles and saw the establishment of the Northern Ireland Assembly, which serves as the devolved legislature of Northern Ireland and makes political decisions that would previously have been made by the UK government in London.

Dissident republican groups opposed the signing of the Good Friday Agreement and as result, republican organizations including the Real IRA and Continuity IRA continued to perpetrate terrorist activities. For example, on July 19, 2000, bombs were discovered at Ealing Broadway Station in West London and Whitehall in Westminster. The devices were intended to disrupt the Queen Mother's centenary birthday pageant. On February 21, 2001, a bomb disguised as a torch exploded when it was picked up by a teenage army cadet outside a British barracks in Shepherd's Bush, West London. The cadet lost his left hand and left eye and suffered other severe injuries. On August 3, 2001, a car bomb exploded in Ealing Broadway, West London, injuring 7 people.[19] The bomb also damaged a nearby shopping center, which was flooded when the explosion ruptured a water pipe.

Devastating IRA attacks such as those on the Baltic Exchange, Bishops-gate, and Canary Wharf caused billions of pounds sterling in damage.[20] However, as major operations, these attacks took the IRA months of plan-ning and preparation. The attacks also relied on sleeper agents and experi-enced bombing teams operating in the UK. Since such attacks required so much preparation, they could be conducted only occasionally. Over time, the UK's authorities learned how to respond, identify, and arrest IRA oper-atives, and the potential for future attacks lessened. In particular, London's Ring of Steel coupled with the police's improved ability to track down most bombers meant that increasingly, IRA attacks became less potent and were viewed almost as distracting irritants.[21]

LONDON AND MIDDLE EAST TERRORISM

London has suffered several terrorist attacks linked to Middle East poli-tics. Following conflicts such as the Bosnian War (1992–1995), London became the hub for jihadist groups operating in Europe. London also served as a temporary location for jihadist recruits heading to Afghani-stan. For these reasons, the French security services dubbed London "Londonistan."[22]

Some academics have suggested that London became a hub for jihadists for a combination of reason: lax British immigration, multiculturalism, and a misplaced focus on the IRA by security services. However, other aca-demics counter these suggestions by pointing out that UK immigration policies were much the same as those of other European nations and that the UK security services did try to mitigate the threat of jihadist terrorists. The prevalence of jihadism in London was likely more the result of high-profile, charismatic individuals such as Egyptian preacher Abu Hamza al-Masri (usually referred to in the UK as Abu Hamza) who were linked to Islamist terrorism and lived in London. Other notable radical preachers operating in London included the Jordanian-Palestinian Abu Qatada and the Syrian Omar Bakri (sometimes called Omar Bakri Mohammed). All three made polemical sermons, ran activist organizations, and helped pro-duce propaganda while networking with extremist groups across Europe and beyond.[23]

Such individuals were able to attract numerous followers, whom they accumulated through Arabic-language newspapers available in the UK, through stressing historical British colonialism that resulted in resent-ment among younger followers, and by delivering inspirational sermons at locations such as Finsbury Park Mosque, in North London. For example, on the first anniversary of the 9/11 attacks, Abu Hamza helped organize a conference at Finsbury Park Mosque to praise the terrorists involved in the attacks. The terrorists who were later convicted of the failed 21/7 London bombings (a failed attempt to bomb the London transport network on July 21, 2005) heard that several of the would-be-attackers had heard Abu Hamza preach, while others convicted of terrorist offenses had links to the mosque.[24]

Since the trio of preachers did not share exactly the same ideologies or aims, they were able to attract different groups of followers. For instance, Abu Qatada was one of many Islamists who found refuge in the UK during the late 1980s and the 1990s. Abu Qatada went on to live in Acton, West London, and gained support among jihadists hailing from the Middle East, North Africa, Bosnia, and Chechnya while also having links to al-Qaida in Afghanistan and across Europe. In 2001, Abu Qatada was arrested in connection with a German terror cell, but charges against him were dropped on the grounds of insufficient evidence. Subsequently, however, recordings of his sermons were found in a flat used by the 9/11 attackers, and the UK's Home Office claimed Abu Qatada was the spiritual guide of the 9/11 ringleader Mohamed Atta. After 9/11, Abu Qatada disappeared, was later detained in prison, and then fought for many years against deportation to Jordan for a retrial in relation to alleged terrorist plots. In 2013, Abu Qatada was expelled from the UK despite years of legal battles involving the European Court of Human Rights. Ultimately, Abu Qatada was acquitted in Jordan of involvement in a plot to target Americans and Israeli tourists. Nonetheless, Abu Qatada was an important player in the London jihadist scene because his credentials as a scholar allowed him to posit his extremist views as philosophical arguments to justify violence. During his time in London, Abu Qatada preached to exiled Islamists at both a community center near Regent's Park and in his own home, justifying suicide bombings and attacks on Jews and civilians in general. A Spanish judge described Abu Qatada as the "spiritual head of the mujahideen in Britain,"[25] and the UK's Security Service and police concluded that Abu Qatada was a threat to national security as he gave religious legitimacy to those intent on committing terrorist attacks, including suicide bombings. Subsequently, Abu Qatada was accused of influencing individuals, among them, Londoner Richard Reid, the so-called "shoe bomber" who tried to blow up an American Airlines flight over the Atlantic Ocean in 2001.

Another London-based radical Islamic cleric, Omar Bakri, sought asylum in the UK, having been expelled from Saudi Arabia. Bakri was involved with the revolutionary Muslim Brotherhood, a large, international organization that promoted Islamist political and religious ideology. Bakri also established the London branch of Hizb ut-Tahrir, an international Islamist movement that sought to unite Muslims under one fundamental Islamic caliphate, as well as the radical British-Islamist group al-Muhajiroun.

Bakri was notorious for making controversial statements in the aftermath of 9/11 and 7/7, the latter a series of coordinated suicide attacks across London's public transport network during rush hour on July 7, 2005.[26] He described the 9/11 attackers as the "magnificent 19."[27] Bakri's proclamations caused public outrage and cast him as a hated figure in the British press, who dubbed Bakri the "Tottenham Ayatollah" because he based al-Muhajiroun in Tottenham, North London. In 2005, Bakri left the UK because he feared the UK government was about to investigate him for committing treason. The then UK home secretary Charles Clarke banned Bakri from returning to the UK on the grounds that Bakri's presence in the UK was not in the interests of the public good. Bakri then moved to Lebanon. In 2010, Bakri was accused of forming a militant group bent on undermining the Lebanese government and was sentenced to life in prison by a Lebanese military court.

The radical cleric who most likely made the biggest impact on the UK's national consciousness was Abu Hamza, who came to England in 1979, where he found work as a nightclub bouncer in London. In 1987, Abu Hamza moved to Afghanistan, where he lost an eye and both his hands under mysterious circumstances. The injuries gave Abu Hamza a very distinct appearance that captured the attention of the British public and led to Abu Hamza being nicknamed "Captain Hook" by the British press. In 1993, Abu Hamza returned to the UK for treatment of his injuries, only to later leave Britain to support Bosnian Muslims fighting in the former Yugoslavia. By 1997, Abu Hamza had become a prominent figure in the British Islamist scene, producing leaflets calling for jihad and preaching at Finsbury Park Mosque. In 1999, Abu Hamza came to national prominence in the UK when he was questioned on suspicion of involvement in alleged bomb plots in Yemen. In 2002, Abu Hamza co-organized a conference at Finsbury Park Mosque and praised the 9/11 attacks. Five years later, a trial heard that the men later convicted of the failed 21/7 London bombings had listened to sermons by Abu Hamza several times. On January 20, 2003, the police raided Finsbury Park Mosque as part of a major investigation into an alleged plot to produce ricin (a highly dangerous toxin). The police sealed off the mosque, but Abu Hamza decided to preach outside its gates, causing a standoff between the cleric and the UK authorities that lasted into 2004. The standoff ended when the United States named Abu Hamza as a "terrorist facilitator with a global reach,"[28] which led to the preacher's arrest pending extradition. He was later charged with 15 UK terror offenses, convicted on 11 counts, and imprisoned for seven years. The United States continued to pursue Abu Hamza's extradition, and in 2012 he was extradited following an eight-year legal battle. Abu Hamza went on trial in the United States, accused of offenses that included a plot to establish a terror camp in Oregon. The preacher denied all the charges but was found guilty nonetheless. In 2014, he was sentenced to life in prison without parole, with his sentence to be served in a Colorado prison.

Following are examples of attacks on London linked to Middle East politics.

In 1980, 6 Iranian gunmen took 26 hostages inside the Iranian embassy in London and demanded the release of Khuzestani prisoners from prisons in Khuzestan as well as their own safe passage from the UK.[29] Khuzestani separatists wished to gain autonomy for Khuzestan, an oil-rich province of Iran. The Khuzestani had long been repressed by the Iranian government, leaving the people marginalized economically and politically. The Khuzestani found it especially galling that Iran profited from Khuzestan's oil while they suffered neglect.

The Iranian embassy siege lasted for five days and ended when the elite British military force the Special Air Service (SAS) stormed the embassy, killing all but one of the gunmen. The siege's resolution was broadcast live in front of millions of bank holiday television viewers. The surviving terrorist went to prison. While the siege brought some attention to the plight of the Khuzestani cause, the Iran-Iraq War (1981) overshadowed their cause, and the Khuzestani remained marginalized in their homeland. Another consequence of the siege was that the SAS raid persuaded many national governments, including that of the United States, to invest in counterterrorist training.

Another infamous event linked to Middle East politics occurred on April 17, 1984, when young police officer Yvonne Fletcher was killed outside the Libyan Embassy in London's St. James's Square in Westminster. Fletcher was killed by shots fired from inside the embassy that were aimed at demonstrators protesting against Colonel Gaddafi, the Libyan leader. A standoff between the Libyan and British governments ensued over the killing, resulting in an 11-day siege that then became a tense standoff between the police and the diplomats. The siege ended when the diplomats walked out of the embassy. Ultimately, the siege resulted in the breaking of diplomatic relations between Britain and Libya, for the diplomats returned to Libya under the protection of diplomatic immunity. A memorial to PC Fletcher stands in St. James's Square.

More recently, incidents perpetrated by Islamist terrorists have occurred in London. For instance, on July 7, 2005, the event usually referred to in the UK as the 7/7 Bombings or, simply, 7/7, saw a series of coordinated suicide attacks occur across London's public transport network during rush hour. The four 7/7 suicide bombers were British citizens who had trained in Pakistan and were linked to al-Qaeda. The bombers carried knapsacks filled with homemade bombs into central London. Three bombs detonated separately in quick succession aboard London Underground trains on the Circle line near Aldgate and Edgware Road, and on the Piccadilly line near Russell Square. A fourth bomb exploded on a double-decker bus in Tavistock Square in Bloomsbury, central London. In addition to the bombers, 52 UK residents belonging to 18 different nationalities died in the attack, while over 700 people were injured in what was the single worst terrorist atrocity on British soil.[30] The 7/7 attack demonstrated al-Qaeda's ability and willingness to create mass civilian casualties. The attack is also important because it focused Britain's authorities on the threat of Islamist extremism.

Islamic State has also attacked London in both mass attacks and assaults on civilian and military individuals. An example of an Islamic State attack on an individual occurred on May 22, 2013, when an off-duty British Army soldier, Fusilier Lee Rigby, was attacked and killed near the Royal Artillery Barracks in Woolwich, South East London. Two British-born converts to Islam drove over Rigby, attempted to decapitate the soldier using knives and a meat cleaver, and then left his body in the street. During their trial, the terrorists described Rigby's murder as an act of war.

Islamist attacks on groups of civilian Londoners have also occurred. For example, on March 22, 2017, a terrorist armed with a knife drove an SUV into pedestrians on London's Westminster Bridge before stabbing a policeman outside the House of Parliament. Six people died in the attack, including the attacker who was shot by the police. At least 50 others were injured.[31] Then, on June 3, 2017, three men inspired by Islamic State donned mock suicide vests to drive a van into numerous pedestrians walking along London Bridge before heading to a nearby London food and dining destination, Borough Market. There the men stabbed several civilians before being shot and killed by the police. In total, 11 people, including the attackers, were killed, while 48 others were injured.[32] Shortly after the London Bridge attack, a van was driven into pedestrians near London's Finsbury Park mosque, an incident that resulted in one death. The incident, which was widely seen as an Islamophobic event, was investigated by counterterrorism police as a terrorist attack. In 2018, the attacker was sentenced to life imprisonment.

On September 15, 2017, a homemade bomb partially exploded on a Tube train at West London's Parsons Green station, leaving 23 people with burns and another 28 suffering crush injuries.[33] The attack, which was perpetrated by a teenage Iraqi, was claimed by Islamic State. Then on August 14, 2018, the Westminster attack saw a car driven into cyclists and pedestrians before crashing into the security barriers outside the Houses of Parliament. Even more recently, on November 29, 2019, London Bridge was targeted again, when a terrorist wearing a fake suicide vest stabbed two people to death at a conference near London Bridge and injured three others. Witnesses attacked the terrorist using random objects, including a narwhal tusk, before the attacker was shot and killed by police. Most recently, on February 2, 2020, three people were stabbed on Streatham High Road in South London. The attacker was shot dead by police.

As well as committing terrorist attacks in London, Islamic State has also made the headlines by recruiting Londoners to their cause. The most famous instance of this is the case of three schoolgirls—Kadiza Sultana (age 16), Shamima Begum, and Amira Abase (both age 15)—who, in 2015, ran away from their homes in Bethnal Green, East London, to marry into Islamic State. It is presumed that Sultana and Abase died while with Islamic State, but Begum was found pregnant in a Syrian refugee camp. Begum asked to return to the UK but was stripped of her UK citizenship by the UK government on security grounds. Under international law, individuals must not be left stateless but in February 2020, a tribunal ruled that Begum's citizenship could be canceled lawfully because her Bangladeshi heritage meant she was a citizen of Bangladeshi descent. Begum's case became a huge talking point in the UK: some people felt Begum was treated badly, as she had been a child when she traveled to join Islamic State; some felt Begum should be tried in Britain for her crimes; and others agreed her citizenship should be removed because they were horrified at Begum's lack of remorse at having joined Islamic State, which they witnessed in her television interviews. In July 2020, Begum's case took another twist when the Court of Appeal in London ruled that Begum should be allowed to return to the UK to fight the decision to remove her British citizenship, prompting the UK's Home Office to appeal the decision.

FUTURE THREATS TO LONDON

UK authorities issue terrorist threat levels. Threat levels are set by the Joint Terrorism Analysis Centre (independent, nonpolitical intelligence experts based at MI5's headquarters at Thames House in London) and the UK's Security Service (MI5). MI5 sets the threat levels with regard to Irish and domestic terrorism in Northern Ireland and Great Britain.

The five levels of threat issued are:

• Low—an attack is highly unlikely
• Moderate—an attack is possible but not likely
• Substantial—an attack is likely
• Severe—an attack is highly likely
• Critical—an attack is highly likely in the near future

When setting a threat level, the authorities take into account factors including the reliability of intelligence gathering, the likelihood of an attack, and the potential scale of an attack. In 2019, the terrorism threat-level system was adjusted to reflect the threat posed by all forms of terrorism. Consequently, there is now a single national threat level for the threat to the UK, which includes Islamist, Northern Ireland, left-wing, and right-wing terrorism. In June 2021, the threat to the UK (England, Wales, Scotland, and Northern Ireland) from terrorism was classed as Substantial, while the threat to Northern Ireland from Northern Ireland–related terrorism was Severe. Threat levels are not time limited but rather can be altered as, and when, intelligence becomes available to authorities.

London's authorities play a key role in the UK government's national counterterrorism strategy known as CONTEST. CONTEST revolves around four main areas: Pursue, Prevent, Protect, and Prepare, as set out by the government, with the boroughs and other London statutory bodies working to reduce the threat of extremist activity. London Boroughs contribute resources that help prevent but also prepare for terrorist attacks on the city. The most high-profile aspect of CONTEST is Prevent, which aims to stop people from becoming terrorists or supporting terrorist activity and from responding to the promotion of terrorist ideology. Prevent aims to safeguard and support people who may be inclined to become terrorists or support terrorism while also supporting the rehabilitation of individuals who are already involved in terrorism. However, critics of Prevent, such as Amnesty International, claim the strategy fosters discrimination against Muslims and inhibits people's right to self-expression. For this reason, in 2019, the UK government announced that an independent review of Prevent would take place to address such concerns. Meanwhile the UK's Home Office said that since 2012, more than 1,200 people had been supported by Channel, the Prevent mentoring program. In 2017–2018, of the 394 people advised by Channel, 179 (45 percent) were referred for concerns related to Islamist extremism while 174 (44 percent) were related to right-wing extremism.[34]

In order to counter extremism, London's authorities have embarked on a program of community-led involvement to work together with communities that may feel marginalized and whose members may be at increased risk of engaging with extremism. In 2018, a grant application process began that invited organizations to bid for grants that they could use to deliver community-led engagement programs. The three winning organizations were:

- Anti-Tribalism Movement (ATM), which focuses on engaging members of the Black and minority ethnic (BAME) communities, particularly young people, parents, the disabled, community workers, and people from East Africa
- Faiths Forum for London (FFL), which received a grant in partnership with the anti-extremism body Integrity UK in order to engage people,

ages 13 to 26 years from London's religious communities, in interfaith dialogue

- Small Steps Community, which works with London's white (though not necessarily British) communities that may be at increased risk of involvement in right-wing extremism

In total, the three grant winners engaged with over 800 Londoners who may have been at elevated risk of being targeted by extremists.[35] Another measure aimed at preventing future extremism is the implementation of citizenship classes. Citizenship is a school subject akin to politics or sociology that teaches children about human rights, the law, and the economy. The subject has been taught in England and Wales since 1991 and has been a compulsory secondary school subject since 2002. Advocates of citizenship classes believe such classes make school pupils more tolerant and therefore less likely to be radicalized.

NOTES

1. Countering Violent Extremism Programme, *A Shared Endeavour: Working in Partnership to Counter Violent Extremism in London* (London: Greater London Authority, June 2019), 16, https://www.london.gov.uk/sites/default/files/cve_strategy_20_8_19.pdf.

2. Reiss Smith, "Remembering the Lives Tragically Lost in the Horrific Nail Bombing Attack at London's Historic Admiral Duncan Gay Bar," Pink News, April 30, 2020, https://www.pinknews.co.uk/2020/04/30/admiral-duncan-pub-soho-bombing.

3. Jonathan Oates, *Attack on London: Disaster, Rebellion, Riot, Terror & War* (Barnsley, UK: Wharncliffe Local History, 2009), 122.

4. Donna Bassett, "UK Parliament Bombing," in *Encyclopedia of Terrorism: Volume 1: A–L*, ed. Peter Chalk (Santa Barbara, CA: ABC-CLIO, 2013), 715.

5. Ibid., 715.

6. Ibid., 716.

7. "A Peaceful Home for Sefton," Horse Trust 1950–2011, http://www.horsetrust.org.uk/history/today/hyde-park-bombing-survivors.

8. "1983: Harrods Bomb Blast Kills Six." BBC: On This Day 1950–2007, December 17, 2008, http://news.bbc.co.uk/onthisday/hi/dates/stories/december/17/newsid_2538000/2538147.stm.

9. Donna Bassett, "Harrods Bombing," in *Encyclopedia of Terrorism: Volume 1: A–L*, ed. Peter Chalk (Santa Barbara, CA: ABC-CLIO, 2013), 286.

10. Ibid., 287.

11. Edward F. Mickolus, "Baltic Exchange Bombing," in *Encyclopedia of Terrorism: Volume 1: A–L*, ed. Peter Chalk (Santa Barbara, CA: ABC-CLIO, 2013), 96.

12. Terry Kirby, "IRA City Bombers Identified by Police," *The Independent*, https://www.independent.co.uk/news/uk/ira-city-bombers-identified-by-police-1533278.html.

13. Mickolus, "Baltic Exchange Bombing," 97.

14. "Bishopsgate Bomb: Photos Issued on 25th Anniversary," *BBC News*, April 24, 2018, https://www.bbc.co.uk/news/uk-england-london-43878479.

15. Edward F. Mickolus, "Bishopsgate Bombing," in *Encyclopedia of Terrorism: Volume 1: A–L*, ed. Peter Chalk (Santa Barbara, CA: ABC-CLIO, 2013), 127.

16. "Bishopsgate Gets Bins Back 20 Years after IRA Explosion," *BBC News*, August 14, 2013, https://www.bbc.co.uk/news/uk-england-london-23695239.

17. Mickolus, "Bishopsgate Bombing," 127.

18. Donna Bassett, "City of London Bombings," in *Encyclopedia of Terrorism: Volume 1: A–L*, ed. Peter Chalk (Santa Barbara, CA: ABC-CLIO, 2013), 166.

19. "London Bomb: Irish Dissidents Blamed," CNN, August 3, 2001, https://edition.cnn.com/2001/WORLD/europe/08/03/london.blast.0900.

20. James Dingley, *The IRA: The Irish Republican Army* (Santa Barbara, CA: Praeger, 2012), 122.

21. Ibid.

22. Petter Nesser, *Islamist Terrorism in Europe*, rev. ed. (London: C. Hurst & Co., Ltd., 2018).

23. Ibid.

24. "Abu Hamza Profile," *BBC News*, January 9, 2015, https://www.bbc.co.uk/news/uk-11701269.

25. Dominic Casciani, "Profile: Abu Qatada," *BBC News*, June 26, 2014, https://www.bbc.co.uk/news/uk-16584923.

26. Karunya Jayasena, "Omar Bakri," in *Counterterrorism: From the Cold War to the War on Terror. Volume 2: Twenty-First Century Counterterrorism Measures*, ed. Frank Shanty (Santa Barbara, CA: Praeger, 2012), 272.

27. "Cleric Bakri 'will return' to UK," *BBC News*, August 9, 2005, http://news.bbc.co.uk/1/hi/uk_politics/4133150.stm.

28. "Abu Hamza Profile."

29. "Iranian Embassy Siege," National Army Museum, https://www.nam.ac.uk/explore/iranian-embassy-siege.

30. Sian Elvin, "7/7 Bombings Victims Remembered 15 Years on as Leaders Pay Tribute," Metro, July 7, 2020, https://metro.co.uk/2020/07/07/tributes-paid-july-7-london-bombings-victims-15-years-12954492.

31. "Westminster Attack: What Happened," *BBC News*, April 7, 2017, https://www.bbc.co.uk/news/uk-39355108.

32. "London Bridge Attack: What Happened," *BBC News*, May 3, 2019, https://www.bbc.co.uk/news/uk-england-london-40147164.

33. "Parsons Green Attack: Iraqi Teenager Convicted over Tube Bomb," *BBC News*, March 16, 2018, https://www.bbc.co.uk/news/uk-43431303.

34. Jamie Grierson and Vikram Dodd, "Prevent Strategy on Radicalisation Faces Independent Review," *The Guardian*, January 22, 2019, https://www.theguardian.com/uk-news/2019/jan/22/prevent-strategy-on-radicalisation-faces-independent-review.

35. Countering Violent Extremism Programme, *A Shared Endeavour*, 25.

FURTHER READING

"Abu Hamza Profile." *BBC News*, January 9, 2015. https://www.bbc.co.uk/news/uk-11701269.

Bassett, Donna. "City of London Bombings." In *Encyclopedia of Terrorism: Volume 1: A–L*, edited by Peter Chalk, 165–66. Santa Barbara, CA: ABC-CLIO, 2013.

Bassett, Donna. "Harrods Bombing." In *Encyclopedia of Terrorism: Volume 1: A–L*, edited by Peter Chalk, 285–88. Santa Barbara, CA: ABC-CLIO, 2013.

Bassett, Donna. "UK Parliament Bombing." In *Encyclopedia of Terrorism: Volume 1: A–L*, edited by Peter Chalk, 715–16. Santa Barbara, CA: ABC-CLIO, 2013.

"Bishopsgate Bomb: Photos Issued on 25th Anniversary." *BBC News*, April 24, 2018. https://www.bbc.co.uk/news/uk-england-london-43878479.

"Bishopsgate Gets Bins Back 20 Years after IRA Explosion." *BBC News*, August 14, 2013. https://www.bbc.co.uk/news/uk-england-london-23695239.

Casciani, Dominic. "Profile: Abu Qatada." *BBC News*, June 26, 2014. https://www.bbc.co.uk/news/uk-16584923.

Clarke, Colin P., ed. *Terrorism: The Essential Guide*. Santa Barbara, CA: ABC-CLIO, 2018.

"Cleric Bakri 'will return' to UK." *BBC News*, August 9, 2005. http://news.bbc.co.uk/1/hi/uk_politics/4133150.stm.

Countering Violent Extremism Programme. *A Shared Endeavour: Working in Partnership to Counter Violent Extremism in London*. London: Greater London Authority, June 2019. https://www.london.gov.uk/sites/default/files/cve_strategy_20_8_19.pdf.

"Counter-Terrorism and Extremism." London Councils. https://www.londoncouncils.gov.uk/node/28115.

Dingley, James. *The IRA: The Irish Republican Army*. Santa Barbara, CA: Praeger, 2012.

Elvin, Sian. "7/7 Bombings Victims Remembered 15 Years On as Leaders Pay Tribute." Metro, July 7, 2020. https://metro.co.uk/2020/07/07/tributes-paid-july-7-london-bombings-victims-15-years-12954492.

Grierson, Jamie, and Vikram Dodd. "Prevent Strategy on Radicalisation Faces Independent Review." *The Guardian*, January 22, 2019. https://www.theguardian.com/uk-news/2019/jan/22/prevent-strategy-on-radicalisation-faces-independent-review.

"Iranian Embassy Siege." National Army Museum. https://www.nam.ac.uk/explore/iranian-embassy-siege.

Jayasena, Karunya. "Omar Bakri." In *Counterterrorism: From the Cold War to the War on Terror. Volume 2: Twenty-First Century Counterterrorism Measures*, edited by Frank Shanty, 72. Santa Barbara, CA: Praeger, 2012.

Kirby, Terry. "IRA City Bombers Identified by Police." *The Independent*, July 15, 1992. https://www.independent.co.uk/news/uk/ira-city-bombers-identified-by-police-1533278.html.

"London Bomb: Irish Dissidents Blamed." CNN, August 3, 2001. https://edition .cnn.com/2001/WORLD/europe/08/03/london.blast.0900.

"London Bridge Attack: What Happened." *BBC News*, May 3, 2019. https://www .bbc.co.uk/news/uk-england-london-40147164.

Mickolus, Edward F. "Baltic Exchange Bombing." In *Encyclopedia of Terrorism: Volume 1: A–L*, edited by Peter Chalk, 96–97. Santa Barbara, CA: ABC-CLIO, 2013.

Mickolus, Edward F. "Bishopsgate Bombing." In *Encyclopedia of Terrorism: Volume 1: A–L*, edited by Peter Chalk, 126–28. Santa Barbara, CA: ABC-CLIO, 2013.

Nesser, Petter. *Islamist Terrorism in Europe*. Rev. ed. London: C. Hurst & Co., Ltd., 2018.

"1983: Harrods Bomb Blast Kills Six." BBC: On This Day 1950–2007, December 17, 2008. http://news.bbc.co.uk/onthisday/hi/dates/stories/december/17 /newsid_2538000/2538147.stm.

Oates, Jonathan. *Attack on London: Disaster, Rebellion, Riot, Terror & War*. Barnsley, UK: Wharncliffe Local History, 2009.

"Parsons Green Attack: Iraqi Teenager Convicted over Tube Bomb." *BBC News*, March 16, 2018. https://www.bbc.co.uk/news/uk-43431303.

"A Peaceful Home for Sefton." Horse Trust 1950–2011. http://www.horsetrust .org.uk/history/today/hyde-park-bombing-survivors.

Smith, Reiss. "Remembering the Lives Tragically Lost in the Horrific Nail Bombing Attack at London's Historic Admiral Duncan Gay Bar." Pink News, April 30, 2020. https://www.pinknews.co.uk/2020/04/30/admiral-duncan -pub-soho-bombing.

"Westminster Attack: What Happened." *BBC News*, April 7, 2017. https://www .bbc.co.uk/news/uk-39355108.

9

Natural Hazards and Emergency Management

London can experience a range of natural hazards, including earthquakes, floods, droughts, heat waves, and other forms of disruptive weather. The degree of risk from various natural hazards is assessed by the London Resilience Forum, a London-wide group of local organizations that can be called upon to respond if a major incident hits the city. The forum oversees the associated London Resilience Group, a body governed by the Greater London Authority (also called City Hall, this is the devolved regional governance body of London), London Local Authorities (responsible for providing public services), and the London Fire Commissioner (London's fire and rescue authority). The London Resilience Group has created the London Risk Register to provide a summary of the main risks affecting Greater London in order to help communities develop coping strategies to deal with emergency situations. Planning for incidents is based on a reasonable worst-case scenario based on historical and technical data, modeling and expert opinion that considers both the probability of an event occurring and the impact such an event would have on London. Individual London Boroughs can also conduct their own additional risk assessments in order to glean additional information on the likelihood of incidents hitting the borough and how their locale would cope. According to the London Risk Register, the highest-risk natural hazards faced by Greater London as a whole come from surface-water flooding, fluvial flooding, severe drought, volcanic eruptions, and space weather. The register classes storms and gales, cold and snow, groundwater flooding, coastal flooding, land movement and heat waves as high risk. Wildfires are deemed a medium-risk natural hazard to London.

LONDON SEISMIC ACTIVITY

Although the United Kingdom is not generally associated with seismic activity, earthquakes are relatively common, with between 50 and 60 quakes experienced by the country annually. Each year in the United Kingdom, several hundred smaller tremors are also recorded. Earthquakes are caused by small shifts along faults in a tectonic plate. The United Kingdom is located in the center of the Eurasian tectonic plate with the nearest plate boundary to the United Kingdom being the mid-Atlantic ridge (a constructive plate boundary located on the floor of the Atlantic Ocean). Presently, the Eurasian plate is being compressed from two sides: northeast along its boundary with northern Africa and eastward along its boundary in the Atlantic Ocean. Previous tectonic movements that occurred during phases of mountain building have resulted in the section of the Eurasian Plate that lies beneath the United Kingdom containing numerous deep faults. The geology of much of the United Kingdom is riddled with these faults, which were once very active but are now almost extinct. However, the constant movement of the earth's tectonic plates means a degree of pressure and strain builds up in these faults. Since the fault lines will never become completely extinct, the faults often shift slightly, thereby triggering small earthquakes. The rocks that make up the plate under the United Kingdom are, however, fairly strong and so can withstand tectonic pressure for a long time.

It is rare for the United Kingdom to experience a severe earthquake. Typically, the United Kingdom experiences one magnitude 3.5 earthquake per year, 10 magnitude 2.5 quakes per year, and around 100 magnitude 1.5 quakes per year. Once per decade, the United Kingdom experiences a magnitude 4.5 earthquake, while a magnitude 5.5 earthquake occurs once per century.[1] The most severe earthquakes experienced by the United Kingdom are the result of movements 6 to 9 miles underground, though some of the faults beneath the United Kingdom reach down 19 miles into the earth's mantle (the layer beneath the earth's crust). Since most of the United Kingdom's earthquakes are not severe, the damage resulting from the quakes tend to comprise falling chimney pots and cracked windows. While such damage does not seem dangerous, many people can be hurt or killed when masonry falls in a heavily populated city. Damaging earthquakes have been felt in London. For example, on April 6, 1580, the

Dover Straits earthquake occurred in an area of northern France and southeastern England that lies 86 miles away from London. This earthquake was likely one of the worst earthquakes ever felt in England. During the earthquake, several of London's chimneys collapsed, a pinnacle fell from Westminster Abbey, and children died when they were struck by stones falling from a hospital roof. At the time, many Puritans (strict Protestant reformers) blamed the earthquake on the emergence of London's theater scene, which they considered the work of the devil. The 1580 earthquake was a virtual repeat of a quake that occurred in 1382, for the earlier quake shared the same epicenter and size and made a similar impact. The most powerful earthquake to hit the United Kingdom occurred in 1884 in the Colchester area, some 50 miles northeast of London. The Colchester quake damaged 1,200 buildings.[2]

There is a feeling among seismologists that the United Kingdom is overdue for a relatively severe earthquake that would cause billions of pounds worth of damage. While such an earthquake might not be very large (because the United Kingdom is far enough away from all tectonic plate boundaries to avoid a very large earthquake), such an earthquake would likely still prove more damaging than those the country usually experiences. Seismologists agree that it is difficult to predict accurately when the next major earthquake to hit London will occur. When it does happen, however, the impact is likely to be more serious than that of previous quakes because London's population is far larger than it was in, say, 1580. The impact of a magnitude 5.5 earthquake in southeastern England would be serious, for while modern office buildings and homes would likely survive relatively intact, the region's older Victorian buildings would be at risk of damage, which in turn could lead to loss of life. Seismologists' belief that London will experience a major earthquake at some point in the future is reinforced by the recent discovery of two fault lines running beneath London. The faults, which are sufficiently large to cause a magnitude 5 earthquake, move at a rate of between 1 and 2 millimeters (between 0.04 inches and 0.08 inches) per year.[3] One fault is located beneath central London. The other fault runs under London's secondary business area, Canary Wharf, which is situated on the Isle of Dogs in central East London and contains the United Kingdom's second-tallest building, One Canada Square.

While London was once considered geologically stable, the area beneath London is now thought to be modestly active in terms of seismic activity to the point that it is probably the most geologically complex area of the country. For this reason, civil engineers suggest that new and renovated London buildings be built to withstand an earthquake registering magnitude 6.5 on the Richter scale. Land movement is another high risk to London. If such an earthquake were to occur, roads would become impassable, thereby hindering the emergency services from reaching the most heavily populated areas of London, and severe congestion would be widespread around the city. A land movement would also cause London to lose its power supplies temporarily, destroy nontransport infrastructure, and hamper essential services from operating over a wide geographical area. There would also be the potential for a high loss of life, and a number of people would be trapped or missing, either in the landslide itself or in collapsed buildings.

While London is seismically active, the city does not contain any volcanoes. That said, London still faces the hazard of volcanic ash, which can enter the atmosphere resulting in the temporary closures of London's airspace. This issue occurred in April 2010 when Iceland's Eyjafjallajokull volcano erupted, hurling a plume of ash seven miles into the atmosphere. Since the volcanic ash could cause aircraft to crash, around 60 percent of flights in European airspace were grounded including those involving London's Heathrow Airport.[4] Dust from the Sahara Desert falls in London frequently but does not tend to cause damage. Saharan dust arrives in London having been whipped up high into the atmosphere and transported northward. The dust then falls to earth in rain—that is, as the raindrops fall, they collect dust particles. When the raindrops land and later evaporate, they leave behind a layer of dust evident on car roofs and other such surfaces in London.

SPACE WEATHER

Another threat from the skies facing London is space weather. During space weather events, magnetic fields, radiation, particles, and matter ejected from the sun interact with the earth's magnetic field and upper atmosphere. There are various types of space weather events. For example, ordinarily the earth is hit constantly by streams of solar particles transported by solar wind, but during periods of heightened solar activity, more solar flares and coronal mass ejections (CMEs, material ejected from the sun into interplanetary space) occur, meaning the impact of the solar particles on earth is greater. Such extreme activity can happen at any point during the 11-year solar cycle. Space weather can impact on national infrastructure, technology, and communications systems. For this reason, in 2011, space weather was added to the United Kingdom's Government National Risk Register of Civil Emergencies, and the Met Office Space Weather Operations Centre (MOSWOC) was founded to provide information to United Kingdom authorities in order to protect the nation from severe space weather events. Even during spells of low solar activity, turbulence in the ionosphere (the layer of the earth's atmosphere that is ionized by solar and cosmic radiation) can disrupt electromagnetic waves that interfere with navigation systems, among them, global positioning systems (GPS) and radio bands. A space weather event would also affect London by disrupting the electricity grid, resulting in substations being disconnected and localized blackouts occurring in urban areas.

LONDON EXTREME WEATHER

Storms

Most of the natural threats facing London are far more mundane than space weather, for they tend to be linked to the earth's weather. Warnings of extreme weather events and their potential impact are provided by the United Kingdom's national weather service, the Met Office, which runs the National Severe Weather Warning Service (NSWWS). The weather warnings are based on a combination of the level of impact that a weather event might cause and the likelihood of that impact occurring. The warnings are coded from yellow to red. A yellow warning is issued when it is likely that the weather will result in low-level impact, including minor travel disruption. An amber warning suggests an increased likelihood of impact from severe weather, which will likely disrupt travel plans more severely by causing road and rail closures. Power outages are also likely to occur with amber warnings, and there is the potential for deaths and property damage to occur. Red warnings indicate that dangerous weather is expected and outlines the measures that should be taken to safeguard lives and possessions from its impact. Red warnings suggest it is highly probable that deaths will occur as the result of the weather and that there will be substantial disruption to transport and power supplies together with widespread damage to infrastructure and property. During times of red warnings, people are told to avoid travel and follow the advice of the emergency services. The Met Office provides warnings for weather including rain, thunderstorms, winds, snow, lightning, ice, and fog and also indicates whether the impact of a weather event will be localized, widespread, prolonged, or short term. The NSWWS, together with Met Éireann (Ireland's national meteorological service) and KNMI (the Dutch national weather forecasting service), also runs a system for naming storms. The system is the single authoritative system for warning the British public of approaching severe weather, which it does through the media and government agencies. By being prepared for storms, the hope is that people can protect themselves, their property, and their businesses from inclement weather.

A storm receives a name when it has the potential to cause an amber or red weather warning. Typically, storm names are suggested by the public, who write to the Met Office and Met Éireann with ideas. The most popular suggestions are chosen, as are names that reflect the diversity of Britain,

Ireland, and the Netherlands. To avoid any confusion over names, if a storm is the remnant of an Atlantic tropical storm or hurricane, then the storm is referred to as "Ex-Hurricane X" as designated officially by the United States' National Weather Service rather than given a new name.

The stormiest period of recent UK weather occurred during the period from mid-December 2013 to mid-February 2014 when at least twelve major winter events occurred. In August 2014, Ex-Hurricane Bertha caused widespread travel disruption across London, when flooding caused numerous Underground stations and Tube lines to close because trees fell across tracks. On January 2 and 3, 2018, Storm Eleanor brought severe gales to the United Kingdom, with gusts of 72 miles per hour recorded at Northolt, in West London.[5] The storm caused major travel disruption, fallen trees, damage to property, and power cuts. On January 14, 2020, Storm Brendan brought travel disruption to London when it blew the roof of Ravenscourt Park station, in West London, causing the suspension of two Tube lines; blew trees onto train tracks between Motspur Park and Chessington, in South West London, caused a landslide in Dorking, around 21 miles south of London, and prompted three flood alerts along an 8-mile stretch of the River Thames between Brentford, in West London, and East Molesey, in Surrey. Meanwhile, on February 9, 2020, the United Kingdom was hit by Storm Ciara, which prompted the Met Office to issue an amber warning. Storm Ciara caused flights to and from Heathrow, Gatwick, and London City airports to be canceled; in addition, numerous London rail and Tube lines were disrupted, and trees were brought down, destroying many parked cars. The strength of Storm Ciara's winds also enabled a British Airways flight to fly from New York to London in just four hours and 56 minutes, reaching speeds of over 800 miles per hour. This meant the flight is likely to have broken the fastest subsonic New York-to-London crossing time.[6]

Flooding

The risk of flooding is both the greatest natural threat to London and the greatest concern surrounding the River Thames. A major flood would threaten London's low-lying land, paralyzing the capital's infrastructure of underground railways, sewers, telephone cables, tunnels, and gas, water, and electricity supplies. The flood risk results from a combination of factors, including the fact that London is sinking at a faster rate than the rest of southeastern England. The reason for the sinking is twofold: First, water extracted from the chalk aquifer (the layer of rock containing groundwater) beneath London is causing the city's underlying clay beds to dry up. Second, the vestiges of the glaciers originating from the last Ice Age that weighed down Scotland while simultaneously raising up southern England have melted. The melting of the glaciers caused London to sink, thus leaving the city increasingly low lying and prone to flooding. The likelihood of the Thames flooding has also increased because the river's tidal rhythm has been intensified by the dredging of the river for navigation as well as by increased embanking of the river's estuary marshes for use in agriculture. Traditionally, walls and embankments were built in London to protect land surrounding the Thames from flooding. Following the Thames Flood Act of 1879, long sections of the Thames's banks were raised up, with further protective measures taken after serious flooding in 1928 and 1953. According to the UK government's latest climate change projections, by the 2050s, it is likely that more Londoners will be living and working in floodplain areas and susceptible to flooding resulting from increased winter rainfall.

According to the London Risk Register, London faces a very high risk of surface-water flooding. Surface-water flooding occurs when so much rain falls that drains and streets fill with water. Such flooding is likely to occur in London during the summer: the atmosphere is unstable but also warmer and able to hold more water, which causes a pattern of convectional rainfall. Convectional rainfall occurs when the land heats up and warms the air above it. The air then expands, rises, cools, and condenses. When this process continues, rain falls. Convectional rainfall is typical of tropical areas but also occurs in southeastern England during spells of warm weather. Since 2016, surface-water flooding has been included on the UK's national risk register. In 2018, the UK Department for Environment, Food and Rural Affairs (Defra) published its Surface Water Management Action Plan to strengthen the current strategies to deal with surface-water flooding.

Urban areas such as London, which contain more concrete, are more susceptible to surface-water flooding than rural areas. Additionally, poor urban areas of London that are characterized by high-density housing are the most susceptible of all urban areas to this type of flooding, because they tend to feature paved areas that do not absorb rainwater. In contrast, more affluent, suburban areas of London tend to contain lawns that can absorb rain. Surface-water flooding is an increasing risk to London, for urban development results in greater use of concrete, which in turn means there is less opportunity for rainwater to drain away. Added to this, climate change will likely cause more frequent and intense rainfall to occur, resulting in flash flooding and the overloading of London's aging sewer system. As London's population grows, more people become at risk of the consequences of surface-water flooding. According to Sir James Bevan, chief executive of the Environment Agency, surface-water flooding threatens more Londoners and London properties than any other form of flood risk.[7] Surface-water flooding damages homes and businesses and can cripple all aspects of London's infrastructure, including utilities and transport networks. A likely scenario sees a thunderstorm over central London result in rainfall that overwhelms the city's drainage system. In turn, this would cause underpasses to flood and make roads impassable, while the London Underground network would also flood and stop running. Very quickly, London would grind to a halt. The situation could then worsen as power outages would occur and water would start to enter people's homes. Basement flats could end up under several feet of water, causing occupants to drown. A similar situation to the one just outlined occurred in Hampstead in North London in 1975, when a thunderstorm caused more than three months' worth of rain to fall in three hours. The intense downpour caused four of London's mainline railway stations to flood, and hundreds of homes were made uninhabitable.[8]

In 2007, England and Wales suffered summer floods that killed 13 people, flooded 44,600 homes and caused £3billion of damage.[9] The event led to the 2008 Pitt Review, which found most of the flooding had arisen from surface water running off the land. The Pitt Review led in turn to the Flood and Water Management Act (2010) that clarified the responsibilities of various entities, including the Environment Agency, local authorities, and water and sewage companies, during periods of flooding. The review also established the Lead Local Flood Authorities, which are responsible for managing the flood risk from local surface water, groundwater, and waterways. In 2008, the Environment Agency produced the first map of areas at elevated risk of surface-water flooding. The following year, the Environment Agency and the Met Office worked together to establish the Flood Forecasting Centre to better improve surface-water flooding forecasting; the Centre provides a 24/7 flood forecasting service to the Environment Agency, the UK government and emergency services. There has also been investment in flood barriers, water pumps, and other equipment so that authorities can respond to surface floods faster. At the same time, civil engineering projects are mindful of the need to lessen the use of concrete and so reduce the risk of surface-water flooding. In order to improve London's resilience to surface-water flooding, Sustainable Drainage Systems (SUDS) have been built into as many London locations as possible. SUDS can take many forms, including various types of paving that allow water to drain away, infiltration systems, living roofs (roofs that are partially or completely covered in vegetation), and green walls (vertical structures intentionally covered in vegetation). Examples of SUDS can be seen across London. For example, London Wall, in the City of London, has had a living roof installed that contains wildflower beds. The planting produces a biodiverse urban habitat, while the roofs are divided into two separate rain-catchment areas. Goods Way, in the London borough of Camden, has a green wall. This new neighborhood is being built in such a way as to preserve as much green space as possible, with more than 400 trees planted in the area and the installation of 656 feet of green wall and living roofs.[10] The green space, green wall, and living roofs will reduce the risk of flooding by intercepting rainwater. Meanwhile, at Streatham Common South in the London Borough of Lambeth, which forms part of the Streatham Critical Drainage Area, a series of measures have been implemented to alleviate the surface-water flood risk. These measures include grass shoulders inserted into pavements in order to replace some concrete, thereby slowing the rate at which surface water drains into the sewer system.

Another type of flooding to face London is fluvial flooding (also called river flooding or riverine flooding). Fluvial flooding occurs when rain saturates river catchment areas, causing river channels to reach their full capacity and then flood. In London, high-intensity, heavy rainfall causes the River Thames's tributaries to exceed their channel capacity. When this happens, flooding ensues rapidly, often without warning, so there is little time to evacuate people and property. London also faces a high risk of groundwater flooding. Groundwater flooding happens when the water table (i.e., the water level within the underground rock or soil) rises to ground level, allowing water to seep through to the surface and then flood. In 2019, following unparalleled levels of extended periods of above-average rainfall over the course of the three winter months, the London Risk Register noted that London's groundwater levels were exceptionally high. South East London was deemed at particular risk of groundwater flooding because here the geology is predominantly chalk.

Coastal or tidal flooding is another high-risk threat facing London. The landscape of the River Thames is characterized by gently rolling lowlands, so tidal surges can have a profound effect on the water level of the Thames's lower course. Along the Thames, the tide is felt intermittently, with high tide experienced for three hours at Teddington, in South West London, which is the upper limit of the tidal Thames. During times of extreme floods (such as those that occurred in March 1947), the Thames may flow far more quickly than normal at Teddington Weir, while high spring tides can flood Teddington Weir, causing the river to flow as far as miles upstream. Such tidal surges can have a catastrophic impact on London's infrastructure, buildings, and people. Consequently, London's authorities have built structures to guard against flood damage; they include the Thames Barrier, in East London, and extensive flood defenses along the river's entire tideway. Localized tidal flooding occurs when London's Thames tidal wall or embankments are breached suddenly, typically when a traffic accident or construction incident occurs or when a tidal floodgate fails during a high tide. Heavy rain in London can also lead to flooding, as can tidal surges. The Environment Agency provides a Flood Warning Service for specific rivers in London and also deals with flooding, should it ensue. The last time central London suffered severe tidal flooding was on January 6 and 7, 1928, when the Thames flooded much of the area, and the flood extended as far west as Putney and Richmond. The 1928 flood resulted from a depression in the North Sea that combined with high tide and high river flows to send a storm surge up the Thames's tidal section, leading to the river bursting its banks in the middle of the night. Most Londoners were asleep as the floodwaters gushed into landmark buildings (including the Houses of Parliament, Charing Cross Station, and the Tower of London), and many of London's narrowest slum streets ended up four feet underwater.[11] Numerous overcrowded basement dwellings that housed London's poorest families in Southwark, Blackfriars, Westminster, and Bankside were deluged by the floodwaters, which led to the drowning of 14 people.[12] Thousands of other Londoners were left homeless. Many priceless artworks that were kept in museum basements were also destroyed by the flood. At that time, there was no early warning system to alert Londoners to the likelihood of flooding. Relief efforts were hampered by the fact that the city had already suffered widespread flooding in the preceding days. Additionally, heavy snowfall had occurred over Christmas, and the melted snow had swelled inland rivers and left much of East London underwater. The tidal flood experienced along the Thames was far worse, however, for the river's flood defenses were designed to cope with a tide of 18 feet above the Ordnance Datum (OD, the height of mean sea level used as the basis for deriving altitudes on maps). During the 1928 tidal surge, however, the floodwaters exceeded this level by 11 inches.[13] Following the flood, London's authorities discussed the need to dredge rivers and whether local or central government should take responsibility for such matters. Additionally, the Thames's embankments were raised to keep larger surges at bay.

It was only after the North Sea flood of 1953, however, that authorities looked into building the Thames Barrier. The 1953 tidal surge was the worst natural disaster in modern British history, and it caused the North Sea to rise to 16 feet above its average on the night of January 31.[14] The flood resulted from several factors, including strong northerly Atlantic winds that occurred alongside a high tide, thereby forcing more water than usual along the narrow north-south stretch of the North Sea into the Straits of Dover on England's south coast. At the same time, the earth's rotation meant that the extra water was redirected west of prevailing tidal currents to hit Britain's east coast. The tidal surge resulted in widespread flooding along the east coast of Britain, with the death toll especially bad on low-lying, reclaimed Canvey Island in the Thames Estuary, for excess water that was forced up the estuary washed away the island's seawall. In total, 307 people in England died, around 30,000 people were evacuated from properties, and 386 square miles of land were flooded. Canvey Island was evacuated during the flood but not before 58 islanders had died.[15] The impact of the flood could have been worse, for the amount of inland rainfall had been below average and rivers on Britain's east coast were lower than usual. Had the rivers been fuller, the loss caused by the tidal surge would have been much more severe, causing far more deaths and much greater damage to London's infrastructure. The potential risk to the London Underground system influenced much of the political debate that followed the flood, and a government inquiry was launched on how best to renew the Thames's flood defenses. The inquiry recommended the creation of a new flood early warning system as well as the building of a retractable barrier to protect London. Eventually, the Thames Barrier and Flood Prevention Act 1972 was enacted, and the Thames Barrier opened in 1982 a few miles east of the Isle of Dogs. The barrier's northern bank is located at Silvertown, in the London borough of Newham, while its southern bank is in the New Charlton area of the Royal Borough of Greenwich.

Today, the Thames Barrier is one of the world's largest movable flood barriers. It is maintained by the Environment Agency, which also maintains London's other flood defenses. The Thames Barrier spans 1,706 feet across the River Thames and is responsible for protecting 48 square miles of central London from flooding caused by tidal surges. The barrier has 10 steel gates that can be raised into position across the River Thames. When

The Thames Barrier, located in East London, is a flood control dam that allows ships to pass through. The barrier, which opened in 1982, protects much of London from flooding caused by tidal surges. (Spiroview Inc./Dreamstime.com)

raised, the main gates are five stories high. Each main gate weighs 3,300 tons.[16] Under storm conditions, the barrier is closed in order to protect London from tidal flooding. The barrier may also be closed during periods of high flow over Teddington Weir so as to reduce the risk of river flooding in parts of West London, including Richmond and Twickenham. Once shut, the Thames Barrier remains closed until the water level downstream of the barrier has reduced to the same level as the level upstream. Once the levels are equal, the Thames Barrier is reopened, thereby allowing the water upstream to flow out to sea.

Partly as a result of the 1953 flood, the River Thames floodplain, 1.25 million people, and £200 billion worth of property are now protected by a warning system and flood defenses.[17] The Thames Estuary 2100 project (TE2100), spearheaded by the Environment Agency, is a comprehensive action plan to manage the flood risk for the tidal Thames area that stretches from Teddington to Sheerness and Shoeburyness, in the counties of Kent and Essex, to the east of London. TE2100 is based on sea-level rise and climate change predictions that suggest a relative sea level rise of 90 centimeters by 2100.[18] The TE2100 Plan can be adapted to cope with various rates of sea level rise as well as an increase of 40 percent in peak river flows by 2080.[19] The Environment Agency has performed extensive research on how future river flows, storm surges, and sea level rise will affect the tidal flood risk in the Thames Estuary. At the same time, the Environment Agency is mindful that London's flood defenses are aging while an increasing number of people live and work on the River Thames floodplain. The Thames Estuary Partnership (TEP), an umbrella organization comprising various bodies—including the Corporation of London (the municipal governing body of the City of London), University College London, the Environment Agency, and Thames Water (the private utility company responsible for much of London's public water supply)—provides a framework for the sustainable management of the River Thames. The TEP organizes talks and open days in order to keep communities and organizations in South and East London, Kent, and Essex up to date on how to prepare for flooding. In 2019, the mayor of London together with the Environment Agency, Thames Water, and the London Resilience Partnership co-organized London Flood Awareness Week. This event ran from November 11 to 17, aimed to improve Londoners' awareness of the flood risk facing the city, and helped them prepare for possible winter floods.

Heat Waves and Drought

While flooding is the greatest threat to London, summer heat is another natural hazard the area faces. In recent years, London has experienced very high temperatures, with heat waves declared in 2003, 2006, 2013, 2018, and 2019. In the United Kingdom, a heat wave is said to occur when a location records a period of at least three consecutive days when daily maximum temperatures meet or exceed the heat wave temperature threshold. The temperature threshold varies across the United Kingdom, with the London threshold being 28 degrees Celsius (82.4 degrees Fahrenheit). Heat waves usually occur in summer, when slow-moving high pressure develops across an area, resulting in persistent dry, settled weather. In 2003, over 2,000 excess deaths occurred in England during a 10-day heat wave that lasted from August 4 to 13, 2003.[20] Meanwhile, in 2020 it was revealed that 892 people died as a result of a record-breaking heat wave experienced in the United Kingdom during the summer of 2019, with all deaths occurring among people over 65 years of age. The heat exacerbated senior Londoners' existing heart or kidney problems and left them at risk of dehydration that in some cases led to dizziness and falls. During the heat wave, temperatures reached a record 38.7 degrees Celsius (101.66 degrees Fahrenheit) on July 25, breaking the record for the highest temperature ever recorded in the United Kingdom.[21] Although the Met Office classifies heat waves as extreme weather events, a Met Office study into the 2018 United Kingdom heat wave revealed that the probability of the country experiencing a summer hotter than 2018 by the mid-twenty-first century is greater than 50 percent.[22] To help England prepare for this eventuality, Public Health England (the expert national public health agency), in association with the Met Office and other organizations, has devised a heat wave plan. The plan relies on coordinated plans being in place to deal with severe hot weather before it occurs as well as on the implementation of a heat wave alert system that operates from June 1 to September 15 using Met Office forecasts. The triggering of a heat wave warning alerts the National Health Service (NHS) and advises health and social care professionals to pay particular attention to at-risk groups (especially the elderly and those with chronic health conditions).

As well as causing illness and death, London heat waves can also disrupt power supplies, telecommunications, and transport infrastructure: during heat waves, transport engineers have to check that Tube tracks are not at risk of bending or buckling, and temporary speed restrictions are imposed as a precautionary measure, so journeys take longer than usual. Another consequence of hot weather in London is that in some instances, vegetation dries out, leading to wildfires. The London Risk Register classifies wildfires as a medium risk to London. A severe wildfire could spread across an area of 1,500 hectares of land on the edge of the metropolis and would likely last for 7 to 10 days.[23] Such a fire would endanger people, particularly firefighters, animals, and property. Recent wildfires that have affected London include those at Epping Forest, in Leytonstone, East London, in

2013 and 2018. The 2018 fire stretched across 100 hectares (247 acres) of forest near Stratford, in East London, as people were warned to evacuate their homes and roads were closed.[24]

The UK government's latest UK climate change projections suggest that by the 2050s, London may experience a 2.7 degree increase in average summer temperatures and a 15 percent increase in average winter rainfall but also an 18 percent decrease in average summer rainfall.[25] Consequently, London is at very high risk of experiencing severe drought. Recent dry London winters mean London is currently experiencing a severe drought situation. The situation was exacerbated by the fact that in 2020, England experienced its driest May since weather records began in 1910 with the Thames receiving just 7 percent of its typical average rainfall.[26] When this occurs, emergency drought orders go into effect, meaning millions of properties face water supply restrictions and low water pressure (this especially affects properties located on higher levels and apartment blocks). If London were to face a severe sudden drought, there would be an increase in rates of illnesses caused by reduced use of water for hygiene reasons. Southeastern England already experiences "water stress" during periods of dry weather, meaning that water consumption outstrips the available water supply. Typically, water shortages result in minor inconveniences such as the so-called hose pipe ban, a British umbrella term for water restrictions placed on water company customers to prevent them from wasting water through the use of hoses, particularly to water gardens. In 2019, Sir James Bevan warned that within 25 years, England would not have enough water to meet demand because of a combination of climate change, population growth, and an aging water supply system featuring leaking pipes.[27]

Thunderstorms

In London, thunderstorms can occur year-round but are most common during warm, humid summers, which is when intense thunderstorms move across the entire United Kingdom. Typically, London's thunderstorms are accompanied by large hail, gusty winds, and torrential rain. Thunderstorms in London can be very localized, particularly in terms of the amount of rainfall they produce, with big differences in rainfall totals occurring over very short distances. In May 2018, southern England experienced an overnight thunderstorm as warm and humid weather broke down into a storm dubbed "the mother of all thunderstorms" by London-based BBC weather forecaster Tomasz Schafernaker. The storm saw southern England hit with between 15,000 and 20,000 lightning strikes. As a result of the storm, the London Fire Brigade received 505 weather-related calls, with the majority asking for help with flooding situations. Kew Gardens, in South West London, received more than a half inch of rain in an hour, and travelers were stranded at Stansted Airport north of London after lightning struck the airport fueling system.[28]

Windstorms, Tornadoes, and Hurricanes

In London, windstorms tend to last for several hours in one location with the aftereffects continuing for longer. If a major windstorm is followed by windy spells, recovery from the original storm is hampered, so the impact of both the original and subsequent winds is prolonged. In London, strong winds often result in trees being damaged or uprooted. Where trees fall determines the severity of tree damage. A tree falling onto a road, railway line, power line, or property in the United Kingdom can cause varying levels of damage: while several trees could fall in a remote rural area of the country with little impact, an uprooted tree falling in a heavily populated part of London can cause severe damage, disruption (e.g., if a tree falls on power lines), or death.

The United Kingdom experiences the most tornadoes per unit area in the world, with around 30 tornadoes occurring each year.[29] The area between London and Reading (in Berkshire) has the highest likelihood of experiencing a tornado in the UK (a 6 percent chance of a tornado per year).[30] However, most tornadoes in the United Kingdom do not cause much damage. That said, the largest tornado in the country's history, which occurred on October 17, 1091 (or October 23, if the date is adjusted to today's Gregorian calendar) caused great damage when it hit London. The then-wooden London Bridge was destroyed, as was St. Mary-le-Bow Church, in the City of London, along with 600 wooden houses. Meteorologists believe the 1091 tornado had a T8 (severely devastating) status on the TORRO tornado scale (which runs from T0 to T10), with winds of up to 240 miles per hour hitting the city.[31] T8 tornadoes are rare in the United Kingdom, but if such a tornado were to hit London today, it would likely result in cars being blown along streets and properties destroyed. Other notable London tornadoes occurred in December 1954, when a tornado caused the roof to blow off Gunnersbury Underground station in West London injuring six people; and on December 7, 2006, when a T4 (or F2 on the Fujita scale of tornado intensity) ripped through several streets in North West London's Kensal Rise area. The tornado damaged up to 150 houses and many cars, and 6 people were injured.[32] The BBC Weather Centre reported that the tornado lasted less than a minute and happened because intense energy in the United Kingdom's air produced widespread heavy thunderstorms and gusty winds that in London resulted in huge updrafts and downdrafts. The drafts spiraled to create a tornado.

The most notorious windstorm in UK history occurred in October 1987, when a powerful nighttime storm hit many parts of the country, London included. During the storm, known to Londoners as the "Great Storm," winds gusted at up to 100 miles per hour and caused large-scale destruction across the country. The storm led to the death of 18 people (some of whom suffocated in building rubble). Fifteen million trees were uprooted, with many falling on to roads and railways and thereby causing major travel disruption. The uprooted trees included historic species in London's Kew Gardens and Hyde Park. Elsewhere in London, many trees lining the city's streets were blown down so that they blocked roads and crushed parked cars. The falling trees also took down electricity and telephone lines, leaving thousands of people without power. Buildings, scaffolding, and billboards were also severely damaged by both the wind and the falling trees. Had the storm hit during the day, it is likely that many more people would have died.[33] Several days before the Great Storm struck, weather forecasters had predicted the approach of severe weather. However, as the storm got closer, weather prediction models suggested the severe weather would pass along England's south coast. At 6:30 a.m. on October 15, however, weather authorities issued the first gale warnings for sea areas in the English Channel (the body of water separating England and France). These were followed four hours later by warnings of severe gales. By 10:35 p.m., Force 10 winds were forecast. On the evening of October 15, radio and TV forecasts told people to prepare for strong winds but also warned that heavy rain would be the storm's main feature. At the same time, however, severe weather warnings had been issued to the London Fire Brigade and other emergency services. At 1:35 a.m. on October 16, however, the Met Office issued warnings of Force 11 winds, as temperatures accompanying the passage of the storm's warm front rose dramatically. It was also at 1:35 a.m. that the United Kingdom's Ministry of Defence warned the impact of the storm would be so great that the military might need to assist the UK's civil authorities. At 2:50 a.m., the London Weather Centre recorded winds measuring 82 knots, while at 4:30 a.m., winds of 86 knots were recorded at London's Gatwick Airport. Ultimately, southeastern England suffered the greatest damage, because gusts of 70 knots or more were constantly logged there for four consecutive hours. During the storm, London experienced winds reaching up to 94 miles per hour.[34] Additionally, the wind direction swung from southerly to southwesterly with damage patterns suggesting that whirlwinds had occurred.

The Great Storm was an exceptional weather event in UK history, but it was not classified officially as a hurricane by weather authorities because it did not originate in the tropics. Nonetheless, according to the Beaufort scale of wind force, hurricane force (Force 12) is a wind of 64 knots or more that lasts over a period of at least 10 minutes. According to this definition of a hurricane, hurricane-force winds had occurred locally during the Great Storm but were not widespread. The Great Storm was also extraordinary for the temperature changes that occurred during the weather event, for during a five-hour period, temperatures rose by more than 6 degrees Celsius per hour.[35]

The 1987 storm was the worst storm experienced anywhere in the United Kingdom since the Great Storm of 1703. The 1703 storm caused extensive damage, including uprooting thousands of trees and blowing the roof off the Houses of Parliament, as well as launching cows and fish into the air, transplanting boats from the River Thames and, most seriously, killing between 8,000 and 15,000 people.[36]

Analysis of historical hourly mean wind speeds and highest gust data suggests that such extreme windstorm conditions will occur overland in southern and southeastern England on average only once every 200 years.[37] In the aftermath of the Great Storm, the Met Office was accused of failing to forecast the storm correctly. Based on the findings of an internal review, several improvements were made to the way in which the Met Office gathered data. For example, observation of the atmosphere over water to the south and west of the United Kingdom was improved by increased use of observational equipment, while computer models used in forecasting were refined.

Snow and Ice

In the past, London experienced far colder winters than today, for from 1300 until 1870, the earth experienced very cold temperatures due to a natural phenomenon called the "Little Ice Age" that was caused primarily by geological climate change combined with volcanic eruptions and very low sunspot activity. The Little Ice Age affected many aspects of everyday London life. During the coldest spells of the period, such as that experienced from 1683 to 1684, the lakes and rivers of southern England froze, as did part of the sea off England's south coast. Indeed, this period was so cold that it was dubbed the Great Frost: England experienced the severest frost ever recorded in London, with the River Thames frozen solid for two months and ice reaching a thickness of 11 inches.[38] The Thames was able to freeze because at that time it was far wider, shallower, and slower flowing than it is today. Additionally, London Bridge was built on numerous arches supported by small piers that broke up the river's flow. Consequently, in winter, when the bridge's arches became blocked with ice and debris, the bridge acted like a dam, slowing the river and assisting the freezing process. The frozen river left hundreds of barge operators and sailors unemployed. Luckily, though, the advent of frost fairs (winter carnival-like events) allowed people who usually worked on the river the chance to earn money by guiding sightseeing tours out on the ice. Other workers fitted runners to their boats, effectively turning them into sleighs and offering rides along the frozen river.

Today in the United Kingdom, daily weather forecasts specifically focused on gritting (salting) and snowplowing needs are used by some organizations to help them decide how to reduce the impact of winter weather. In London, when snow is accompanied by strong winds, the snow can drift and cause large variations in snow depth that make it hard for authorities to clear roads, railways, and airports. Snow and cold temperatures can also increase the chance of Londoners suffering from hypothermia; wrist (and other) fractures, caused when people use their hand to break a fall while slipping on ice; and other health issues. The effect of snow and ice on roads can be alleviated by treating roads with salt or grit. However, in London, it is impossible to treat all of the hundreds of thousands of miles of roads, cycle paths, or pavements; to do so would cost authorities hundreds of millions of pounds. Also, some of London's roads are too narrow or steep for gritting lorries (salt trucks) to navigate. Consequently, icy patches can form on untreated roads and pavements. Another problem faced by London's authorities is that sometimes the grit used to treat roads and pavements is washed away by rain. Occasionally, freezing rain can fall in London. Freezing rain occurs when rain freezes immediately on contact with very cold surfaces, such as roads and vehicle windshields. Freezing rain results in very dangerous icy conditions that disrupt travel and puts a strain on emergency services.

When snow falls in London, travel disruption can rapidly ensue. Road and air transport organizations help mitigate possible disruption by performing winter weather maintenance duties such as salting and snowplowing. Despite planning, however, snow can make London grind to a halt. Indeed, the phrase "the wrong type of snow" (or "the wrong kind of snow") has been in circulation in the United Kingdom since 1991, when severe winter weather disrupted many national train services. A train company press release implied that the management and engineering staff had been unaware of the different types of snow and therefore could not prepare for it. Since then, the phrase has been used in the United Kingdom to symbolize euphemistic excuses. In 2009, thousands of Londoners were again unable to travel when up to eight inches of snow brought the city's transport network to a standstill.[39] On this occasion, very few bus routes were able to run in central London, Tube lines were suspended, stations closed, rail routes (including international Eurostar services) were interrupted, and flights to and from Heathrow Airport, London City Airport and Luton Airport were disrupted. Roads into and out of the capital were also affected, including the M25 freeway that encircles London. The London Ambulance Service received more than 650 calls for help but were only able to respond to life-threatening situations because the weather put the service under severe pressure. Similarly, the NHS in London was also impacted, with outpatient clinics and nonemergency surgeries closed for two days. Meanwhile, over 260 schools across London closed for health and safety reasons and the fact that staff could not travel to school.[40] The wintry conditions led the Met Office to issue an extreme weather warning for London and southeastern England.

The following December, snow and ice again caused major transport problems in and around London. No flights were able to land at Heathrow Airport, and few were able to take off, so thousands of travelers were stranded at the airport. Numerous train operators, including Eurostar, were forced to cancel or change their schedules, and the London Underground network ran with severe delays. The M25 was also closed in both directions after a liquid petroleum gas tanker overturned. The disruption came despite Transport for London's fleet of gritters working to spread hundreds of tons of grit across the road network. London water supplier Thames Water also reported a fourfold increase in burst pipes caused by the subzero temperatures.

In February 2018, London experienced the "Beast from the East" cold weather event: high pressure over Scandinavia caused polar continental air to extend south to the United Kingdom, while at the same time, cold air was drawn to the United Kingdom from the Eurasian landmass, creating very cold, wintry conditions. During the Beast from the East, major routes around London ran fairly smoothly, as London's authorities heeded past experience of winter disruption and ensured the routes were treated. London's side roads and pavements fared less well, however, as many remained untreated. The rail networks also suffered disruption as Network Rail (the public body that oversees Britain's rail system) implemented its severe winter strategy. Some rail services that were able to run were reduced to allow more deicing trains to run and thereby ensure some passenger trains could operate.

In 2019, heavy snow fell in southern England; London City Airport closed its runway, and British Airways canceled flights from Heathrow. Since so many of London's natural hazards involve the weather, it is no surprise the weather is one of Londoners' favorite topics of conversation.

NOTES

1. Alok Jha, "London Is Overdue for a Major Earthquake, Warns Seismologist," *The Guardian*, September 16, 2010, https://www.theguardian.com/science/2010/sep/16/british-science-festival-2010-british-science-festival.

2. "Earthquakes in the UK," British Geological Survey, 2020, https://www.bgs.ac.uk/discoveringGeology/hazards/earthquakes/UK.html.

3. Jasper Hammil, "London at Risk of Earthquake after Two Faultlines Are Found beneath the City," Metro, June 1, 2018, https://metro.co.uk/2018/06/01/london-risk-earthquake-two-faultlines-found-beneath-city-7597704.

4. "Volcanic Ash: Flight Chaos to Continue into Weekend," BBC News, April 16, 2010, http://news.bbc.co.uk/1/hi/8623534.stm.

5. "A History of UK Named Storms," BBC, June 14, 2018, https://www.bbc.co.uk/weather/features/44481058.

6. Isha Sesay, "Storm Ciara's Powerful Winds Help British Airways Flight from New York to Heathrow Break 800mph Speed Record," Euro Weekly News, February 9, 2020, https://www.euroweeklynews.com/2020/02/09/storm-ciaras-powerful-winds-help-british-airways-flight-from-new-york-to-heathrow-break-800mph-speed-record.

7. Environment Agency, "Surface Water: The Biggest Flood Risk of All," speech by Sir James Bevan KCMG, chief executive, Environment Agency, CIWEM Surface Water Management Conference, October 17, 2018, https://www.gov.uk/government/news/surface-water-the-biggest-flood-risk-of-all.

8. Ibid.

9. Ibid.

10. Transport for London and Mayor of London, SUDS in London: A Guide, November 2016, 36, http://content.tfl.gov.uk/sustainable-urban-drainage-november-2016.pdf.

11. Shari L. Gallop, "Historic Events: Severe Coastal Flooding and Damage in Central London on 6th and 7th January 1928," Surge Watch, November 5, 2015, https://www.surgewatch.org/historic-events-severe-coastal-flooding-and-damage-in-central-london-on-6th-and-7th-january-1928.

12. Ibid.

13. Jon Kelly, "The Great 1928 Flood of London," BBC News Magazine, February 16, 2014, https://www.bbc.co.uk/news/magazine-26153241.

14. Matthew Kelly, "1953 Storm Surge: How Britain's Worst Natural Disaster Kicked Off the Debate on Climate Change," The Conversation, January 16, 2017, http://theconversation.com/1953-storm-surge-how-britains-worst-natural-disaster-kicked-off-the-debate-on-climate-change-71310.

15. Ibid.

16. Tom De Castella, "How Does the Thames Barrier Stop London Flooding?" BBC News Magazine, February 11, 2014, https://www.bbc.co.uk/news/magazine-26133660.

17. Environment Agency, TE2100 5 Year Review Non-Technical Summary, July 2016, 1, https://assets.publishing.service.gov.uk/government/uploads/system/uploads/attachment_data/file/558631/TE2100_5_Year_Review_Non_Technical_Summary.pdf.

18. Ibid.

19. Environment Agency, TE2100: Managing Flood Risk through London and the Thames Estuary, November 2012, 28, https://assets.publishing.service.gov.uk/government/uploads/system/uploads/attachment_data/file/322061/LIT7540_43858f.pdf.

20. Public Health England, Heatwave Plan for England: Protecting Health and Reducing Harm from Severe Heat and Heatwaves, May 2018, https://assets

.publishing.service.gov.uk/government/uploads/system/uploads/attachment_data/file/801539/Heatwave_plan_for_England_2019.pdf.

21. Naomi Ackerman, "Summer 2019 Heatwaves Killed Almost 900 People across UK, Data Says," *Evening Standard*, January 7, 2020, https://www.standard.co.uk/news/summer-2019-heatwaves-killed-almost-900-people-across-uk-official-data-suggests-a4328566.html.

22. Mark McCarthy et al., "Drivers of the UK Summer Heatwave of 2018," in "Heatwave and Drought in 2018," special issue, *Weather* 74, no. 11 (November 2019): 390.

23. London Resilience Partnership, *London Risk Register*, version 8.1, January 2019, 1, https://www.london.gov.uk/sites/default/files/london_risk_register_2019.pdf.

24. Mattha Busby, "Firefighters Tackle Large Grass Fire in East London," *The Guardian*, July 15, 2018, https://www.theguardian.com/uk-news/2018/jul/15/firefighters-tackle-large-grass-fire-east-london-wanstead-flats.

25. Mayor of London/London Assembly, "Chapter One: Context and Strategy," 2020, https://www.london.gov.uk/what-we-do/planning/london-plan/past-versions-and-alterations-london-plan/london-plan-2016/london-plan-chapter-one-context-and-strategy-6.

26. David Jones, "Summer Drought Risk Increases Despite Recent Rain," *Farmers Weekly*, June 17, 2020, https://www.fwi.co.uk/arable/summer-drought-risk-increases-despite-recent-rain.

27. Roger Harrabin, "Climate Change: Water Shortages in England 'within 25 Years,'" *BBC News*, March 19, 2019, https://www.bbc.co.uk/news/uk-47620228.

28. Press Association and Helena Horton, "'Mother of All Thunderstorms' Delivers Up to 20,000 Lightning Strikes—as Stansted Fuel System Hit," *The Telegraph*, May 27, 2018, https://www.telegraph.co.uk/news/2018/05/27/mother-thunderstorms-lights-skies-london.

29. Kate Ravilious, "Weatherwatch: Britain's Earliest Recorded Tornado," *The Guardian*, October 19, 2011, https://www.theguardian.com/news/2011/oct/19/weatherwatch-tornado-london-britain.

30. Sean Coughlan, "UK's 'Tornado Alley' Identified," *BBC News*, June 15, 2015, https://www.bbc.co.uk/news/education-33136737.

31. Mike Rowe, "Tornado Extremes in the United Kingdom: The Earliest, Longest, Widest, Severest, and Deadliest," in *Extreme Weather: Forty Years of the Tornado and Storm Research Organisation*, ed. Robert K. Doe (Chichester, UK: John Wiley & Sons, 2016), 77.

32. "Six Hurt as Tornado Hits London," *BBC News*, December 7, 2006, http://news.bbc.co.uk/1/hi/england/london/6217514.stm.

33. "The Great Storm of 1987," Met Office, https://www.metoffice.gov.uk/weather/learn-about/weather/case-studies/great-storm.

34. Tanya Gupta, "Great Storm 1987: The Day 18 People Were Killed," *BBC News*, October 15, 2017, https://www.bbc.co.uk/news/uk-england-kent-41366241.

35. "The Great Storm of 1987."

36. Lucy Jones, "In 1703, Britain Was Struck by Its Worse Ever Storm," *BBC Earth*, 2020, http://www.bbc.com/earth/story/20170309-in-1703-britain-was-struck-by-possibly-its-worst-ever-storm.

37. "The Great Storm of 1987."

38. Martin Holman, "Frost Fairs and the Frozen Thames," Art UK, January 11, 2017, https://artuk.org/discover/stories/frost-fairs-and-the-frozen-thames.

39. "UK Prepares for Freezing Weekend," *BBC News*, February 2, 2009, http://news.bbc.co.uk/1/hi/uk/7864395.stm.

40. "Heavy Snow Disrupts London Travel," *BBC News*, February 2, 2019, http://news.bbc.co.uk/1/hi/england/london/7864315.stm.

FURTHER READING

Ackerman, Naomi. "Summer 2019 Heatwaves Killed Almost 900 People across UK, Data Says." *Evening Standard*, January 7, 2020. https://www.standard.co.uk/news/summer-2019-heatwaves-killed-almost-900-people-across-uk-official-data-suggests-a4328566.html.

Corton, Christine L. *London Fog: The Biography*. Cambridge, MA: Belknap of Harvard University Press, 2015.

Coughlan, Sean. "UK's 'Tornado Alley' Identified." *BBC News*, June 15, 2015. https://www.bbc.co.uk/news/education-33136737.

De Castella, Tom. "How Does the Thames Barrier Stop London Flooding?" *BBC News Magazine*, February 11, 2014. https://www.bbc.co.uk/news/magazine-26133660.

"Earthquakes in the UK." British Geological Survey, 2020. https://www.bgs.ac.uk/discoveringGeology/hazards/earthquakes/UK.html.

Environment Agency. *TE2100 5 Year Review Non-Technical Summary*. July 2016. https://assets.publishing.service.gov.uk/government/uploads/system/uploads/attachment_data/file/558631/TE2100_5_Year_Review_Non_Technical_Summary.pdf.

Gallop, Shari L. "Historic Events: Severe Coastal Flooding and Damage in Central London on 6th and 7th January 1928." Surge Watch, November 5, 2015. https://www.surgewatch.org/historic-events-severe-coastal-flooding-and-damage-in-central-london-on-6th-and-7th-january-1928.

"The Great Storm of 1987." Met Office. https://www.metoffice.gov.uk/weather/learn-about/weather/case-studies/great-storm.

Gupta, Tanya. "Great Storm 1987: The Day 18 People Were Killed." *BBC News*, October 15, 2017. https://www.bbc.co.uk/news/uk-england-kent-41366241.

Hammil, Jasper. "London at Risk of Earthquake after Two Faultlines Are Found beneath the City." Metro, June 1, 2018. https://metro.co.uk/2018/06/01/london-risk-earthquake-two-faultlines-found-beneath-city-7597704.

Harrabin, Roger. "Climate Change: Water Shortages in England 'within 25 Years.'" *BBC News*, March 19, 2019. https://www.bbc.co.uk/news/uk-47620228.

"Heavy Snow Disrupts London Travel." *BBC News*, February 2, 2019. http://news.bbc.co.uk/1/hi/england/london/7864315.stm.

"A History of UK Named Storms." *BBC*, June 14, 2018. https://www.bbc.co.uk/weather/features/44481058.

Holman, Martin. "Frost Fairs and the Frozen Thames." Art UK, January 11, 2017. https://artuk.org/discover/stories/frost-fairs-and-the-frozen-thames.

Jha, Alok. "London Is Overdue for a Major Earthquake, Warns Seismologist." *The Guardian*, September 16, 2010. https://www.theguardian.com/science/2010/sep/16/british-science-festival-2010-british-science-festival.

Jones, Lucy. "In 1703, Britain Was Struck by Its Worse Ever Storm." *BBC Earth*, 2020. http://www.bbc.com/earth/story/20170309-in-1703-britain-was-struck-by-possibly-its-worst-ever-storm.

Kelly, Jon. "The Great 1928 Flood of London." *BBC News Magazine*, February 16, 2014. https://www.bbc.co.uk/news/magazine-26153241.

Kelly, Matthew. "1953 Storm Surge: How Britain's Worst Natural Disaster Kicked Off the Debate on Climate Change." The Conversation, January 16, 2017. http://theconversation.com/1953-storm-surge-how-britains-worst-natural-disaster-kicked-off-the-debate-on-climate-change-71310.

London Environment Strategy. https://www.london.gov.uk/sites/default/files/adapting_to_climate_change.pdf.

"London Gears Up for Cold Weather." Transport for London, November 25, 2010. https://tfl.gov.uk/info-for/media/press-releases/2010/november/london-gears-up-for-cold-weather.

London Resilience Partnership. *London Risk Register.* Version 8.1. January 2019. https://www.london.gov.uk/sites/default/files/london_risk_register_2019.pdf.

London Resilience Partnership. *Severe Weather and Natural Hazards: Response Framework.* Version 1. June 2017. https://www.london.gov.uk/sites/default/files/severe_weather_and_natural_hazards_framework_v1.0.pdf.

Mayor of London/London Assembly. "Chapter One: Context and Strategy." 2020. https://www.london.gov.uk/what-we-do/planning/london-plan/past-versions-and-alterations-london-plan/london-plan-2016/london-plan-chapter-one-context-and-strategy-6.

McCarthy, Mark, Nikolaos Christidis, Nick Dunstone, David Fereday, Gillian Kay, Albert Klein-Tank, Jason Lowe, Jon Petch, Adam Scaife, and Peter Stott. "Drivers of the UK Summer Heatwave of 2018." In "Heatwave and Drought in 2018," special issue, *Weather* 74, no. 11 (November 2019): 390–96.

Press Association and Helena Horton. "'Mother of All Thunderstorms' Delivers Up to 20,000 Lightning Strikes—as Stansted Fuel System Hit." *The Telegraph*, May 27, 2018. https://www.telegraph.co.uk/news/2018/05/27/mother-thunderstorms-lights-skies-london.

Public Health England. *Heatwave Plan for England. Protecting Health and Reducing Harm from Severe Heat and Heatwaves.* May 2018. https://assets.publishing.service.gov.uk/government/uploads/system/uploads/attachment_data/file/801539/Heatwave_plan_for_England_2019.pdf.

Ravilious, Kate. "Weatherwatch: Britain's Earliest Recorded Tornado," *The Guardian*, October 19, 2011. https://www.theguardian.com/news/2011/oct/19/weatherwatch-tornado-london-britain.

Rowe, Mike. "Tornado Extremes in the United Kingdom: The Earliest, Longest, Widest, Severest, and Deadliest." In *Extreme Weather: Forty Years of the Tornado and Storm Research Organisation*, edited by Robert K. Doe, 77–90. Chichester, UK: John Wiley & Sons, 2016.

Sesay, Isha. "Storm Ciara's Powerful Winds Help British Airways Flight from New York to Heathrow Break 800mph Speed Record." *Euro Weekly News*, February 9, 2020. https://www.euroweeklynews.com/2020/02/09/storm-ciaras-powerful-winds-help-british-airways-flight-from-new-york-to-heathrow-break-800mph-speed-record.

"Six Hurt as Tornado Hits London." *BBC News*, December 7, 2006. http://news.bbc.co.uk/1/hi/england/london/6217514.stm.

"Surface Water: The Biggest Flood Risk of All." Speech by Sir James Bevan KCMG, chief executive, Environment Agency, CIWEM Surface Water Management Conference, October 17, 2018. https://www.gov.uk/government/news/surface-water-the-biggest-flood-risk-of-all.

Transport for London and Mayor of London. *SUDS in London: A Guide.* November 2016. http://content.tfl.gov.uk/sustainable-urban-drainage-november-2016.pdf.

"UK Prepares for Freezing Weekend." *BBC News*, February 2, 2009. http://news.bbc.co.uk/1/hi/uk/7864395.stm.

"Volcanic Ash: Flight Chaos to Continue into Weekend." *BBC News*, April 16, 2010. http://news.bbc.co.uk/1/hi/8623534.stm.

10

Culture and Lifestyle

London is a vibrant, cosmopolitan city that is rich in culture and in which no one particular lifestyle predominates. It is home to numerous ethnicities and nationalities, something that is reflected in the huge range of cultural and religious venues, foods, shops, and activities available in the city. London contains an array of green spaces and historical sites as well as a wide range of sporting and fitness centers, with some municipal parks incorporating outdoor gyms. London also contains numerous sports venues, most particularly those focused on soccer, cricket, rugby, and tennis. London can boast thirteen professional football clubs (Chelsea, Arsenal, West Ham, Millwall, Leyton Orient, Tottenham Hotspur, AFC Wimbledon, Fulham, Brentford, Queens Park Rangers, Crystal Palace, Sutton United, and Charlton Athletic). Some sports venues are private enterprises, but there are many public facilities. Famous sporting events that have occurred in London include the Summer Olympic Games, the Wimbledon Lawn tennis championship, cricket matches at Lords and the Oval, and rugby at Twickenham. Every year, over 35,000 runners compete in the London Marathon,[1] which finishes in the Mall, a road that links Buckingham Palace to Trafalgar Square in central London.

London contains hundreds of famous landmarks, including four UNESCO World Heritage Sites: the Tower of London; the Royal Botanic Gardens, Kew; the Palace of Westminster and Westminster Abbey (including St. Margaret's Church); and Maritime Greenwich (the buildings, including the Royal Observatory, which symbolize the English artistic and

---

DID YOU KNOW?

THE BLESSING OF THE THROATS

St. Etheldreda's Church, in Holborn, is the oldest Catholic church in England and one of only two remaining buildings in London from the reign of King Edward I. The church is named after Princess Etheldreda of East Anglia (630–679), who wanted to become a nun but agreed to a marriage of political convenience on condition she could remain a virgin. She later established a monastic community. Shortly before Etheldreda's death, a tumor was removed from her neck. Etheldreda considered her tumor a divine punishment for her previous love of expensive necklaces. As well as being a patron of chastity, Etheldreda is also invoked for help against infections of the throat and neck. To this day, the Blessing of Throats is an important annual service at St. Etheldreda's Church. However, the blessing is specifically associated with St. Blaise, a fourth-century Armenian bishop reputed to have saved the life of a boy who had a fishbone stuck in his throat. The Blessing of the Throats takes place on or immediately after February 3, St. Blaise's Day. During the service, two candles are held in the form of a crucifix to the throat of an afflicted person, and a blessing is said as the individual kneels on a step.

---

scientific undertakings of the seventeenth and eighteenth centuries). UNESCO considers these locations to be of "outstanding universal value" (OUV) and international importance. The Darwin Landscape Laboratory in the borough of Bromley, where Charles Darwin developed his theory of evolution, is a proposed addition to the UNESCO list.

Other famous London landmarks include Buckingham Palace, in Westminster, which since 1837 has served as the official residence of the reigning UK monarch; St. Paul's Cathedral, which is the headquarters of the Diocese of London; Tower Bridge, which is a combined bascule and suspension bridge; and the London Eye, a giant observation wheel situated on the south bank of the River Thames.

MULTICULTURAL LONDON

Each area of London tends to have its own community and way of life, though, generally, Londoners are tolerant and open-minded. Indeed, London is so multicultural that it has been described as "super-diverse."[2] In several ways, however, London differs from most other global cities in terms of migration. London's history of immigration reaches back through millennia to the city's founding during Roman times. Also, unusually, two of London's most significant immigrant populations, the Irish and Jewish communities, have existed in London for centuries; thus these immigrant groups are ingrained in the city's life. While immigrants to London once tended to settle in East London, immigrant communities now exist across the capital and have found employment on all levels and not just those deemed undesirable by city dwellers, as occurs in many other world cities. London, then, has become a melting pot of different lifestyles, ranging from that of the descendants of nineteenth-century Irish laborers who helped excavate the London Underground lines to the uber-wealthy Russian oligarchs who call modern London home.

London's ethnic diversity is reflected linguistically: more than 300 languages are spoken across London, which is more than in any other city in the world.[3] Indeed, while according to the 2011 UK Census, 78 percent of Londoners speak English as their first language, more than 100 languages are spoken in almost every London borough. After English, the most commonly spoken language is Polish, which is the first language for 2 percent of London's residents. The next most spoken languages are Bengali, Gujarati, French, Urdu, and Arabic. Hillingdon is the most linguistically diverse London borough, for 107 languages are spoken there. Similarly, 104 languages are spoken in Newham. London is home to a well-established French community. Traditionally London's French population has been concentrated around the French embassy in South Kensington, but today there are growing numbers of French communities living throughout London to the extent that more French people live in London than in the major French cities of Bordeaux, Nantes, or Strasbourg. For this reason, London is sometimes regarded as France's sixth biggest city in terms of population.[4] The geographic distribution of various ethnicities and nationalities in London means that certain languages predominate in certain London Boroughs. For example, Polish is spoken widely in Ealing, Turkish in Haringey, Gujarati in Brent and Harrow, and Arabic in Westminster. The borough of Kensington and Chelsea has the highest proportion of French, Spanish, Italian, German, and Filipino speakers.[5]

London's multiculturalism is also reflected in terms of religion. London contains more than 2,200 religious buildings and is home to more religious groups than any other city in the world.[6] This variety of faiths has led to the formation of numerous different communities throughout London, each with its own diverse lifestyles and traditions.

According to the UK's 2011 Census, 71 percent of Londoners held some kind of religious belief. Almost 4 million Christians and 1 million Muslims live in London, along with 411,000 Hindus, 148,600 Jews, 126,000 Sikhs, and 82,000 Buddhists. While the number of Christian Londoners has decreased over time, the number of Muslim, Sikh, Hindu, and Buddhist Londoners has increased.[7] Christian Londoners tend to live in such Outer London Boroughs as Croydon, Bexley, Havering, Sutton, Merton, Barking and Dagenham, Richmond, and Enfield. Christian communities also exist in more central parts of London, in the boroughs of Kensington and Chelsea, Hammersmith and Fulham, and Wandsworth, as well as in the Inner London Boroughs of Lambeth, Greenwich, Lewisham, and Southwark. Since 2001, the number of Muslim Londoners has increased, and their population has become more widely spread across multiple London Boroughs. The boroughs with the largest proportion of Muslim residents are Barking and Dagenham, Newham, Tower Hamlets, Redbridge, Waltham Forest, Westminster, Kingston, and Haringey. Indeed, between 2001 and 2011, the size of Barking and Dagenham's Muslim population more than tripled in size, from 7,148 to 25,520, while the Muslim population of Hillingdon more than doubled in size, from 11,258 to 29,000. The boroughs of Westminster, Barnet, Hounslow, Bexley, and Brent saw their Muslim populations almost double in size during the same period. At the same time, the size of London's Jewish population has fallen slightly. London's largest Jewish communities are located in the boroughs of Hackney, Camden, Harrow, Redbridge, and Westminster. Golders Green, in the North West London borough of Barnet, is synonymous with London's Jewish population and has fast-growing Charedi and Israeli communities. Golders Green is home to 30 Jewish schools, more than 40 synagogues, and 50 kosher restaurants and shops.[8]

Since 2001, London's Hindu population has increased in size by 41 percent. Most Hindus in London live in the North West London Boroughs of Harrow and Brent, and the East London Boroughs of Redbridge and Barking and Dagenham. In Barking and Dagenham, the Hindu population more than doubled in size, from less than 2,000 to over 4,400.[9] The Shri Swaminarayan Mandir, in Neasden, North West London, once held the distinction of being the largest Hindu *mandir* (temple) built outside of India. London's Sikh population has increased since 2011, with large Sikh communities living in the West London Boroughs of Ealing, Hounslow, and Hillingdon as well as in Redbridge and Newham. In 2019, approximately 50,000 Sikhs took part in the Southall Nagar Kirtan, in Ealing.[10] This was the UK's largest Sikh procession to date and marked 550 years after the birth of Guru Nanak, the founder of Sikhism. London's Buddhist population has grown in size by almost a third since 2001. Most Buddhist communities in London are found in the Outer London Boroughs of Barnet, Brent, and Ealing, as well as in Westminster. There are significant Buddhist communities in the Inner London Boroughs of Greenwich, Southwark, Lewisham, and Hackney too. In recent years, the outer London Boroughs of Hounslow and Hillingdon have seen large increases in their Buddhist population.

LONDON ETIQUETTE

The British place great store on good manners, and Londoners are no different. Like other Brits, Londoners tend to be punctual, say "please" and "thank you" and display fairly reserved body language. Most London-specific etiquette concerns conduct on public transport, for public transport is of great importance to Londoners, many of whom use the system daily.

On the London Underground and buses, the unspoken rule is that passengers keep themselves to themselves. Typically, Londoners do not strike up conversations with strangers while on buses or the Tube, and while this behavior can seem standoffish to outsiders, the lack of conversation is really just born of Londoners' respect for people's right to travel undisturbed. For the same reason, many trains include a quiet zone, a car in which passengers are not supposed to make or receive cell phone calls and all electrical equipment should be used in silent mode. Despite their preference to not talk on public transport, Londoners are usually more than happy to help someone with directions if an individual is lost or does not understand the city's transport network.

When traveling, Londoners frown upon travelers boarding a train before passengers wishing to disembark have had an opportunity to do so. If a passenger stands by a Tube door and people are trying to disembark, then it is expected that the person by the door gets off the train, lets the disembarking passengers pass, and then gets back onto the Tube. If a Tube is very crowded, it is expected that people standing on the station platform will wait to board the next train, which is often very close behind. Once on the Tube, it is considered rude to place a bag on an adjacent seat, as this prevents passengers from sitting. This is especially true at peak travel times. Londoners also frown upon their fellow passengers eating on the Tube, especially smelly foods that can permeate an entire car. It is usual for Tube passengers to offer their seat to pregnant people, the elderly, and the disabled. Londoners who are less able to stand can apply for badges supplied by Transport for London that say, "Please offer me a seat." A similar badge declaring "Baby on Board" is available to pregnant people. Often it is the case that when someone wearing a badge enters a Tube car, several seated passengers all offer the badge-wearer their seat as they each wish to help the badge-wearer be seated.

When traveling on a station escalator, the left-hand side of the escalator should be kept clear, as this side is reserved for people who prefer to walk up the escalator as if it were a staircase. Travelers who prefer to stand and be transported by the escalator should keep to the right-hand side of the escalator. Once at the ticket gate, passengers should have their Oyster Cards or travel cards ready to tap out of the station, as this reduces queuing time at the barriers and so prevents delays.

LONDON SHOPPING

London takes the form of numerous small towns linked together. Each of these settlements has at least one shopping street and supermarkets. London is home to an extraordinary array of shops, ranging from iconic department stores to independent boutiques and ethnic food shops. The city also boasts many indoor or outdoor markets, including food markets, vintage and antique markets, artisan markets, and general street markets. Several areas of London are synonymous with certain types of shops or products. For instance, Hatton Garden in Holborn is synonymous with jewelers, and Goldhawk Road in Shepherd's Bush (in West London) is famous for its many fabric shops. Similarly, certain London markets are synonymous with certain products. For example, Billingsgate Fish Market in Canary Wharf is the UK's largest inland fish market. The market takes its name from Billingsgate, in the City of London, where the market began. Similarly, the 800-year-old Smithfield market in the City of London is the UK's largest wholesale meat market and is closely associated with selling meat and poultry. Columbia Road Flower Market in Bethnal Green, East London, is one of London's most photogenic attractions, filled with flower vendors and plants for sale.

The City of London is not really a shopping destination, however, for on weekends, there are few office workers around, so shops tend to be closed. However, the One New Change shopping center near St. Paul's Cathedral is known for selling luxury goods. Similarly, the Royal Exchange shopping mall and office complex located near the Bank of England contains high-end shops that are popular with white-collar workers. To the west of St. Paul's Cathedral is the Hatton Garden jewelry district. A little farther west is Lamb's Conduit Street, which contains historic independent shops and restaurants. To the east of there is Commercial Street in Shoreditch, which is a mecca for vintage lovers. The area also contains numerous pop-up stores and the Spitalfields antiques market. To the north is the Columbia Road Flower Market.

In contrast to the City of London, Oxford Street in London's West End area is arguably the most famous shopping destination in London if not the whole of the UK. At some 1.5 miles long, the street runs from Tottenham Court Road to Marble Arch via Oxford Circus and is the world's largest shopping street. Oxford Street is home to more than 90 flagship stores selling everything from fashion to technology and home goods. There are also 500 restaurants in the vicinity.[11] The abundance of shops and restaurants on and around Oxford Street means the area is Europe's most visited shopping street, attracting 200 million shoppers annually.[12] The westernmost end of Oxford Street at Marble Arch is the location of the high-end Selfridges department store, which was opened by the American businessman Harry Gordon Selfridge in 1909.

Walking along Oxford Street going east toward Tottenham Court Road, the shops tend toward the budget end with a plethora of souvenir shops. The area was notable as the location for Topshop's Oxford Circus flagship store in the UK, which was the biggest Topshop branch in the world. The

Oxford Circus store was spread across 90,000 square feet and three floors[13] and welcomed 28,000 shoppers, who were attracted by the store's pop-up boutiques, beauty counters, cafes, and DJ-ing area.[14] However in May 2021 Topshop's Oxford Circus store was put up for sale as a symbol of upheaval on Oxford Street that will also see Marks & Spencer and John Lewis redesign their flagship shops situated on the thoroughfare in light of the shift to online shopping.

To the north of Oxford Street is the chic Marylebone area that runs roughly from Marylebone Underground station in the north, south to Oxford Street, and from Edgware Road in the west, east to Oxford Circus. Marylebone features luxury shops, boutiques, cafes, and restaurants located on and around Marylebone High Street. The area is popular with West Londoners but little known by visitors. Consequently, despite its proximity to hectic Oxford Street, Marylebone has a low-key atmosphere. The area of Marylebone known as Marylebone Village runs through Marylebone High Street and is home to a mix of fashion and housewares retailers, beauty and well-being shops, cafes, restaurants, and pubs. One of the most notable Marylebone shops is Daunt Books, which is thought to be the world's first custom-built bookshop.[15] On Sundays, Marylebone Farmers' Market operates, featuring stalls selling organic and locally grown produce, fresh juices, and cheese. Farmers markets are very popular in London, as they allow Londoners to buy quality foodstuffs produced within 100 miles of the M25 freeway, straight from the producers. Many British towns hold a weekend famers market, with around 20 official markets in London established by the London Farmers Markets organization.

Regent Street, which curves east between Oxford Street and Piccadilly, tends to contain high-end stores offering affordable luxury. However, the area is most notable for the world-famous Liberty department store with its distinctive mock Tudor, beamed frontage. Liberty opened in 1875 as a furnishings shop specializing in oriental fabrics. Today it sells designer brands, furniture, and textiles. Regent Street is also the location of Hamleys, the world's largest and oldest toy shop, which opened in 1881.[16]

Running parallel to Regent Street is the Bond Street area that links Oxford Street to Piccadilly. The Bond Street area, which comprises New Bond Street and Old Bond Street, is synonymous with luxury fashion, international designers, and jewelers. Nearby Dover Street Market is a designer shop selling various fashion brands. The Fenwick of Bond Street department store is known for stocking merchandise by famous fashion designers.

Close to Oxford Street is Carnaby Street, a pedestrianized area that is home to fashion retailers, including many independent boutiques. In the 1960s, Carnaby Street was a mecca for fashionable Londoners, especially

LIBERTY PRINTS

The Liberty department store is famous for producing its Liberty print fabrics. The shop started out selling imported oriental fabrics, but when demand for the oriental fabrics grew, Liberty decided to import undyed cloth that they then had hand printed in England with their own designs. Liberty prints first went on sale in the 1920s. Typically, Liberty print fabric is decorated with small florals and abstract prints and has a distinctly vintage vibe. Today, 120 new Liberty prints are released annually, and Liberty Tana lawn cotton fabric is a best-selling fabric. The Liberty Archive contains around 40,000 Liberty prints.

those who identified with the Mod and hippie subcultures. Designers based in Carnaby Street at that time included Mary Quant, who is often credited as the inventor of both the miniskirt and hotpants. Burlington Arcade is a glass-roofed shopping arcade that runs parallel to, and east of, Bond Street from Piccadilly to Burlington Gardens. The arcade, which opened in 1819, is England's oldest and longest shopping arcade.[17] Ever since its opening, Burlington Arcade has been seen as an exclusive, upscale shopping location with such luxury goods as jewelry, fashion, art, perfume, antiques and fine foods proffered by mahogany-fronted boutiques. Such is the arcade's reputation for wealth that it has its own security force: top-hatted guards known as Beadles who are members of the Burlington Beadle Guard, the world's smallest private police force.[18] Almost opposite the Piccadilly end of the Burlington Arcade is the luxury department store Fortnum and Mason. Dating from 1707, Fortnum and Mason is known for its extensive food hall and provision of gourmet gift baskets. The store also contains several eateries, including an ice cream parlor and afternoon tea salon. North of Burlington Arcade is Savile Row, an area of Mayfair famous for its connections to the tailoring industry.

London's West End borders two very different shopping areas: Soho, which is noted for its concentration of sex shops, and Covent Garden, where everything from fashion to food, toys, and books are for sale. From the 1950s to the early 1980s, Soho's sex shops were notorious for their seediness. By 1982, the area contained 54 sex shops, 39 sex cinemas and 12 licensed massage parlours.[19] From 1982, however, the new Miscellaneous Provisions Act required all sex shops to be licensed, and later amendments to the Act allowed local councils to determine how many of such shops should be allowed to open in an area. Consequently, the number of Soho sex shops fell dramatically. Today, Westminster City Council allows no more than 16 sex shops to operate in Soho.[20] However, there remains a high concentration of sex shops, erotic boutiques, and strip clubs located within a half-mile area. This situation is unusual for the UK, where such establishments are usually relegated to peripheral city areas.

Covent Garden began as a fruit-and-vegetable market in 1654. However, the early marketplace overflowed its boundaries and was subsumed by the surrounding area. Consequently, Covent Garden today is divided by the road known as Long Acre, to the north of which are the Neal's Yard and Seven Dials areas that are home to numerous independent shops. Nearby Charing Cross Road is celebrated for its many secondhand bookshops and Foyles, a large bookstore founded in 1903.

Not far from the West End of London is the South Bank area of the River Thames. South Bank is home to Gabriel's Wharf, which has an eclectic mix of artisan shops and cafes. The nearby Oxo Tower and Hay's Galleria house a selection of upscale shops. Farther along the South Bank toward Tate Modern is Borough Market, a famous London foodie destination filled with food stalls and eateries.

Farther west, Portobello Market, in Notting Hill, attracts lovers of antiques and vintage clothing. There are many boutiques and independent shops in the area too. These tend to sell vintage items, unusual housewares, and music. West London is also home to the Westfield London and Whiteleys shopping malls (in Shepherd's Bush and Bayswater, respectively). Whiteleys is currently undergoing redevelopment, while Westfield London has recently been enlarged. Westfield London has five large department stores as well as around 265 luxury and discount shops. Westfield London also contains roughly 50 eateries, a cinema, a children's entertainment zone, and a bowling alley. Farther west still, boroughs such as Ealing have notable shopping areas such as Pitshanger Lane, which in 2016 won the title of London's Best High Street in the Great British High Street awards on account of its many independent shops, amenities, and eateries.

South West London has many notable shopping areas, among them, Knightsbridge, which is the home of the Harrods department store. Opened as a wholesale grocery in 1834 by Charles Harrod, in 1849 the grocery relocated to the Brompton area of London on the site of what is now the department store. In 1883, Harrods burned down, only to be reconstructed on a grander scale. In 1898, Harrods unveiled the world's first escalator, which shoppers initially viewed with suspicion. Harrods offers an extremely extravagant shopping experience, for the ornately decorated store is focused on exclusive merchandise. However, the shop is particularly popular with tourists who buy inexpensive Harrods-brand souvenirs that they take home as mementos of their visits.

Traditionally, Sloane Street, near Knightsbridge, is considered a designer area, but today the area is populated by higher-end discount chains rather than designer boutiques. Nearby is Beauchamp Place, which contains

The food hall at London's Harrods department store. Founded in the nineteenth century, Harrods is the largest department store in Europe. The store has survived two IRA bombing attacks. (Andersastphoto/Dreamstime.com)

high-end shops. Farther along Brompton Road is Brompton Cross, which is a trendy area containing designer shops. Walton Street, which runs from Brompton Cross back toward Kensington's museum quarter specializes in luxury shops. Close by is the famous King's Road, in Chelsea, that like Carnaby Street is synonymous with the Swinging London of the 1960s through its association with designers such as Mary Quant and Vivienne Westwood. During the 1970s, impresario Malcom McLaren (manager of the Sex Pistols punk band) had a boutique on the King's Road. The shop attracted punks and resulted in the road becoming associated with punk counterculture. King's Road has since undergone a process of gentrification and is now a haven for shops selling designer clothing and housewares. The museums of South Kensington, including the Victoria and Albert, the Natural History Museum, and the Science Museum all contain their own shops and sell museum merchandise and other items.

Across London to the east is the Westfield Stratford City, which is located in Stratford next to the main venue of the London 2012 Olympic and Paralympic Games. Westfield Stratford City opened in 2011 and is now one of Europe's biggest urban shopping malls, for it houses 250 shops, over 70 eateries, a 17-screen cinema, a casino, and a bowling alley. Also in East London is the East Shopping Centre, in Upton. This is London's first Asian shopping center. East Shopping Centre contains a wide range of clothes and shoe shops, luxury jewelers, and boutiques featuring leading Asian fashion designers. Greenwich hosts flea and artisan markets, with Greenwich Market itself containing stalls selling global art and crafts.

North London tends to be known for two main types of shopping, for Camden is associated with heavy metal and goth retailers, while the Primrose Hill area is known for its small, independent shops. Camden Market opened in 1973 and since then has attracted both tourists and Londoners in search of unconventional clothing. Camden is home to many residents who follow an alternative lifestyle, so the area contains shops that sell goth clothing or offer such services as tattooing and body piercing. Since being damaged by fire in 2008, Camden Market has become somewhat smarter but is still known for its alternative stalls. To the north of Camden, is picturesque, upscale Primrose Hill which contains designer stores, art galleries, and high-end boutiques. To the southeast of Camden is Angel in Islington, which contains independent, vintage and luxury shops. Nearby Camden Passage is also a vintage shopping destination.

LONDON CULTURAL LANDMARKS

London is renowned for its many museums, art galleries, theaters, and music venues. In some ways, the city is itself a giant museum, for it contains numerous historic buildings. London's museums are among the city's most popular destinations, visited by both Londoners and tourists. In 2019, Tate Modern, a modern art gallery on London's South Bank, was the UK's most popular visitor attraction, visited by 5.9 million people. The rest of the UK's top 10 most popular visitor attractions for 2019 were all located in London: the British Museum, National Gallery, Natural History Museum, Southbank Centre arts venue, Victoria and Albert Museum, Science Museum, Somerset House cultural venue, the Tower of London, and the Royal Museums Greenwich.[21]

Tate Modern took over the top spot as the UK's most visited attraction from the British Museum, which had held the position for a decade. The British Museum, in London's Bloomsbury area, which opened in 1759, is dedicated to human history, art, and culture. Notable artifacts held within the museum include the Rosetta Stone, which held the key to deciphering hieroglyphics; the Elgin Marbles, from the Parthenon in Athens; and the twelfth-century chess set known as the Lewis Chessmen.

The South Kensington area of London is especially associated with museums, for it is home to the Science Museum, Victoria and Albert Museum, and the Natural History Museum. The Science Museum, founded in 1857, contains such famous exhibits as Puffing Billy (the oldest surviving steam locomotive), the first jet engine, and the Apollo 10 command module. The museum also has numerous interactive exhibits as well as an IMAX 3D cinema that shows science and nature documentaries. The museum's Wellcome Wing focuses on digital technology.

The nearby Natural History Museum includes a permanent dinosaur exhibition as well as such earth science specimens as a life-size blue whale and a 40-million-year-old spider. The Victoria and Albert Museum (often known as the V&A), founded in 1852, is dedicated to applied and decorative arts and design around the world. The museum houses a permanent collection of 2.3 million objects spanning over 5,000 years of artistic endeavor, including paintings, sketches, furniture, sculpture, metalwork, and textiles.[22] The Victoria and Albert Museum also runs the V&A Museum of Childhood in Bethnal Green, East London, which is the UK's National Museum of Childhood. This is the largest institution of its kind in the world and is dedicated to engaging visitors in the material culture and experiences of childhood.[23]

The Royal Museums Greenwich is home to the Royal Observatory Greenwich, the historic sailing ship *Cutty Sark*, the National Maritime Museum, and the Queen's House Art Gallery. The Royal Observatory, founded in 1675, is dedicated to the history of astronomy and navigation. Famously, the prime meridian line (which divides the earth's eastern and western hemispheres) passes through the Observatory. As the prime meridian line indicates 0 degrees longitude, it once marked the start of the universal day, hence times were given as Greenwich Mean Time (GMT).

Other popular London museums include the Imperial War Museum, which tells the story of conflict from World War I to the present; the Museum of London, which is the world's largest urban museum[24] and relates London's history through artifacts and exhibits; the London Transport Museum, which investigates the importance of transport to London's social and cultural history; and the Design Museum, which is the world's leading collection of contemporary design.[25] Less well-known London museums include the Museum of Brands, in Notting Hill, which explores consumer society through branding and packaging; the Cartoon Museum, in Fitzrovia, which showcases British comics, caricatures, and animation; the Old Operating Theatre Museum & Herb Garret, in Southwark, South East London, which gives insights into medical history; and the London Museum of Water and Steam, housed in the former Kew Bridge Waterworks, in Brentford, West London, which tells the story of how water shaped London's history.

As well as museums and art galleries, London contains numerous music venues both large and small. Major music venues include the impressive Royal Albert Hall, a concert hall in South Kensington that is the venue for the Henry Wood Promenade Concerts (usually called the Proms), which take the form of a summer season of concerts celebrating all genres of music; the Hammersmith Apollo, in West London, which has hosted performers including the Beatles, the Rolling Stones, Bob Marley, and Elton John; and Wembley Stadium, a multipurpose stadium in Wembley, North West London, that, while most noted for hosting sporting events such as English soccer matches, also holds music concerts including, most famously, Live Aid in 1985. More intimate London music venues include Ronnie Scott's Jazz Club, which opened in Soho in 1959; the Old Blue Last, in Shoreditch, East London, which is a small, trendy venue located in a former brothel; and Paper Dress Vintage, in Hackney, East London, which plays vintage rock and roll, soul, reggae, blues, and swing.

London's theaters, known collectively as Theatreland, range from such famous West End venues as the Palladium, Her Majesty's Theatre, and the Theatre Royal Drury Lane to more intimate venues such as the Donmar Warehouse, in Covent Garden; the Almeida, in Islington; and the Jermyn Street Theatre, which is London's smallest West End theater. London also boasts numerous pub theaters. Although these hark back to Shakespearean times, pub theaters as known today are a relatively modern innovation. They arose in the twentieth century, when pubs phased out renting rooms to travelers and, needing to fill empty upstairs rooms, decided to create intimate theater and cabaret venues. The earliest modern pub theater was likely the King's Head, in Islington, which was established in 1970.

The history of London's Theatreland area dates back to at least 1663, when the Theatre Royal Drury Lane was founded. Today, the Theatre Royal is the West End's oldest theatre. Shaftesbury Avenue, the heart of London Theatreland, is home to many iconic theatres, the oldest of which is the Lyric Theatre, founded in 1889. By the time the Theatre Royal was built, London already had a buzzing theater scene, for the theater was popular with many of London's social classes and theatergoing was part of everyday London life. Aristocrats in London enjoyed the theater, as they were familiar with plays from acting parts at school and seeing plays as part of the monarch's court, while the merchant classes would take the afternoon off work to see a play. Therefore, when William Shakespeare began to work in London circa 1588, there was great demand for new plays. Indeed, in London between 1567 and 1622, nine new outdoor playhouses were built. Shakespeare became part of a company of actors called the Lord Chamberlain's Men (later called the King's Men), a theater troupe that first performed in the playhouses called The Theatre and the Globe; a reconstruction of the original Globe theater can be found on London's South Bank. The King's Men performed to audiences of around 3,000 people.[26] This required a varied repertoire of plays, for each day they would perform in a different play in order to keep their audience interested. The ever-changing repertoire of plays is very different from today, when one play can be performed for years at the same theater. For instance, the longest-running play in the West End and indeed the world, is *The Mousetrap*, a murder mystery by

Agatha Christie, which opened in the West End in 1952 and ran continuously until March 16, 2020, when all London theater productions had to close due to the COVID-19 pandemic. Over the play's 68 years of performances, more than 10 million *The Mousetrap* tickets were sold,[27] and it is a London tradition that nobody reveals the identity of the murderer. Performances of *The Mousetrap* restarted in May 2021 after the relaxation of COVID-19 restrictions allowed London's theaters to reopen with social distancing measures in place.

While plays such as *The Mousetrap* and West End musicals are very popular with tourists, Londoners themselves also visit London's theaters, for ticket prices are kept fairly affordable for many city dwellers. For example, ticket prices for London's prestigious, publicly funded Royal National Theatre (usually called simply the National Theatre) start at just £5 ($6.54), and there are regular £15 ($19.66) ticket seasons. The National Theatre, which actually consists of three individual theaters, was founded by legendary actor Sir Laurence Olivier and opened on London's South Bank in 1976–1977.

LONDON FOOD AND DRINK

London is home to numerous places to eat and drink, including 3,500 pubs.[28] Eateries range from "greasy spoons" (cheap and cheerful cafés serving very basic, comforting meals such as English breakfasts and mugs of tea) to 67 Michelin-starred, fine-dining restaurants.[29] London has three 3-star Michelin restaurants: The Lecture Room & Library at Sketch, in Mayfair; Alain Ducasse at the Dorchester, also in Mayfair; and Gordon Ramsay, in Chelsea. There are also ten 2-star London restaurants.

While London has a long history of coffee drinking, it has not traditionally had a European café culture, though there have always been a few coffeehouses and patisseries that aimed to capture a continental atmosphere. Recently, however, a growing number of cafés have opened in London that blend the European-style café with something more typical of London. While many Londoners frown upon shopping district coffee chains, as they feel these establishments have driven out traditional London tea shops and independent cafes, the coffee chains have increased the number of coffee-drinking Londoners who, in turn, seek out better-quality coffee at independent coffee shops. London's multicultural population means there is a ready market for such cafes. For example, in areas such as South Kensington, which is home to many French people, there is a constant demand for high-quality cafes serving good coffee. In 2020, researchers found that London had experienced a 700 percent rise in the number of independent coffee shops over the past decade (from 50 in 2010 to more than 400 in 2020). At the same time, the number of branches belonging to international coffee chains such as Starbucks and Costa rose by 57 percent rise to 2,195 over the same period. Researchers also found that Londoners' favorite coffee is the latte, which is preferred by 51.4 percent of Londoners, followed by the cappuccino, which is ordered by 35 percent of Londoners. Only one in four Londoners order a flat white. There is also a trend among Londoners to add alternative milks to their coffees, with oat milk being the most popular alternative to cow's milk. The move to alternative milks is not shared by the UK as a whole, however, for while one in five Londoners prefer oat milk in coffee, only 9 percent of Brits nationwide share this preference.[30]

Despite Londoners' love of coffee, afternoon tea remains a favorite treat among Londoners. Afternoon tea usually takes the form of beautifully presented pots of tea, finger sandwiches, scones, and dainty cakes (and sometimes a glass of champagne) served on a tiered stand amid elegant surroundings. To this end, afternoon tea is served by most luxury London hotels (most famously at the Ritz and the Savoy), shops (most especially Fortnum and Mason), and cafés. In London it is even possible to enjoy afternoon tea on a vintage double-decker bus or at Lord's cricket ground.

ENGLAND'S WORLD CUP CRICKET WIN

DID YOU KNOW?

On July 14, 2019, Lord's cricket ground in St. John's Wood, North West London, played host to one of the most memorable moments in British sporting history and arguably the greatest one-day international cricket match. The 2019 Cricket World Cup began on May 30, with games played across England and Wales. Ten teams played each other once in a round-robin competition, and eventually England came to play New Zealand (runners-up in the previous World Cup) in the final. It was the fifth time Lord's had hosted the Cricket World Cup Final, the most of any cricket ground. At the end of the match England and New Zealand were tied on 241 runs each, meaning a Super Over (where both teams play a single, additional over of six balls to determine the match winner) had to be played to break the tie. On the final ball of New Zealand's Super Over, having equaled the runs England made during their Super Over, batsman Martin Guptill tried to score the winning run but was run out by the England wicketkeeper, meaning that the Super Over was also tied. With the Super Over also drawn, England's superior boundary count (26 to New Zealand's 17) meant England won the match. It was England's first World Cup title despite having reached the final four times. Ironically, New Zealand–born England cricketer Ben Stokes was named Man of the Match for his batting. The match was the first time a Super Over had been played during a One Day International final and also the first time a boundary count had decided a final. Meanwhile, across London that day the first Wimbledon tennis final decided by a final-set tiebreak occurred when Novak Djokovic beat Roger Federer 7-6, 1-6, 7-6, 4-6, 13-12.

London tends to establish the food trends followed, in time, by the rest of the UK.[31] At present there is a trend toward serving local, seasonal, sustainable ingredients and offering more vegan dishes. It is possible to find virtually all global cuisines in London, with some areas of the city particularly associated with certain regional cuisines: Chinatown, near Leicester Square in central London, contains numerous Chinese restaurants, many of which serve regional Chinese foods. Other cuisines served in Chinatown include Korean, Malaysian, Vietnamese, and Japanese. Brick Lane, in London's East End, is synonymous with Indian cuisine, for in the 1960s and 1970s, newly arrived Bengali immigrants established Indian restaurants there. Today, the area still has many Indian restaurants, but there has also been an explosion in other types of restaurants, including vegan eateries, fried chicken restaurants, and even a café that specializes in breakfast cereal. Similarly, the plethora of Indian restaurants in Southall, West London, means the area is sometimes called "Mini Punjab," though Southall is also home to eateries serving Pakistani, Afghan, and Somalian foods. Marylebone, in West London, is home to the Swedish embassy, a Swedish church, and many Swedish shops and eateries, while so-called Turkish London, in North London, stretches from Dalston and Stoke Newington to Haringey. Green Lanes, in Haringey, is known as Little Istanbul because it is home to 200,000 Turkish speakers (from Cyprus, Turkey, and Kurdish areas), who have established numerous Turkish restaurants, bars, and bakeries in the area.[32]

Since London's cuisine is so varied, it is difficult to pinpoint any one dish as being quintessentially representative of London food. However, two iconic London dishes are pie and mash, and jellied eels. Pie and mash is a traditional staple dish of working-class Londoners living in the East End. Traditionally, the dish comprises a pastry pie filled with meat scraps and vegetables that is baked and served with mashed potatoes. The pie and mash are accompanied by "liquor," a thin, green parsley sauce. Today, pie and mash can feature chicken or vegetarian pies. Although eaten less regularly than in earlier times, there are still pie-and-mash shops throughout London, particularly in the East End. Liquor is also the traditional accompaniment to another London food, jellied eels. During the eighteenth century, eels were plentiful in the River Thames and provided working-class Londoners in the East End with cheap, bountiful food. The eels were easy to prepare, for they just needed to be chopped and boiled with herbs, onion, vinegar, peppercorns, and salt. As the eels cooled, they produced so much of their own gelatin that a soft jelly formed around the individual pieces of eel, hence the familiar name of the dish. When the first pie-and-mash shops opened in the nineteenth century, jellied eels were served alongside the pies. Traditionally, Londoners sprinkle their jellied eels with spicy chili vinegar. Jellied eels were especially popular during World

War II, when food was scarce, and by the end of the war, London had more than 100 shops selling jellied eels.[33] Over time, jellied eels fell out of fashion among Londoners, but some pie-and-mash shopkeepers and other London food markets continue to sell jellied eels, particularly in London's East End.

ATTENDING THE LONDON 2012 OLYMPICS AND PARALYMPICS

LIFE IN THE CITY

I had tickets to the Olympic Women's Hockey on day 10 of the Olympics, at the Riverbank Arena at the Olympic Park, and on day 15, I saw the Women's Handball gold medal match in which Norway beat Montenegro to retain its title. The handball was at the Basketball Arena at the Olympic Park. To get to the Olympic Park, I traveled by Tube from Boston Manor to Stratford; although this meant traveling across London from west to east, the journey only took about a half hour. I also went to Earl's Court for the quarterfinal of the Olympic Women's Volleyball between Russia and Brazil, which was much nearer to home.

Buying London 2012 tickets took a lot of planning—almost like a military operation—as you had to apply via a website. Tickets were released for certain sports at various times of day, so you had to be on the ball to get the tickets for the sports you wanted to see. I deliberately tried to get tickets for sports I thought would be interesting to see live but at the same time might not appeal to the majority of spectators, as this allowed me a greater chance of getting tickets. This was especially true of the handball because I had enjoyed watching handball on TV but guessed that demand for the handball tickets would be less than for some other sports. I applied for tickets several months before the events. From looking at my bank account, I could tell my application for some tickets had been successful, but I did not know which events I had bought tickets for until about a month later, when tickets were sent out. In the spring of 2012, I applied for Paralympic tickets, too, and was successful in my application, because I won tickets to Paralympic Swimming on day 9 at the Aquatic Centre in the Olympic Park. I remember that the swimming events were very noisy, as the sound of the crowd reverberated around the arena.

I also went to the final evening of the Paralympic Athletics on day 10 at the Olympic Stadium in the Olympic Park. I saw Tatyana McFadden compete for the United States, the Women's Shotput F40 final, and saw Oscar Pistorius win the T44 400 meter in the last race of the Games. As a sports statistician by profession, for years I had seen sporting events held in other cities, and I felt proud to have the world's biggest sporting event in my hometown. All the events had an amazing atmosphere, but on the last night of the Paralympic Athletics, being in the stadium near the Olympic flame and under lights, there was an extra special atmosphere. I still have the programs from each day I attended as well as the event tickets, as these are mementos of a special time in London's sporting history.

—Matthew Davis

NOTES

1. Roman Adrian Cybriwsky, *Capital Cities around the World: An Encyclopedia of Geography, History, and Culture* (Santa Barbara, CA: ABC-CLIO, 2013).

2. Panikos Panayi, *Migrant City: A New History of London* (New Haven, CT: Yale University Press, 2020).

3. "A Student City: Top Reasons to Be a Student in London," London School of Economics and Political Science, 2020, https://www.lse.ac.uk/student-life/London-life/A-student-city.

4. Lucy Ash, "London, France's Sixth Biggest City," *BBC News Magazine*, May 30, 2012, https://www.bbc.co.uk/news/magazine-18234930.

5. "Census Data Shows 100 Different Languages Spoken in Almost Every London Borough," *Evening Standard*, January 30, 2013, https://www.standard.co.uk/news/london/census-data-shows-100-different-languages-spoken-in-almost-every-london-borough-8472483.html.

6. "Assessment of the GLA's Impact on Faith Inequality," December 2014, 1, https://www.london.gov.uk/sites/default/files/assessment_of_the_glas_impact_on_faith_equality.pdf.

7. Ibid.

8. Rosa Doherty, "Golders Green: Clocking Up a Growth in Numbers," *Jewish Chronicle*, March 29, 2018, https://www.thejc.com/community/special-reports/golders-green-clocking-up-a-growth-in-numbers-1.461649.

9. "Assessment of the GLA's Impact on Faith Inequality," p. 3.

10. Qasim Peracha, "Huge Procession through Southall Will Be 'Biggest Sikh Festival This Millennium,'" My London, November 3, 2019, https://www.mylondon.news/whats-on/whats-on-news/huge-procession-through-southall-biggest-17188358.

11. "Oxford Street," Visit London, https://www.visitlondon.com/things-to-do/place/5042973-oxford-street.

12. "Oxford Street," WestEnd, 2020, https://www.westend.com/oxford-street.

13. "Topshop: Oxford Circus," TopShop, https://stores.topshop.com/london/214-oxford-street.

14. "Your Guide to Topshop in London: Store Opening Times & Details," LDN Fashion, July 11, 2017, https://ldnfashion.com/features/topshop-london-opening-times.

15. George Hoole, "The Picture-Perfect Bookshop That's Designed for Travellers: Daunt Books," Secret London, February 15, 2019, https://secretldn.com/daunt-book-shop.

16. "Hamleys History," Hamleys, 2020, https://www.hamleys.com/history.

17. "Burlington Arcade," WestEnd, 2020, https://www.westend.com/burlington-arcade.

18. Ibid.

19. Erin Sanders-McDonagh, *Immoral Geographies and Soho's Sex Shops: Exploring Spaces of Sexual Diversity in London*, https://bura.brunel.ac.uk/bitstream/2438/19272/1/FullText.pdf.

20. Kate Hill, "How Many Sex Shops in Soho?" Estate Agents London News, June 21, 2018, https://www.greaterlondonproperties.co.uk/how-many-sex-shops-in-soho.

21. "Tate Modern Overtakes British Museum as Top UK Visitor Attraction," *BBC News*, March 27, 2019, https://www.bbc.co.uk/news/entertainment-arts-47711540.

22. "About Us," Victoria and Albert Museum, 2020, https://www.vam.ac.uk/info/about-us.

23. "About Us," Victoria and Albert Museum of Childhood, 2020, https://www.vam.ac.uk/moc/about-us.

24. "Top 10 Museums in London," Visit London, https://www.visitlondon.com/things-to-do/sightseeing/london-attraction/museum/best-museums-in-london.

25. Ibid.

26. "Elizabethan London," Royal Shakespeare Company, 2020, https://www.rsc.org.uk/shakespeares-life-and-times/elizabethan-london.

27. "Agatha Christie's *The Mousetrap*," UK, https://uk.the-mousetrap.co.uk/about-the-show.

28. Kate Hill, "How Many Pubs in London," Estate Agents London News, August 31, 2018, https://www.greaterlondonproperties.co.uk/how-many-pubs-in-london.

29. "Michelin-Star Restaurants in London," Time Out, November 20, 2019, https://www.timeout.com/london/restaurants/michelin-star-restaurants-in-london.

30. Naomi Ackerman, "London Sees 700% Surge in Independent Coffee Shops since 2010," *Evening Standard*, February 5, 2010, https://www.standard.co.uk/go/london/restaurants/london-sees-700-surge-in-independent-coffee-shops-a4354216.html.

31. Laura Mason, "Great Britain," in *Food Cultures of the World Encyclopedia: Volume 4*, ed. Ken Albala (Santa Barbara, CA: Greenwood, 2011), 156.

32. Stuart Husband, "Little Istanbul," *Evening Standard*, June 27, 2002, https://www.standard.co.uk/news/little-istanbul-7223100.html.

33. Tony Dunnell, "Jellied Eels," Atlas Obscura, 2020, https://www.atlasobscura.com/foods/jellied-eels-london.

FURTHER READING

"About Us." Victoria and Albert Museum of Childhood, 2020. https://www.vam.ac.uk/moc/about-us.

Ackerman, Naomi. "London Sees 700% Surge in Independent Coffee Shops since 2010." *Evening Standard*, February 5, 2010. https://www.standard.co.uk/go/london/restaurants/london-sees-700-surge-in-independent-coffee-shops-a4354216.html.

Ash, Lucy. "London, France's Sixth Biggest City." *BBC News Magazine*, May 30, 2012. https://www.bbc.co.uk/news/magazine-18234930.

"Assessment of the GLA's Impact on Faith Inequality." Greater London Authority, December 2014. https://www.london.gov.uk/sites/default/files/assessment_of_the_glas_impact_on_faith_equality.pdf.

"Burlington Arcade." WestEnd, 2020. https://www.westend.com/burlington-arcade.

"Census Data Shows 100 Different Languages Spoken in Almost Every London Borough." Evening Standard, January 30, 2013, https://www.standard.co

.uk/news/london/census-data-shows-100-different-languages-spoken-in
-almost-every-london-borough-8472483.html.

Cybriwsky, Roman Adrian. *Capital Cities around the World: An Encyclopedia of Geography, History, and Culture.* Santa Barbara, CA: ABC-CLIO, 2013.

Doherty, Rosa. "Golders Green: Clocking Up a Growth in Numbers." *Jewish Chronicle,* March 29, 2018. https://www.thejc.com/community/special -reports/golders-green-clocking-up-a-growth-in-numbers-1.461649.

Dunnell, Tony. "Jellied Eels." Atlas Obscura, 2020. https://www.atlasobscura.com /foods/jellied-eels-london.

"Elizabethan London." Royal Shakespeare Company, 2020. https://www.rsc.org .uk/shakespeares-life-and-times/elizabethan-london.

"Hamleys History." Hamleys. https://www.hamleys.com/history.

Harrison, Anna. "Six Interesting Facts about Liberty of London Fabric." Holme & Moss, March 23, 2018. https://holmeandmoss.com/blogs/posts/six-interesting -facts-about-liberty-of-london-fabric.

Hill, Kate. "How Many Pubs in London." Estate Agents London News, August 31, 2018. https://www.greaterlondonproperties.co.uk/how-many-pubs-in -london.

Hill, Kate. "How Many Sex Shops in Soho?" Estate Agents London News, June 21, 2018. https://www.greaterlondonproperties.co.uk/how-many-sex-shops-in -soho.

Hoole, George. "The Picture-Perfect Bookshop That's Designed for Travellers: Daunt Books." Secret London, February 15, 2019. https://secretldn.com /daunt-book-shop.

Husband, Stuart. "Little Istanbul." *Evening Standard,* June 27, 2002. https://www .standard.co.uk/news/little-istanbul-7223100.html.

Mason, Laura. "Great Britain." In *Food Cultures of the World Encyclopedia: Volume 4,* edited by Ken Albala, 147–59. Santa Barbara, CA: Greenwood, 2011.

"Michelin-Star Restaurants in London." Time Out, November 20, 2019. https://www .timeout.com/london/restaurants/michelin-star-restaurants-in-london.

"Oxford Street." Visit London. https://www.visitlondon.com/things-to-do/place /5042973-oxford-street.

Panayi, Panikos. *Migrant City: A New History of London.* New Haven, CT: Yale University Press, 2020.

Peracha, Qasim. "Huge Procession through Southall Will Be 'Biggest Sikh Festival This Millennium.'" My London, November 3, 2019. https://www.mylondon .news/whats-on/whats-on-news/huge-procession-through-southall-biggest -17188358.

Sanders-McDonagh, Erin. *Immoral Geographies and Soho's Sex Shops: Exploring Spaces of Sexual Diversity in London.* https://bura.brunel.ac.uk/bitstream /2438/19272/1/FullText.pdf.

"A Student City: Top Reasons to Be a Student in London." London School of Economics and Political Science, 2020. https://www.lse.ac.uk/student-life /London-life/A-student-city.

"Tate Modern Overtakes British Museum as Top UK Visitor Attraction." *BBC News*, March 27, 2019. https://www.bbc.co.uk/news/entertainment-arts -47711540.

"Top 10 Museums in London." Visit London. https://www.visitlondon.com /things-to-do/sightseeing/london-attraction/museum/best-museums-in -london.

"Topshop: Oxford Circus." TopShop. https://stores.topshop.com/london/214 -oxford-street.

"Your Guide to Topshop in London: Store Opening Times & Details." LDN Fashion, July 11, 2017. https://ldnfashion.com/features/topshop-london-opening -times.

11

The City in Popular Culture

As a major global city, London has long been depicted in film, literature, and art.

LONDON FILMS

London is frequently used as both a filming location and as the setting for films ranging from period dramas, romantic comedies, and crime capers, to spy thrillers, science fiction, horror movies, and musicals. London's long history means that versions of the city during various time periods have been re-created including Tudor, Victorian, Edwardian, and wartime London.

Historic London: From Shakespeare to Margaret Thatcher

Elizabethan London (the period from 1558–1603) has been depicted in numerous films, including *Fire over England* (1937), starring Sir Laurence Olivier and Vivien Leigh; *The Private Lives of Elizabeth and Essex* (1939), starring Bette Davis and Errol Flynn; and *Elizabeth* (1998), starring Cate Blanchett, which focus on the court of Queen Elizabeth I. Elizabethan London is also portrayed in *Shakespeare in Love* (1998), the award-winning romantic comedy revolving around the fictional exploits of William Shakespeare. *Orlando* (1992) is also set partly at the London court of Elizabeth I. A number of films have looked at the restoration of the monarchy under Charles II, including *Nell Gwyn* (1937) and *Stage Beauty* (2003), which sees a female theater dresser cause a stir in seventeenth-century London by appearing in a production of Shakespeare's play *Othello*. *Restoration* (1995) also encompasses the Great Plague and the Great Fire of London.

The London of the eighteenth and early nineteenth centuries appears in several films, including *Lady Hamilton* (1941), *Princess Caraboo* (1994), the Oscar-winning Jane Austen adaptation *Sense and Sensibility* (1995), and versions of *The Scarlet Pimpernel*, based on Baroness Orczy's novel of the same name, which was written after the author visited Temple Underground station. Some of the most enduring cinematic depictions of London appear in films set during Victorian times (1837–1901), especially adaptations of the novels of Charles Dickens, Sherlock Holmes stories, retellings of Bram Stoker's novel *Dracula*, and dramas based on the Jack the Ripper murders.

There are numerous film adaptations of Charles Dickens's novels. These range from the silent short film *Death of Nancy Sykes* (1897), director David Lean's fairly faithful adaptations of *Oliver Twist* (1948) and *Great Expectations* (1946), and *David Copperfield* (1935 and 1969), *Nicholas Nickleby* (1947 and 2002), *The Pickwick Papers* (1952), *Little Dorrit* (1987), *Great Expectations* (2012), and *The Personal History of David Copperfield* (2019). The life of Charles Dickens was itself the subject of *The Invisible Woman* (2013), which was set and filmed partly in London. There have also been numerous recent BBC television adaptations of the Charles Dickens's novels *Our Mutual Friend* (1998), *Bleak House* (2005), and *Little Dorrit* (2008). Other less faithful, but no less enjoyable, Dickens adaptations include the Oscar-winning musical *Oliver!* and the very many versions of Dickens's *A Christmas Carol*, the best known of which include *Scrooge* (1951) and *The Muppet Christmas Carol* (1992), in which Gonzo the Great plays Charles Dickens.

Other films set in Victorian London that are adapted from nineteenth-century literature include the many cinematic retellings of *Dracula*. Although much of *Dracula* takes place in London, it is not often that films of the novel are set extensively in London. Two *Dracula* films that do use Victorian London as a setting are the Hammer film *Taste the Blood of Dracula* (1970), which has several scenes located in London cemeteries, and the opulent *Bram Stoker's Dracula* (1992). The Hammer Studio's *Dracula AD 1972* is unusual in that it is set in 1970s London, where Count Dracula is resurrected and fights the descendant of his nemesis, Van Helsing.

There have been numerous film and television offerings based on Sir Arthur Conan Doyle's character Sherlock Holmes, including the iconic

Basil Rathbone film series (1939 to 1946) that saw London (both Victorian and modern) re-created on Hollywood lots. Other notable Sherlock Holmes films to feature London include *The Private Life of Sherlock Holmes* (1970), *Young Sherlock Holmes* (1985), *Without a Clue* (1988), *Sherlock Holmes* (2009), and the BBC television series *Sherlock* (2010–2017), which updated Conan Doyle's character to modern times.

In both *A Study in Terror* (1965) and *Murder by Decree* (1978), Holmes is responsible for tracking down serial killer Jack the Ripper. Most films inspired by the London killings are set at least partly in the city, among them, *Pandora's Box* (1929), *Jack the Ripper* (1958), and the Hammer films *Dr. Jekyll and Sister Hyde* (1971) and *Hands of the Ripper* (1971), as well as *From Hell* (2001). A memorable TV miniseries, *Jack the Ripper* (1988), made great use of its London setting with depictions of city slums, debauched taverns, and lavish theaters. London-born film director Sir Alfred Hitchcock depicted a foggy London in his silent film classic *The Lodger*, which is about the hunt for a Jack the Ripper–like killer. Hitchcock revisited the Jack the Ripper theme in *Frenzy* (1972), which focuses on the hunt for a London serial killer. *Frenzy* features many London locations, including Covent Garden, the Hilton Hotel on Park Lane, and the area around County Hall. Other notable films set in Victorian London include adaptations of *The Picture of Dorian Gray* (1945 and 2009), *Gaslight* (1940 and 1944), *Topsy-Turvy* (1999), adaptations of the Oscar Wilde plays *The Importance of Being Earnest* (1952 and 2002) and *An Ideal Husband* (1999), adaptations of Jules Verne's novel *Around the World in Eighty Days* (1956 and 2004), and *The Elephant Man* (1980).

Edwardian London (the era from 1901 to 1910) is less frequently depicted on screen than the Victorian era is. Nonetheless, a number of memorable films have been set in London during this era, including the Academy Award–winning *My Fair Lady* (1964), *Mary Poppins* (1964), and *The King's Speech* (2010); the classic Ealing Studios comedy *Kind Hearts and Coronets* (1949); and the award-winning Merchant Ivory adaptations of E. M. Forster's novels *A Room with a View* (1985) and *Howards End* (1992). The 1997 adaptation of Henry James's novel *The Wings of the Dove* provides a rare re-creation of the London Underground network during Edwardian times.

Wartime London has appeared in many films, though the London of World War I has been featured less often than World War II London has been. That said, *The Life and Death of Colonel Blimp* (1943) looked back over 40 years of London life and included World War I. Numerous films have been made featuring the London of World War II, including such documentaries on wartime life as *London Can Take It!* (1940), narrated by U.S. war correspondent Quentin Reynolds. Similarly, London-based U.S. journalist Edward R. Murrow made numerous London war reports, especially during the Battle of Britain. The reports, which began with Murrow's signature opening line, "This is London ... ," crossed the Atlantic via shortwave radio and were then relayed across the United States by CBS. In time, Murrow's reports became the United States' link to wartime events in London.[1]

A huge number of films have been set in the London of World War II. For example, the Blitz features in the British films *Hope and Glory* (1987), a comedy-drama war movie based on director John Boorman's own experiences of growing up in the Blitz in London; *Mrs. Henderson Presents* (2005), about the real-life Windmill Theatre's struggle to remain open during the bombing; and the Ealing Studios film, *The Bells Go Down* (1943), which included shots taken at actual fires caused by the Blitz air raids. Similarly, the docudrama *Fires Were Started* (1943) features real firefighters who re-created scenes from actual London bombings. Hollywood of the 1940s made many London-set films, including *Forever and a Day* (1943), which followed several generations of owners of a London home. Later films set in World War II London include the thrillers *The Man Who Never Was* (1955) and *I Was Monty's Double* (1958), which are based on true events; and *Hanover Street* (1979) and *The End of the Affair* (1999), which use wartime London as the backdrop to romance.

Some of the most famous depictions of postwar London occur in the films of Ealing Studios that were made during the 1940s and 1950s. For example, *Hue and Cry* (1947) and *Passport to Pimlico* (1949) are both set amid the bomb sites of postwar London. In the 1950s and 1960s, Ealing released the comedy *The Lavender Hill Mob*, which made extensive use of London locations, as did the studio's dramas *The Blue Lamp* (1950) and *Sapphire* (1959). The latter is unusual for being an early British film to look at London race relations.

The London of the 1960s—a time often referred to as the Swinging Sixties—has long proven popular with filmmakers for during this period, London was the site of exciting new developments in society, music, and fashion, as well as the center of an energetic urban youth culture. Films set in Swinging Sixties London include the acclaimed *Blowup* (1966), a thriller revolving around a day in the life of a London fashion photographer. The same year, another seminal British film, *Alfie*, was released and starred Sir Michael Caine as an arrogant East End lothario. In 1970, *Performance*, about a London gangster, starred Sir Mick Jagger of the Rolling Stones. More recent films to depict actual 1960s London events include *Scandal* (1989) a fictionalized account of the Profumo affair that shook the British government, and *The Krays* (1990), which looked at the crimes of the criminal Kray twins, who were also the subject of *Legend* (2015). The Ealing Studios drama *Victim* (1961) broke barriers by looking at contemporary homophobia at a time when homosexuality was illegal in Britain.

London of the 1970s was less often depicted on screen than that of the 1960s. However, the gangster film *The Long Good Friday* (1979) and the Hammer horror film *Straight On till Morning* (1972) paint vivid portraits of the city in the 1970s.

Many films set in modern London explore contemporary issues. For example, *Up the Junction* (1968) looks at class, economic depression, and abortion; *My Beautiful Laundrette* (1985) is a comedy-drama that explores race and homosexuality during the premiership of Margaret Thatcher; coming-of-age comedy *Beautiful Thing* (1996) focuses on gay teenagers in South London; *Nil by Mouth* (1997) concentrates on a dysfunctional working-class London family; *Dirty Pretty Things* (2002) looks at the plight of illegal immigrants in London; and *Eastern Promises* (2007) investigates sex trafficking and prostitution in London.

Genre Films: From Jack the Ripper to the Spice Girls

London's varied landscape presents filmmakers with myriad locations that can be incorporated into a wide variety of film genres. For instance, London is often the setting for screen romances including *Spring in Park Lane* (1948), a hit British romantic comedy, and *Indiscreet* (1958), starring Hollywood icons Cary Grant and Ingrid Bergman. More recently, British screenwriter Richard Curtis has set some of the most successful recent British films either wholly or partly in London, including *Four Weddings and a Funeral* (1994), *Notting Hill* (1999), and *Love Actually* (2003). Other romantic films set in London include *Jack and Sarah* (1995); *Sliding Doors* (1998); *Martha, Meet Frank, Daniel and Laurence* (1998); *Bridget Jones's Diary* (2001); *About a Boy* (2002); *Wimbledon* (2004); *Closer* (2004); and *Match Point* (2005).

Sir Alfred Hitchcock set many of his thrillers in the city of his birth, using famous London landmarks as the backdrops for film finales. For instance, the dome of the British Museum appears in Hitchcock's *Blackmail* (1929). The British Museum also appears in the classic horror film *Night of the Demon* (1957), the Cold War thriller *The IPCRESS File* (1965), and the blockbuster *The Mummy Returns* (2001), which also features a chase across Tower Bridge aboard a London bus. Other Hitchcock thrillers set at least partly in London include the remake of *The Man Who Knew Too Much* (1956), *The 39 Steps* (1935), *Sabotage* (1937), *Foreign Correspondent* (1940), and *Stage Fright* (1950), as well as the aforementioned *Frenzy* and *The Lodger*. Other London-based thrillers include *Night and the City* (1950), *23 Paces to Baker Street* (1956), *Peeping Tom* (1960), *Bunny Lake Is Missing* (1965), *Repulsion* (1965), and *The Spy Who Came in from the Cold* (1965).

Many blockbuster films have been set in London. For instance, James Bond films tend to have at least one scene set in London, for this is where

Bond's boss, M, is based. In *On Her Majesty's Secret Service* (1969), Bond visits the College of Arms, and in *For Your Eyes Only* (1981), Bond is taken on a helicopter flight over London's Docklands. The new MI6 building on the River Thames at Vauxhall was featured in the films in which Pierce Brosnan plays Bond. For example, *The World Is Not Enough* (1999) opens with a lengthy boat chase that travels from the MI6 building down the river to the Millennium Dome. London also features heavily in *Skyfall* (2012), as it does in *Spectre* (2015), the climax of which is a car chase that takes in Admiralty Arch, the MI6 building, and Westminster Bridge. The London Underground appears in numerous films. For example, catching/missing the Tube is an integral part of the plot of *Sliding Doors* (1998), while the thriller *Séance on a Wet Afternoon* (1964) and the horror films *An American Werewolf in London* (1981), *Creep* (2004), and *28 Weeks Later* (2007) all include sequences on the Underground. Almost all of *Death Line* (1972) takes place on the London Underground as a cannibal stalks the tunnels looking for victims, all the while intoning the chilling refrain "mind the doors" (the message repeated over Tube train speaker systems). The *Battle of Britain* (1969) shows how Underground tunnels sheltered Londoners during the Blitz, while excavation work on the Underground unearths an alien spacecraft in *Quatermass and the Pit* (1967) and sleeping dragons in *Reign of Fire* (2002).

The British thriller *Seven Days to Noon* (1950), about a scientist who threatens to destroy London with a nuclear bomb, is notable for containing numerous scenes of an evacuated London. *Seven Days to Noon* foreshadowed later films' depictions of a deserted London as seen in the horror film *28 Days Later* (2002), which begins with the hero wandering along a desolate Westminster Bridge. The nuclear threat was also at the heart of the atmospheric British sci-fi thriller *The Day the Earth Caught Fire* (1961), which sees nuclear testing knock the earth off its axis, thereby causing its climatic zones to shift. *The Day the Earth Caught Fire* contains many notable scenes of London suffering extreme weather, including depictions of the River Thames running dry. The film is also famous for including scenes shot inside the former offices of the *Daily Express* newspaper on Fleet Street, which added to the film's air of authenticity. London landmarks St. Bride's Church, Battersea Park, Parliament Square, Trafalgar Square, and Piccadilly Circus also appear in the film. London is the setting for apocalyptic events in the horror comedy *Shaun of the Dead* (2004), in which suburban London is overrun by zombies; the juxtaposition of mundane London life with the extraordinariness of the film's events creates a darkly comic film.

The *Quatermass* films (*The Quatermass Xperiment*, 1955, *Quatermass 2*, 1957, and *Quatermass and the Pit*, 1967) and the *Quatermass* television series (1953 and 1979) helped build on the popularity of London as a setting for science fiction. For example, the finale of *The Quatermass Xperiment* takes place in Westminster Abbey, while *Quatermass and the Pit* starts with the discovery of an alien spacecraft under a Tube station. In 1962, a film adaptation of John Wyndham's novel *The Day of the Triffids* was released that featured several scenes set in London. Aliens also attack London in the Dr. Who–inspired *Daleks' Invasion Earth: 2150 A.D.* (1966). The London of the future features in *V for Vendetta* (2006); based on the graphic novel of the same name written by Alan Moore, the film depicts a mysterious anarchist who hopes to destroy a fascist regime. Futuristic London is also depicted in the apocalyptic *Children of Men* (2006), which includes London landmarks Tate Britain, Battersea Power Station, and Admiralty Arch. *Star Trek into Darkness* (2013) is also set partly in a futuristic London.

London's long history allows criminality from various historical periods to be portrayed. For example, in addition to films focused on the Kray twins and 1960s gangsters, *Where's Jack?* (1969) focuses on an eighteenth-century highwayman, *The First Great Train Robbery* is set in Victorian London, *Chicago Joe and the Showgirl* (1990) is a crime drama set during World War II, and *10 Rillington Place* (1971) re-creates the killings of the 1940s' London serial killer John Christie. Other films looking at London's contemporary underbelly include *Villain* (1971), which focuses on a sadistic East End gangster, and *Mona Lisa* (1986) about an ex-gangster's relationship with a prostitute. In the late 1990s and early 2000s, a number of crime films were released that explored London's underworld. These include the dark comedies *Lock, Stock and Two Smoking Barrels* (1998), *Snatch* (2000), and *Sexy Beast* (2000). These films build on a long line of London-set crime comedies that include the Ealing comedies *The Lavender Hill Mob*, *The Ladykillers*, and *Kind Hearts and Coronets*; *The Green Man* (1953), about an assassin, and *Carry On, Constable* (1960), the fourth in the much-loved *Carry On* film series. More recently, the Hatton Garden robbery in which a gang of elderly thieves stole millions of pounds worth of valuables from safe deposits inspired several films, such as *The Hatton Garden Job* (2017) and *King of Thieves* (2018), starring Sir Michael Caine. These films were populated by older casts and so are reminiscent of the British crime film classic *The League of Gentlemen* (1960), in which a group of retired soldiers plan a London bank heist.

London has long been a popular setting for children's films. Indeed, a number of animated Disney films are set against a London backdrop: *Peter Pan* (1953), *One Hundred and One Dalmatians* (1961), and *The Great Mouse Detective* (1986), among others. Disney's live-action films *Mary Poppins* (1964), *Bedknobs and Broomsticks* (1971), and *One of Our Dinosaurs Is Missing* (1975) also feature London. Other live-action children's films set in London include *A Kid for Two Farthings* (1955), in which an East End boy mistakes a sick goat for a unicorn; *John and Julie* (1955), about two children who run away to London to see Queen Elizabeth II's coronation; *101 Dalmatians* (1996); and *The Parent Trap* (1998). *Stormbreaker* (2006), about a child spy, features such London locations as Hyde Park, Piccadilly Circus, and the Science Museum, while *Paddington* (2014) includes the Shard skyscraper and the London Eye. The Muppets moved to London for *The Great Muppet Caper* (1981) and for *The Muppet Christmas Carol*. Several *Harry Potter* films also make use of London as a setting, for Platform 9¾, from which pupils depart for Hogwarts, is a fictional part of London's King's Cross station.

Like *The Muppet Christmas Carol, Oliver!* was also set in Victorian London and, while not quite a children's film, it is a rousing musical featuring numerous child actors. Victorian London was also the setting for the melodramatic musical *Sweeney Todd: The Demon Barber of Fleet Street* (2007), based on the fictional serial killer Sweeney Todd. Indeed, London's musical heritage means the city often acts as a backdrop to musical films. For example, the UK's first Technicolor musical film, *London Town* (1946) revolves around a comedian in London. The film is considered one of British films' worst flops, but this did not put an end to the British musical, for during the 1960s, a slew of London-set British musicals was released. For example, British singing star Sir Cliff Richard starred in several musical comedies, the first of which, *The Young Ones* (1961), was set in London. Another Sir Cliff Richard musical film, *Summer Holiday* (1963), sees a London bus driven across Europe. Another British singer, Joe Brown, starred in *Three Hats for Lisa* (1965), about young Cockneys who take a day off work to meet a film star at Heathrow Airport. The film includes a chase against a background of 1960s London. In 1964, two acclaimed big-budget London-set musicals were released: *Mary Poppins* and *My Fair Lady*. The latter was based on the George Bernard Shaw play *Pygmalion*, itself filmed in 1938. Other musical literary adaptations set in London include two more Dickens adaptations: *Scrooge* (1970), adapted from *A Christmas Carol*, and *Mr. Quilp* (1975), adapted from *The Old Curiosity Shop*. Meanwhile, the musical adaptation of H. G. Wells's *Goodbye, Mr. Chips* used several London locations, including the Savoy Hotel, while *Absolute Beginners* (1986), starring David Bowie and set in late 1950s London, was adapted from Colin MacInnes's book. *Quadrophenia* (1979), a musical drama based on The Who's 1973 rock opera of the same name, focuses on a London Mod who sets off on his scooter to Brighton.

Punk music has a long history in London, starting with such mid-1970s bands as the Sex Pistols and the Ramones. Punk is the inspiration for *Sid and Nancy* (1986), which is a biopic of Sid Vicious, the Sex Pistols' bassist. Pop stars the Spice Girls played themselves in the hit caper film

---

JIM MARSHALL: THE FATHER OF LOUD

DID YOU KNOW?

Marshall (1923–2012) was a drummer, teacher, businessman, and, most famously, the founder of the music equipment company Marshall Amplification. Born in Acton, West London, as a child, Marshall spent many years in hospital. Exempted from military service during World War II on health grounds, Marshall became a singer and drummer. He also worked as an electrical engineer, and as such he devised a portable music amplification system. From 1960, Marshall owned a successful music store, Jim Marshall and Son, at 76 Uxbridge Road in Hanwell, Ealing, which sold drums and guitars to customers including Pete Townshend of The Who. When customers asked for a new type of amplifier, Marshall created a new amp.

In 1962, Marshall founded Marshall Amplification. The same year, the Marshall amp known as "Number One" went on sale and would become the first of many JTM45 amps. In 1965, Marshall went further when Townshend demanded a louder amp, and he created the 100-watt Marshall amplifier, the Super 100 head, and the Marshall 8x12 speaker cabinet. The Marshall 8x12 proved too bulky to transport, however, so it was replaced by two stacked 4x12 cabinets. This innovation gave rise to the iconic Marshall Stack, in which cabinets are stacked on top of each other. The vertical look became the norm and was adopted by bands including Led Zeppelin. In 1984, Marshall was awarded the Queen's Award for Export in recognition of Marshall Amplification's outstanding export achievement. The following year, Marshall was included in the Hollywood Rock and Roll Walk of Fame. In 2003, Marshall received an OBE for services to the music industry. After Marshall's death, a blue plaque honoring him was unveiled at the site of his Hanwell shop. The annual Hanwell Hootie music festival celebrates Marshall's legacy.

Spice World (1997), which made use of multiple London landmarks, as the film depicts a series of events leading up to a Spice Girls concert at the Royal Albert Hall. *Spice World* was in the vein of *A Hard Day's Night* (1964), a caper movie filmed throughout London, in which the Beatles starred as themselves.

London Film Studios

One of the reasons London has appeared in so many films is that over the years, London has been home to several film studios, including Gainsborough Studios, based in North London; and Isleworth Studios and Twickenham Film Studios, both in West London. In 2018, 70 percent of all UK film companies were based in London, where they generated 79 percent of the UK film industry's turnover.[2] Today, London is home to the world's oldest continuously working film studio film, Ealing Studios in Ealing, West London. Ealing Studios has made films since 1902 but is most famous for its "golden age," starting in 1938, when film producer Michael Balcon (grandfather of actor Daniel Day Lewis) took over the studios. Ealing Studios is best known for creating a string of 1940s and 1950s comedies, including *The Ladykillers* (1955), *The Lavender Hill Mob* (1951), *Kind Hearts and Coronets* (1949), and *The Man in the White Suit*, which were either heartwarming commentaries or darkly comic satires on British society. However, Ealing also made a number of important wartime propaganda films such as *Went the Day Well* (1942), epics such as *Scott of the Antarctic* (1948), the East End–set thriller *It Always Rains on Sunday* (1947), the horror film *Dead of Night* (1945), and the ghost story *Halfway House* (1944). During the 1960s, 1970s, and 1980s, innumerable BBC television shows were made at Ealing Studios, among them, *Dr. Who*. Today, Ealing Studios still produces such acclaimed feature films as *The Theory of Everything* (2014) and *The Darkest Hour* (2017), while major British television series, such as *Downton Abbey* (2010–2015), are also filmed there. Even after more than a half century, Ealing Studios' comedies remain iconic to the extent that they are often simply referred to as "Ealing comedies," a genre of their own and a sort of cinematic shorthand for ideas about quirky Britishness as depicted in the films. Indeed, Ealing comedy is still one of British cinema's most powerful brands, enjoying enduring fame and affection alongside Hammer Studio's horror films, the James Bond franchise and the *Carry On* films.

LONDON IN LITERATURE

London has long inspired writers, with the city appearing in prose, poetry, and plays.

Shakespearean London: History, Royalty, and Poverty

William Shakespeare (1564–1616) is probably the most famous playwright associated with London. London is the setting for several of Shakespeare's history plays, including *Henry IV, Richard III*, and *Henry VIII* (cowritten by Shakespeare and John Fletcher). It is, though, in *Henry IV Parts I* and *II* that Shakespeare paints an especially intense portrait of all aspects of London life, from the brothels and taverns to aristocratic society and the royal court. London also inspired Shakespeare's contemporaries Ben Jonson (1572–1637) and Thomas Dekker (1572–1632), who were known for writing "city comedies," satirical comedy-dramas that looked at contemporary urban issues and middle-class concerns, and were produced in London theaters during the early 1600s.

Technological advances made during Shakespearean times allowed plays, poems, and pamphlets to be printed quickly and in volume. The literature was then sold by booksellers to patrons throughout London, including the nobility, wealthy middle classes, and the literate poor. In Shakespearean times, however, most poor people were illiterate and so were unable to record their life experiences. Consequently, much that is known of the poor of those times has been obtained from government records, such as legislation providing poor relief and the laws regarding vagrancy. However, John Stow's *Survey of London* (1598), the first detailed description of London's history and the city's suburbs, records in detail various initiatives to provide refuge for sick, poor Londoners. As well as recording the plight of the poor, Stow also provided a vivid depiction of the River Thames, which he posited as a major reason for London's emergence as Europe's most important city. In Shakespearean times, London Bridge over the Thames was lined with hundreds of shops, houses, and stalls in which Londoners took much pride. One of Shakespeare's contemporaries, Michael Drayton, summed up Londoners' pride in the city's river in his poem "The Thames," in *Polyolbion* (1622): "most costly bridge that doth him most renown / By which he clearly puts all other rivers down" (lines 23–24).

Literary London: Romanticism and Revolution

The Industrial Revolution (1760–1840) meant that in London, extreme wealth existed alongside extreme poverty, while at the same time, an air of political radicalism was palpable, thanks to the French Revolution, which began across the English Channel in 1789. It was amid this politically charged atmosphere that the London-based poet and artist William Blake composed his poem "London" (written in 1792 and published in 1794). As a Londoner, Blake writes about the city as a resident rather than as an outsider, and through the poem, he tackles the city's social issues—poverty, child labor, repression by religious authorities—as well as the power of imagination. The poem depicts London as a city of dirty streets that reflect the fallen state of a society caught up in a spiritual blindness; its moral and physical degeneration is exemplified by bleeding walls, disease-ridden prostitutes, and suffering chimney sweeps. However, Blake's accompanying illustration suggests that hope for salvation remains, as a child gestures an old man toward an open door through which light is shining.

Blake was a seminal figure of the Romantic Age (ca. 1800–1890) and the first of the English Romantics, poets and artists inspired by a desire for freedom who denounced the exploitation of the poor and emphasized the importance of individual expression. The Romantics stressed the need to express personal feelings and felt responsibility for others, believing it was their duty to use poetry and art to inform, inspire, and bring about reform. The Romantics idealized the concepts of liberty and social justice that had given rise to revolution. Chief among the Romantics was the poet William Wordsworth, who was passing through London when he wrote one of his most famous poems, "Composed upon Westminster Bridge, September 3, 1802." In this poem, however, Wordsworth describes as serenely beautiful an early morning view of the Thames. Here, London appears as stunning as any natural landscape, made beautiful by the morning light and seemingly empty of people. The reference to "smokeless air" (line 8) alerts the reader that the poem depicts London very early in the day before household fires are lit and enshrouding the city in smoke. The poem's setting and subject matter are atypical of Wordsworth's work, which tends to reject urbanization in favor of country life. Indeed, it is ironic that the poem has become a famous portrayal of London, for Wordsworth claimed to be appalled by London, preferring the poetic refuge of the Lake District in northern England.

In his famous poem, "Composed upon Westminster Bridge, September 3, 1802," the Romantic poet William Wordsworth describes the beauty of the River Thames. The poem is atypical of Wordsworth's work, for the poet rejected London's city life in favor of a rural existence in northern England. (Library of Congress)

Pierce Egan's monthly publication *Life in London* chronicles the misadventures of the central characters Tom, Jerry, and Logic, wealthy young men-about-town who wish to experience the poorer areas of London. The publication captures the diversity and inequality of 1820s London by contrasting the city's rich and poor societies. Accounts of London's poor are fairly scarce before the nineteenth century, so *Life in London* is unusual for depicting the urban poor and showing the contrasting elements of London society at this time. While the serial is fictionalized and somewhat sensationalized, it contains sufficient detail to suggest the publication presents an authentic picture of both spheres of London society. Also, by representing London's urban poor, Egan's serial helped pave the way for authors such as Charles Dickens, who depicted various aspects of London life.

Victorian London: Dickens, *Dracula* and the Dark Side of the City

Arguably, no author captured the social landscape of Victorian London better than Charles Dickens, who drew inspiration from long walks through the city. In his *Sketches by Boz* (anthologized short pieces published originally in periodicals between 1833 and 1836), Dickens follows the fictional Boz as he wanders around London observing different neighborhoods in such a way that the stories act as a tour of the city. The popularity of *Sketches by Boz* resulted in Dickens being commissioned to write his first novel, *The Pickwick Papers* (1837). As a former journalist, Dickens's novels are rooted in realism, and although he fictionalized reality, his contemporaries felt he captured the London they knew. Other writers had examined London's history or used the city as a setting, but none had made the city a subject in its own right as did Dickens. Indeed, in novels such as *Our Mutual Friend* (1865), London and the Thames, along with death, are the mutual friends known to all readers. Fascinated, amused, and angry at London life, in many ways the London Dickens describes resembles London today—crowded with people from different backgrounds and classes.

In several of his novels, Dickens examines the various backgrounds of Londoners as well as the social issues affecting them. For example, in *Oliver Twist*, Dickens tells the story of orphaned Oliver who becomes part of a London pickpocketing gang. The novel can be read as a response to the Poor Law Amendment Act (1834) that aimed to reduce the cost of caring for the poor by stopping money being given to them except in exceptional circumstances. Instead, the poor had to live in workhouses where they were given clothes and food in exchange for several hours of daily manual labor. Many Victorian Londoners disapproved of this treatment of the poor for they felt workhouses were akin to prisons and criminalized the needy. Similarly, Dickens's *Little Dorrit* (1857) focuses on Amy Dorrit, who is raised in London's Marshalsea prison for debtors, in which Dickens's own father had been incarcerated from 1824. *Little Dorrit* satirizes the inadequacies of authorities and society, including the concept of debtors' prisons, where people who had fallen into debt were imprisoned until they repaid their debts yet were prevented from working to earn money.

Writing at a time when public executions were legal in England, Dickens felt all Londoners were at risk either from crime or punishment. Indeed, it is known that Dickens remembered the humiliation he felt when his own father was imprisoned for debt, meaning that as a boy Dickens was sent to work and in so doing became aware of London's darker side. In his Oliver character, Dickens explored the idea that but for the grace of God, he might easily have ended up on the wrong side of the law. In *Oliver Twist*, Dickens depicts London's criminal underbelly, populating the story with pickpockets, prostitutes, murderers, and thieves to the horror of many of his readers, including the then prime minister, Lord Melbourne. In the preface to the 1841 edition of *Oliver Twist*, Dickens recognized the potential shock value of the story but argued that he must portray London's poor and criminal classes in order to help London's society improve. Indeed, in *Oliver Twist*, Dickens presents perhaps his most corrupt vision of London, yet the city is also depicted as a place where ultimately good prevails.

Other Dickens's novels offer different perspectives on London. For example, in Dickens's last completed novel, *Our Mutual Friend*, one of the heroines, Lizzie, and her companion Jenny live together in a part of London described as something out of a fairy tale, as though the architecture of London is enchanted and thus able to ward off dangers. Meanwhile, many of the events that affect Pip, the hero of *Great Expectations*, occur in London, with the city representing Pip's adolescence and journey toward adulthood as Pip overcomes the conflict between his social aspirations and his personal morality. In *Great Expectations*, London is depicted as dark and overcrowded, yet it is also the place where Pip realizes his ambitions. In *Great Expectations*, the London that Pip describes is the city that Dickens remembered from the 1830s, which existed before the advent of the railways, the sewer system, and embankments along the Thames, and where luxury, crime, and poverty coexisted. This dual-natured London is often referred to as Dickensian London because Dickens portrayed the city of this time in such an evocative manner. Although much of the London of *Great Expectations* draws on real life, Dickens at the same time embroidered reality and created places that never existed.

It was not, however, just novelists who wrote about the dark side of London life, the city's slums, and urban poverty. For instance, in his *London Labour and the London Poor* (1865), the journalist and reformer Henry Mayhew (1812–1887) interviewed London street-sellers, road sweepers, prostitutes, and mudlarks so that he could share their stories with his readers. The interviews, in Londoners' own words, make for an especially vivid account of the lives of the city's poor. At almost 2 million words long, the book is a comprehensive anecdotal report on working-class London life. In 1885, another journalist, W. T. Stead (1849–1912) famously wrote a multipart article called "The Maiden Tribute of Modern Babylon," in which he graphically detailed the ways in which young girls were acquired for sex by wealthy London men. For this piece, Stead interviewed girls who had been enticed to enter the homes of the wealthy men or had been recruited by brothel keepers and by employment agencies that were actually fronts for prostitution rackets, all with the knowledge of the police. In order to show how easily a man could acquire a girl for sex, Stead procured a 13-year-old girl for himself. Although he did so for the sake of his investigative reporting, the authorities swooped on Stead, and he had to serve three months in prison for abduction. Ultimately, however, Stead's journalism mobilized support for a parliamentary bill that raised the age of sexual consent for girls from 13 to 16.

The later Victorian period also saw writers that included Robert Louis Stevenson (in *The Strange Case of Dr. Jekyll and Mr. Hyde*) and Oscar Wilde (in *The Portrait of Dorian Gray*) investigate the dual nature of London through the use of literary doubles: the scientist/monster and gentleman/portrait. Few late-nineteenth-century writers are as closely associated with London, however, as Sir Arthur Conan Doyle, whose Sherlock Holmes character famously lived at 221B Baker Street in London's West End. Many of the London locations named in the Sherlock Holmes stories still exist, including Simpson's-in-the-Strand restaurant on the Strand, the British Museum, the Lyceum Theatre, and the Royal Opera House.

Another enduring literary character, Count Dracula, also lives in London. His creator, Bram Stoker, who worked at the Lyceum Theatre that the character Sherlock Holmes was said to frequent, used London as the secondary setting in *Dracula* (1897), for it is where the Count buys property and other characters live.

As an Eastern European, Dracula is associated with the East: he buys a house in Purfleet, on the eastern fringe of the Thames, and his association with London's East End links the Count with all things foreign, as well as with an area associated with criminality, transgression, and violence. Dracula also has his coffins sent to an address in Whitechapel, an area of London that the novel's readers would associate with Jack the Ripper, poverty, prostitution, disease, and foreignness. While Jonathan and Mina Harker live in London, through the course of the novel, various other characters converge on London. For example, Arthur Holmwood stays at a hotel in Piccadilly, Jack Seward runs the asylum at Purfleet, and Lucy stays in Southwark. Once in London, Dracula preys on Londoners, and his minions encircle the city: a wolf operates in the west, Renfield the lunatic lives in the east, and vampiric Lucy resides in a North London graveyard.

London in Twentieth-Century Literature: Ambiguity, Modernity, and the Great War

Joseph Conrad's novel *The Secret Agent* (1907), which is set in late Victorian London, deals broadly with the themes of revolution, espionage, and terrorism. The novel's gloomy portrait of London was influenced by that in Charles Dickens's novel *Bleak House.* In *The Secret Agent*, a detective tries to discover the truth behind a plot to blow up the Greenwich Observatory. Conrad's London is described in terms of fluidity, as a slimy, mud-like place where a character could drown amid the landscape. Such descriptions are apt, for in the novel, London is depicted as an unruly place where even the street numbers are askew. In addition, the novel itself has a fluid form that experiments by confusing the order of its chapters. Hitchcock's film *Sabotage* was based on *The Secret Agent* and features a darkly powerful sequence in which a boy unwittingly causes a bomb to explode on a London bus.

The inconsistency of Conrad's London echoes the fogginess of London depicted by Dickens, Stevenson, Conan Doyle, and Stoker, all of whom present London as unsettlingly unknowable. Similarly, in E. M. Forster's novel *Howards End* (1910), the author presents London ambivalently as a city in flux. London represents different things to the novel's various characters: it is at once a home of culture and humanity but also a place of deficiency and hopelessness. Furthermore, Howards End, the family home that gives the novel its name and serves as the story's moral core, is threatened by the encroaching city in the form of urban dust that creeps toward the house.

The association of London with the unhealthy environment is echoed by the poet T. S. Eliot (1888–1965) in his poem *The Waste Land* (1922), in which London is described as the "Unreal City" (line 60) and home to "brown fog." On the one hand, *The Waste Land* describes the mundanity of London life in the form of, for example, the daily commute, but the anonymity of the commuters also suggests uneasily that the commuters lack their own autonomy. This recalls the status of the soldiers who died in World War I: ordered into battle and not free to refuse. For Eliot, then, London is a place of both adventure and anxiety. The Londoners Eliot describes in the poem—the workers, the typists, the pub drinkers—are oblivious to their fate.

To Virginia Woolf (1882–1941), London was both a source of inspiration and a symbol of the culture in which she lived and worked. Consequently, London was the setting for much of her writing. Moreover, Woolf was a member of the Bloomsbury Group, the name given to a group of English writers, philosophers, and artists who between 1907 and 1930 frequented the homes in London's Bloomsbury district belonging to Clive and Vanessa Bell and Vanessa's brother and sister Adrian and Virginia Stephen (later Virginia Woolf). The Bloomsbury group considered aesthetic, intellectual, and philosophical questions in order to arrive at definitions of the good, the true, and the beautiful.

Woolf loved London; hence her novel *Mrs. Dalloway* (1925) begins with the titular Clarissa Dalloway walking through the city, which the narrator describes dreamily yet also as distinctly modern (home to cars, advertisements, and the trauma of modern warfare). London is also central to Woolf's *Jacob's Room* (1922), which tells the story of Jacob Flanders. As a young man, Jacob arrives in London and takes rooms in Bloomsbury. His London is depicted as a place of culture, learning, and hopes. However, Woolf also highlights that aspirations can die just as Jacob's life is ended by World War I. Indeed, *Jacob's Room* is both a love letter to London and an elegy for an era that ended with the advent of war.

Such was Woolf's love of London that she was heartbroken to see the city reduced to rubble by the Blitz. Visiting London's landmarks was one of Woolf's favorite pastimes, and she enjoyed walking the metropolis's teeming streets. Woolf's delight in London is evident in *The Years* (1937), which focuses on an upper-middle-class London family during the period from 1880 to 1937. Each chapter of *The Years* begins with a panoramic description of fields, lanes, and damp London streets that leads the reader from one part of London to the next: from dingy Westminster back streets, to lavish parties in Kensington, through city slums, train compartments, halls of residences, and gardens. However, the narration flits about so the reader never spends long enough in one location to get a true sense of it. Instead, London as a whole looms large throughout the novel. The novel moves forward in time until the reader approaches the threshold of London and the beginning of modernity.

Despite her admiration for London, Woolf also felt that the city symbolized the patriarchal repression of women and as such was a place of limitations. This belief is evident in *Three Guineas* (1938), in which Woolf examines the influence of men who held power in London's banks, courts, and political institutions. In *Jacob's Room* and *The Years*, Woolf questions what London's monumental buildings really represent while also exposing London's social inequalities. All but two of Woolf's works of fiction are set in London, and in every one of Woolf's other novels, the injustices of London life are revealed to the reader in the form of the homeless, prostitution, and disparities of wealth. In short, Woolf's London is a place of contradictions, splendid yet also the home of the desperate and disillusioned. For all Woolf's acknowledgment of London's darker side, however, her love for the city shines through in her writing.

London in Postwar Literature: Spies, the Future, and Multiculturalism

In contrast to Woolf's delight in London, Len Deighton's first novel, *The IPCRESS File* (1962), begins and ends in London and gives a sense of the city in decline. In his disorienting retelling of his story, the novel's narrator traces his journey across London and elsewhere. Deighton's London is post–World War II, the fading center of the faltering British Empire that has been displaced as a superpower by the United States and the Soviet Union. Deighton grew up in London, but, having worked as cabin crew, he recognized London's links to the rest of the world. Moreover, Deighton gives an insider's insight into postwar London's need for the Clean Air Act, for he depicts London as gray, sooty, and soiled, a city yet to experience the psychedelia of the Swinging Sixties.

A London that is not merely declining but apocalyptic is depicted in *London Fields* (1989), often considered the middle part of Martin Amis's London trilogy, along with *Money* (1984) and *The Information* (1995). *London Fields* provides an innovative vision of London as the narrator Samson Young, a terminally ill American writer living in London searches for inspiration for his last novel. The title of the novel is paradoxical, both urban (London) and rural (fields), with the ambiguity indicating to the reader the uncertainties inherent in the novel's imagined city. *London Fields* is set in the Notting Hill area of West London. However, despite the novel's compact geography, Amis presents a varied view of London from the affluent townhouses of Notting Hill itself to the bohemian air of Portobello Road to the dingier canal-side buildings. Other examples of visionary London novels include *Mother London* by Michael Moorcock (1988). Moorcock's novel follows three London mental patients through various periods of London's history—from the bombings of World War II to the late 1980s—and in so doing provides an impressionistic portrait of the city.

Angela Carter, who is perhaps best known for her magic realism novels, spent much of her life in South London. In her last novel, *Wise Children* (1991), Carter offers up a nostalgic view of the city that mourns for a lost era while presenting London as carnivalesque and ever-changing. *Wise Children* is a novel of opposites, for it starts with an account of the divide between London's north and south, rich and poor. The city's geographical split reflects the contrasts between low and high culture (in the forms of music hall and Shakespeare) and illegitimacy and legitimacy that lie at the heart of the novel. London's music hall tradition is also at the heart of Peter Ackroyd's *Dan Leno and the Limehouse Golem* (1994), which follows the hunt for a serial killer in 1880 with the plot revolving around the real-life Victorian music hall star, Dan Leno. Ackroyd brings Victorian London to life, transporting the reader from the seedy glamour of the music hall to the squalid East End slums.

In the 1990s, there were few English-language novels about growing up as a mixed-race child. Hanif Kureishi's *The Buddha of Suburbia* (1990) is important for opening the debate about postwar immigration and multiculturalism, paving the way for such writers as Zadie Smith. *The Buddha of Suburbia* tells the story of Karim, a bisexual, mixed-race teenager growing up in 1970s suburban London who is yearning to escape to the city. The novel is a postmodern coming-of-age tale examining gender, class, sexuality, and race through the prism of postwar multicultural Britain, a discussion that Kureishi establishes through numerous sets of oppositions. The novel's most obvious opposition is in the representation of place, for the novel is structured in two parts: "In the Suburbs" and "In the City." The novel portrays suburban London as dour and repressive. For this reason, Karim yearns to move to urban London, which to Karim embodies freedom and sophistication. Ultimately, the anonymity of London provides Karim with an escape from suburban racism and snobbery but reveals to him a world of social transgression, radicalism, and sexual experimentation.

Published in 2000 by mixed-race author Zadie Smith, *White Teeth* is a groundbreaking look at multicultural London during the period from the 1970s to the late 1990s. The novel focuses on first-generation immigrants and their relationship with Britain's colonial past. Set against a backdrop of multiracial London, *White Teeth* rejoices in the mishmash of people that is modern London. Much of the novel focuses on a patriarchal Bangladeshi family headed by a father who is failing to pass on his culture. By mixing-up cultures and ethnicities, Smith is able to depict the various histories, traditions, and vocabularies that coexist in London.

LONDON ART

London has long been a source of inspiration to artists, whether they've wished to paint beautiful views of famous landmarks, depict modernity, or comment on social issues.

Early Depictions of London Landmarks

Many depictions of London in art are of famous London landmarks. For example, the Dutch artist Claude de Jongh (ca. 1600–1663), who specialized in refined cityscapes, painted *View of Old London Bridge from the West* (1650), which is housed in the Victoria and Albert Museum. The oil painting is one of the three versions of old London Bridge that de Jongh painted that year, all of them variants of de Jongh's earlier work *Old London Bridge* (1630). The earlier painting is based on a series of drawings (now kept in London's Guildhall Library) that de Jongh likely drew when he stayed in England during the 1620s. The same drawings may well have inspired de Jongh's later series of paintings. The painting kept in the Victoria and Albert Museum is notable for its treatment of the River Thames, the water reflecting the gray clouds above while the variations of tone de Jongh employs enhance the painting's sense of depth. Almost a century later, Balthasar Nebot painted *Covent Garden Market and St. Paul's*

Church, London (ca. 1737), which shows the bustling Covent Garden marketplace looking west toward St. Paul's Church. In the 1730s, the market was located at the heart of London's artistic community. The market was also a constant source of inspiration for artists in London, for each day the market had a diverse collection of sellers, visitors, and produce on display. Nebot painted two versions of this scene: one is displayed in London's Guildhall Art Gallery and the other is on display at Tate Britain.

Giovanni Antonio Canal (1697–1768), usually referred to as Canaletto, was one of the most important members of the eighteenth-century Venetian school of art. Canaletto was particularly famous for his cityscapes of Venice, Rome, and London. From 1746 to 1756, Canaletto painted many London scenes. In *A View of Greenwich from the River* (ca. 1750–1752), Canaletto depicts the Greenwich riverfront with the Royal Naval Hospital and the Queen's House. The imposing hospital building is visible on the far hill.

Another Canaletto work, *London: The Thames from Somerset House Terrace toward Westminster* (ca. 1750–1751), shows the view from the terrace of the old Somerset House, the skyline dominated by St. Paul's Cathedral. Canaletto altered the cathedral's dome so that it is viewed from slightly below and thus is made more imposing. Beyond the dome, the horizon is dominated by the steeples of London's churches, mainly those designed by Christopher Wren following the Great Fire of London. To the right of the painting, the Monument to the Great Fire is visible. Elsewhere the Old London Bridge is viewable, as well as part of the Thames's South Bank.

Hogarthian London: Brothels and Bedlam

The work of London-born artist and satirist William Hogarth (1697–1764) ranged from realistic portraits to comical pictures examining modern morality. At the time Hogarth was active, London was a place of paradoxes: the City of London was a commercial hub but also associated with poverty and crime; the West End was fashionable and genteel, yet pockets of great deprivation existed nearby. Hogarth's artworks of London are bustling, to the point of claustrophobia, while presenting Londoners in a way that was far removed from the decorum portrayed in conventional engravings of city life or the polite topographical paintings of Nebot and Canaletto. Hogarth depicted London as a paradoxical place where high and low cultures interacted.

In Hogarth's celebrated drawing *Gin Lane* (1751), Hogarth shows the evils of gin drinking on the residents of the St. Giles slums. The picture was part of a campaign against the uncontrolled production of cheap gin that led, ultimately, to the Gin Act of 1751, which greatly reduced the number of gin shops in London. However, Hogarth is probably most famous for his series *A Harlot's Progress* and *A Rake's Progress*. *A Harlot's Progress* (1732) consists of six prints that together tell the cautionary tale of Moll, who becomes a London prostitute after arriving in the city from the countryside. The prints show Moll's journey from innocent to harlot. The first print shows Moll being praised for her beauty by a disease-ridden brothel keeper as an aroused gentleman looks on. The second print shows Moll, no longer innocent, distracting one of her lovers by exposing her breast so that her other lover can leave her bedroom. By the third picture, Moll is no longer a kept woman but a common prostitute, about to be arrested. The following drawings show Moll in prison and then dying from syphilis. The final print shows Moll dead in her coffin at age 23, surrounded by her fellow prostitutes as a clergyman pleasures a woman with his hand.

When Hogarth began his *A Rake's Progress* (series of eight paintings produced in 1732–1734, engraved in 1734, and published in print in 1735), the concept of the rake was a well-known symbol of male depravity who would fritter away his fortune on sex, drink, and gambling while accruing crippling debts. In scene 1 of *A Rake's Progress*, the fictional Tom arrives home, having inherited a fortune from his father. The scene shows Tom trying to pay off his pregnant lover Sarah, who stands weeping and holding a wedding ring. Scene 2 shows Tom has adapted to his new life of luxury and is surrounded by a crowd of people vying for his attention. The scene is deliberately absurd, for it satirizes high society as well as the members of the middle class, who aspire to join the upper classes. In scene 3, Tom is shown drunk at a Covent Garden brothel-tavern. In the next scene, Tom is on his way to be presented at the royal court at St. James's Palace but is stopped by a bailiff who wants to arrest him on account of his debts. On this occasion, Tom is saved by the intervention of Sarah, whom he had rejected previously. Scene 5 is set in Marylebone Old Church, which was infamous for performing clandestine weddings. Having lost his fortune, Tom now marries a rich old maid while Sarah arrives, holding Tom's child. Any hope of Tom's salvation seems to have disappeared. Next, a distraught Tom is shown kneeling on the floor of a dingy gambling den after amassing more debts. By scene 7, all hope is lost, for Tom is now held in London's notorious Fleet debtors' prison, where neither Sarah nor his new wife can help him. In the final scene, Tom is shown incarcerated as a madman in London's infamous mental asylum Bethlem Hospital (known as "Bedlam"). Sarah tries to comfort him, but Tom ignores her. Here, Tom is stripped of his clothes and, therefore, of his social pretensions. At that time, asylums welcomed paying visitors, and Tom is shown being viewed by a fine lady and her maid. The irony is that, while Tom wished to ape the aristocratic lifestyle, he is now merely one of high society's amusements. By depicting the harlot and the rake, Hogarth focused on two of London's social archetypes, made use of identifiable London locations, and incorporated real-life London characters and events. Such references gave Hogarth's work both topicality and an air of authenticity as records of the darker side of London life.

Rival Romantics: Turner and Constable

Born in Covent Garden, J. M. W. Turner (1775–1851) was an English Romantic artist best known for his expressive landscapes. For his *Old London Bridge* (ca. 1794), Turner adopts a low viewpoint that suggests he may have painted the bridge from the riverbank. As a lad, Turner was fascinated by the busy waterborne industry of the Thames, but in this painting, Turner focuses on the bridge's architecture, carefully replicating the bridge's Gothic arches and brickwork. In contrast, Constable uses a few sparse brush marks to distinguish the coachmen crossing the bridge. As such, *Old London Bridge* is a record of London's infrastructure.

In *The Burning of the Houses of Parliament* (ca. 1834–1835), Turner painted the 1834 fire at the Houses of Parliament, which Turner is said to have witnessed. The watercolor looks over Old Palace Yard from Abingdon Street, with St. Margaret Street beyond. On the painting's left is the Henry VII Chapel at the east end of Westminster Abbey, while to the east, the central third of the composition shows the committee rooms adjoining part of Westminster Hall, which is distinguished by its pinnacles. Turner shows the fire burning inside the buildings with the outer shell surviving. By highlighting the rectilinear lines of the building's architecture on the left side and center, Turner is able to stress the untamed nature of fire to the painting's right. The semicircular openings visible against the flames at the far right of the painting are also apparent in Robert William Billings's 1834 watercolor *House of Lords from Old Palace Yard*.

Turner knew the Tower of London well and painted *Fire at the Grand Storehouse of the Tower of London* (1841), which is thought to document a catastrophic fire that destroyed part of the Tower of London on October 30, 1841. William Oliver depicted the same fire in his lithograph *Conflagration of the Tower of London, on the Night of the 30th of October 1841*, which shows flames and smoke pouring from the windows' of the Grand Storehouse and obscuring the White Tower.

Turner's rival landscape painter, John Constable, was another influential exponent of Romanticism, emphasizing an emotional response to nature by concentrating on acute observations of clouds, trees, and light. In 1832, Constable painted *The Opening of Waterloo Bridge ("Whitehall Stairs, June 18th, 1817")*, which was influenced by Canaletto's paintings of the Thames. The painting commemorates both the opening of Waterloo

Bridge and the second anniversary of the Battle of Waterloo on June 18, 1817. This was a day of tremendous pomp that Constable attempted to capture on canvas. Constable was a royalist, so the subject also allowed him the opportunity to document for posterity an important historical event attended by the prince regent, who Constable shows about to board the royal barge at Whitehall. The painting also depicts several other London landmarks, among them, St. Paul's Cathedral and Somerset House. The painting's combination of dark foreground and high viewpoint draws the eye to the bridge in the distance and the gathering clouds.

Impressions of London

In the 1870s, France was embroiled in the Franco-Prussian War, and Paris was gripped by insurrection. Consequently, many French artists fled across the English Channel to London. The artists' experiences in London and the friendships they developed there influenced their work and also contributed to British art in general. While in London, the French Impressionists (artists who liked to work in the open air so that they could capture fleeting impressions of scenes) interacted with other French people as well as British artists, thereby creating a community of French exiles centered around Soho that was nicknamed the "French ghetto." At the heart of the French ghetto was the Café Royal, which was founded by a French wine merchant. In time, the Café Royal became the meeting place for artists including Camille Pissarro and Claude Monet. Meanwhile, the artist Alphonse Legros (1837–1911) gained support from London-based artists James Abbott McNeill Whistler, Dante Gabriel Rossetti, and Edward Burne-Jones. Other French artists in London regarded Legros as a success story and asked him for advice when they were in London.

The Impressionist artists were fascinated by London for several reasons. For one, the Impressionists admired Turner and Constable who they believed painted outdoors rather than in a studio. Also, while living in London, the Impressionists were inspired to paint certain subjects, especially London's crowds and parks, which they saw as symbolic of freedom. Above all, however, the Impressionists enjoyed painting the River Thames and the Palace of Westminster, which they considered symbols of Britain.

Pissarro arrived in London in 1870 and that year painted *Fox Hill, Upper Norwood*. The painting shows a frosty London suburb surrounded by snow. The snow is depicted through loose brush work that mirrors the icy blues of the sky. Upper Norwood had become Pissarro's home after he fled the Franco-Prussian War in France, and the painting conveys a sense of tranquility and contentment. In the artist's later *Charing Cross Bridge* (1890), distinct traces of pointillism are evident, for tiny, distinct, contrasting dots of color are used to portray passengers on a steamer. Pissarro painted the work from Waterloo Bridge; to the painting's right is Cleopatra's Needle (an obelisk next to the Thames), to the center of the painting is the clock tower popularly known as Big Ben, and to the left are the Houses of Parliament.

Like Pissarro, Monet found himself in London in the early 1870s due to the outbreak of war in France. However, while Pissarro tended to paint London's suburbs, Monet stuck to more conventional subjects such as London's landmarks. Monet was also captivated by the city's fog and its effect on light. Between 1899 and 1901, Monet produced almost one hundred views of the River Thames; he also painted Waterloo Bridge and Charing Cross Bridge from his room at the Savoy Hotel and painted the Houses of Parliament from St. Thomas' Hospital across the river.

Monet's *The Port of London* (1871) shows a view of the River Thames and the Houses of Parliament from Victoria Quay. In the painting, Monet uses individual brush marks to give the impression of moving river water. Monet's *The Thames below Westminster* (1871) gives a hazy view of the Houses of Parliament from the banks of the Thames. The picture focus on the everyday activity of the river—a jetty dominates the foreground while working boats travel toward the bridge. The painting is an exercise in light and dark, and Monet would return to the same location frequently in order to capture the scene at different times and in different light. Most of Monet's paintings of the Houses of Parliament share the same viewpoints, either looking out from Monet's window or a terrace at St. Thomas' Hospital overlooking the Thames. The paintings were painted during different times of the day and weather conditions, however, so each is different.

The only British artist to be considered an Impressionist (though he was Paris-born), Alfred Sisley painted *View of the Thames: Charing Cross Bridge* (1874). Sisley, who is famed for his colorful landscapes informed by natural light, visited London in 1874, and although he painted several works near Hampton Court, this is Sisley's only picture of the Thames in central London. The painting is bathed in soft pastel tones that give the Thames a near-exotic look, while the river's shoreline is depicted as though on a Mediterranean evening. In the background, however, is the dome of St. Paul's Cathedral silhouetted against the pink sky, so the location of the painting is undeniably London. Individual brushstrokes give the impression of the river's flowing water.

Another French Impressionist in London, James Jacques Joseph Tissot, created playful portraits of modern London life. In particular, Tissot painted the balls, holidays, and afternoon teas enjoyed by London's high society. Tissot rose quickly through the ranks of London society despite claims that he parodied the subjects he depicted, such as in *The Gallery of HMS Calcutta, 1876*, which shows a lady seemingly flirting with a sailor.

Indeed, Tissot began his London career by creating caricatures for the magazine *Vanity Fair*. However, the ambiguity of Tissot's pictures prevents them from being simply scenes from everyday life, and that piques viewers' curiosity. As a Frenchman in London, Tissot's paintings provide a richly detailed visual account of Victorian London's high society and include such details as luxurious teapots, ribbons, and rugs that artists more familiar with London might overlook and consider too mundane to add to the artworks.

The British artist George Hyde Pownall (1866–1939) was best known for his depictions of such London locations as Piccadilly Circus, Leicester Square, Westminster Bridge and the Parliament Buildings. Pownall specialized in paintings of London streets at night, and since the streets at this time were lit by gas lanterns, Pownall's pictures often have a warm, ethereal feel created by the soft lamplight. The paintings, which typically show horse-drawn carriages and motor vehicles sharing London's streets, are imbued with an Impressionist air that give the sense of a snapshot of nocturnal London.

Aesthetic London

The London-born artist Dante Gabriel Rossetti was one of the most significant members of the Pre-Raphaelites, an artistic movement founded in London in 1848 that was an important precursor of the Aesthetic movement. Inspired by the critic and artist John Ruskin's theory that artists aim for truth to nature, the Pre-Raphaelites thought art should focus on serious subjects treated realistically. For this reason, the Pre-Raphaelites tended toward religious and literary themes, particularly those dealing with love and death. However, the Pre-Raphaelites also considered modern social issues, as seen in Rossetti's unfinished painting *Found* (started in 1853). *Found* looks at the theme of the "fallen woman," for it shows a young female prostitute crouching against the wall of a London cemetery. Here the sickly prostitute has thrown herself to the pavement because she recognizes a young man coming toward her. The man has grabbed the woman by the wrists, but she refuses to follow him. There are many interpretations of *Found*. Some regard the painting as simply an examination of urban prostitution, others consider the picture an investigation on the relationship between the countryside and cities, or as an allegory on nature/heaven and urban society/hell.

American-born artist James Abbott McNeill Whistler studied painting in Paris before moving permanently to London in 1860. Whistler was a proponent of the Aesthetic movement, which placed greater focus on beauty than on subject matter. Whistler's *Nocturne: Blue and Gold— Old Battersea Bridge* (ca. 1872–1875), is one of several night scenes (or nocturnes). Whistler preferred the calm of the nighttime Thames to the bustling Thames by day, and so he created the painting in his studio from memory, having sketched London at night from a boat in the middle of the Thames. In this work, Whistler exaggerates Battersea Bridge's proportions so that it looms large, with Chelsea Church and the lights of the new Albert Bridge visible in the distance. Overall, the painting conveys a sense of the beauty and tranquility of the Thames at night. However, despite the painting's peaceful air, it is one of Whistler's most controversial works, for it was produced as evidence in an infamous 1878 trial between Whistler and John Ruskin that saw Whistler sue Ruskin for writing inflammatory remarks about his work. Whistler won the case but received only one farthing (Britain's smallest coin at the time) in damages.

In 1882, Whistler took as an apprentice the British artist Walter Sickert. Over time, however, Sickert moved away from Whistler's style to paint from nature using a wet-in-wet technique and focused on studio-based painting from drawings made in situ. Sickert took rooms in Camden Town and began to hold soirees in his studio which, in 1911, became the London Post-Impressionist artistic group known as the Camden Town Group. This group also included Spencer Frederick Gore, Wyndham Lewis, and Augustus John. Although the Camden Town Group held only three exhibitions (in 1911 and 1912), the group's name is synonymous with a distinctive period in British art history that occurred shortly before World War I. The group aimed to reflect the realities of modern London life through realistic city scenes and post-Impressionist landscapes. Sickert's contributions to the group's exhibitions were very different both from the group's usual subject matter and appearance. For example, Sickert exhibited several low-toned pictures portraying nude women on an iron bedstead in a dingy boardinghouse, sometimes watched by a dressed man. The paintings formed Sickert's *Camden Town Murder* series, and while the realistic paintings do not depict any violence, some commentators have suggested the paintings point toward Sickert being Jack the Ripper.

Modern London Art: War, Industrialization, and the Shock of the New

The short-lived fauvism movement (from the French *les fauves*, translating to "wild beasts," 1905–1910) was an early twentieth-century art movement whose members emphasized painterliness and the use of strong color. When one of the movement's leaders, André Derain, was commissioned to paint a London scene, the artist produced the cityscape *Charing Cross Bridge* (1906). Here Derain depicts a scene from the south shores of the River Thames during the winter of 1906. On the far left of the painting is a blue building; to its right, short brushstrokes represent the rippling river. The distant buildings and landscape are painted smoothly, their soft lines contrasting with the sharp lines in the foreground. While in most paintings the London sky is painted a dull gray, here the London sky is depicted using the dramatic color of the fauvist palette.

During World War II, the sculptor Henry Moore was appointed by the War Artists Advisory Committee to document life in London's shelters. Consequently, Moore produced many powerful drawings of Londoners sheltering in the London Underground during the Blitz. Moore's Underground sketches are often viewed as propaganda pieces that symbolize Londoners' enduring resistance in the face of adversity. However, the drawings also express claustrophobia and fear, as indistinguishable figures are glimpsed massed in dimly lit tunnels. Moore's *Shelterers in the Tube* (1941) was inspired by an evening in 1940, when the artist took shelter from an air raid in Belsize Park. The sight of so many frightened Londoners grouped together had such a profound effect on Moore that he was able to draw the event from memory.

The British artist L. S. Lowry also portrayed a dark, disquieting London in his *View of Deptford Power Station from Greenwich* (1959). Lowry tended to paint the industrial North of England, but here the artist focuses on urban London life. The painting documents the huge power station at Deptford, in South East London, as seen from across the Thames in Greenwich. As a chronicler of industrial areas, here Lowry ignores Greenwich's famous historic buildings but instead shows cranes rising from mist and chimneys belching black smoke into a sky bleached of color. Lowry's interpretation of London reveals a sense of alienation and the inconsequential nature of human life against a backdrop of industrialization. The painting's sense of desolation is emphasized by the lack of color, by black shapes, and by the absence of human figures.

LONDON ART NOW: PICKLED SHARKS, FROZEN BLOOD, AND RATS

From the 1980s to the late twentieth century, London art was dominated by a group of London artists known as the Young British Artists (YBAs), most of whom were educated at Goldsmiths College of Art, University of London, and whose work examined the darker aspects of modern life. The group was most active during the 1990s, with the name of the group deriving from a series of exhibitions mounted at London's Saatchi Gallery. The chief members of the group consisted of artists who participated in Damien Hirst's *Freeze* exhibition (1988), which launched a trend for art exhibitions to be held in East London factories and warehouses. These artists included Damien Hirst himself, Gary Hume, and Sarah

Lucas, though such artists as Tracey Emin, Rachel Whiteread, and Jake and Dinos Chapman were also considered YBAs. In fact, Damien Hirst and Tracey Emin are now household names in the UK. The YBA exhibition *Sensation* (1997), held at London's Royal Academy of Arts, is often cited as one of its most controversial art exhibitions and a landmark in modern British art history. The exhibition featured 110 artworks by over 40 artists associated with the YBA movement. The works included *The Physical Impossibility of Death in the Mind of Someone Living*, by Damien Hirst, which took the form of a shark preserved in formaldehyde; *Self*, a self-portrait cast from pints of artist Mark Quinn's own frozen blood; and *Myra*, Marcus Harvey's portrait of serial child killer Myra Hindley that comprised numerous children's handprints. The exhibition triggered protests and generated much media attention while also proving to be one of the Royal Academy's most popular exhibitions.

The street artist Banksy is known for his controversial pieces that combine freehand work with stencils and slogans. Banksy rose to prominence in the late 1990s, when his work became widely recognized around Bristol in southwestern England and then in London. Banksy's artwork tends toward the satirical, critiquing politics, war, and capitalism, with frequent subjects including rats, policemen, the British royal family, and children. Banksy's street artworks are visible throughout London, though some are in better condition than others. Rats are a particular subject in Banksy's London works and are dotted around London like a miniature rodent army. For example, Banksy's rats can be seen on Tooley Street near London Bridge, in Steelyard Passage underneath Cannon Street station, and on Chiswell Street in Islington. The controversial nature of Banksy's works has resulted in some of Banksy's original pieces falling foul of authorities. For example, his work *The Royal Family* (a cartoon of British royals) on Stoke Newington Church Street in Hackney was almost lost forever in 2009, when workmen from the local council began to paint over the piece. The work was saved, however, when local residents protested, and most of it has survived.

LIFE IN THE CITY   DANCING WITH THE *STRICTLY* PROS AT TRAFALGAR SQUARE

In 2006, I was one of more than 1,000 dancers gathered together to dance at Trafalgar Square in central London for BBC One's *Dancing in the Street* event, during which six new world records were set. The program was broadcast live on BBC One and hosted by television presenters Sir Bruce Forsyth and Zoe Ball.

For some time, I had been part of a semiprofessional flamenco dancing troupe based in Greenford, West London. In the summer of 2006, we were asked to be part of 800 dancers performing *Big Dance*—a new world record featuring 45 different dance styles performed to the same piece of music—which would be the finale to *Dancing in the Street*. Among the other dance troupes were belly dancers, Lindy hoppers, Argentine tango dancers, and even synchronized swimmers who performed in the famous Trafalgar Square fountains.

All the amateur dancers spent many weeks rehearsing separately for the event. Nearer the time, we had to go to rehearsals in a warehouse near the Thames Barrier that was large enough to hold all the dancers rehearsing en masse. By the end of those rehearsals, everyone felt filthy because the warehouse was dirty, complete with decomposing rats.

When performing, the flamenco dancers were positioned on the main stage, which overlooked the rest of Trafalgar Square, with the other dancers and National Gallery in front of us. We shared the stage with professional dancers from *The Rocky Horror Picture Show* and the BBC program *Strictly Come Dancing*—known in the United States as *Dancing with the Stars*—with whom we had to rehearse numerous times. In real life, some of the professional dancers were not as they seemed on television, but the former World Amateur Latin American champion Matthew Cutler was absolutely lovely and asked the flamenco dancers to clap time for him when he practiced. For *Big Dance*, everyone performed to a special arrangement of Junior Senior's *Move Your Feet*. Each of the different dance groups could choose their own costumes, so the flamenco dancers chose long black skirts and tops with red accessories.

On the day of *Dancing in the Street*, the flamenco dancers were based at Canada House, the Canadian embassy at Trafalgar Square. We had a lengthy dress rehearsal before the show that was watched by lots of tourists. Then, just before the broadcast began, it started to rain, which meant the stage was quite slippery. By the time the show started, the sun had set so we danced under lights; this made all the costumes look amazing and created a buzzy atmosphere. After the event, all the dancers received a certificate to say they had been part of the *Big Dance* world record. Later, the BBC asked the flamenco dancers to be on their quiz show *Eggheads*, and we were invited to perform at Earl's Court exhibition center and at Spanish centers in London. Even now, whenever I hear *Move Your Feet*, I instantly think back to dancing at Trafalgar Square. There is footage from *Big Dance* on YouTube at https://www.youtube.com/watch?v=GqjXGb4UGZ8.

—*Victoria Williams*

Working at Wembley

LIFE IN THE CITY

I started working at the Wembley complex in January 1987, providing the telecommunications for musical acts appearing at the stadium and conference center, and for sporting events. At Wembley, musical acts always brought huge amounts of telecommunication equipment with them—telephones, fax machines, and so on—and journalists would bring with them laptops and other IT equipment. During my time at Wembley, I worked with acts including the Rolling Stones, Michael Jackson, Madonna, the Spice Girls, Elton John, and Rod Stewart. Sometimes I would have to go into stars' dressing rooms to sort out the electrics and telephones. During a Guns N' Roses concert, I was stationed under the stage, which was incredibly noisy! I also had to liaise with the police providing security for sporting events such as NFL matches and the Euro '96 soccer championships. I could see how the police cameras were able to zoom in on individuals among the huge crowds. Sometimes, people would phone fake bomb threats into the Wembley switchboard. Stupidly, the hoaxers would often use the public pay telephones dotted around the stadium and so could be located quickly by the switchboard and, presumably, arrested by the police. Before major soccer events such as the FA Cup final, the switchboard would receive calls from members of the public asking to pass messages to players and team managers. People would also confuse Wembley with Wimbledon and phone the switchboard asking what the tennis scores were. A standout funny moment occurred when a very drunk Scottish soccer fan fell face first into a pile of manure deposited by a police horse—I remember thinking that the fan would have to travel back to Scotland smelling awful.

—Bill Barrett

NOTES

1. Victoria Williams, "Murrow, Edward R. (1908–1965)," in *100 Entertainers Who Changed America: An Encyclopedia of Pop Culture Luminaries: Volume II: M–Z* (Santa Barbara, CA: ABC-CLIO, 2013), 413.
2. British Film Institute, *BFI: The UK Film Economy*, 20, https://www2.bfi.org .uk/sites/bfi.org.uk/files/downloads/bfi-uk-film-economy-2019-01-30.pdf.

FURTHER READING

Barr, Charles. *Ealing Studios: A Movie Book*. 3rd ed. Berkeley: University of California Press, 1998.

Morrison, Spencer. "Geographies of Space: Mapping and Reading the Cityscape." In *The Cambridge Companion to* The Waste Land, edited by Gabrielle McIntire, 24–38. Cambridge: Cambridge University Press, 2015.

Richardson, LeeAnne M. "The Journalist Who Exposed the Jeffrey Epsteins of Victorian London." The Conversation, August 12, 2019. https://theconversation.com/the-journalist-who-exposed-the-jeffrey-epsteins-of-victorian -london-121409.

Williams, Victoria. "Dickens' Use of the Fairy Tale in *Our Mutual Friend*." *Pennsylvania Literary Journal: British Literature* 2, no. 2 (Winter 2010): 47–75.

Williams, Victoria. "Great Expectations." In *Literary Geography: An Encyclopedia of Real and Imagined Settings*, edited by Lynn Marie Houston, 111–14. Santa Barbara, CA: Greenwood, 2019.

Williams, Victoria. "Murrow, Edward R. (1908–1965)." In *100 Entertainers Who Changed America: An Encyclopedia of Pop Culture Luminaries: Volume II: M–Z*, 411–18. Santa Barbara, CA: ABC-CLIO, 2013.

Wolfreys, Julian. *Dickens's London: Perception, Subjectivity and Phenomenal Urban Multiplicity*. Edinburgh: Edinburgh University Press, 2012.

12

The Future

At the time of writing, London, like the rest of the UK, is experiencing a historic crisis resulting from the COVID-19 pandemic. Indeed, the combined forces of COVID-19 and Brexit have created a perfect storm of uncertainty over the city's future. It is likely that, in at least the short term, the future of London will be tumultuous, shaped by the intertwined factors of COVID-19, the post-Brexit economy, and public transport issues.

The COVID-19 pandemic is a major negative economic shock unlike anything London has experienced in living memory. Overall, London's job market is performing less well than that of other UK cities despite the fact that many Londoners can work from home. In 2021, the Centre for Cities independent think-tank stated that London is one of the UK locations hardest hit economically by COVID-19.[1] Some Londoners, those who work in services that rely on footfall and workers with fewer qualifications or little work experience, have been impacted particularly badly by the city's worsening labor market. Nearly one in eight Black Londoners (12 percent) were unemployed in the three months to September 2020, more than double the rate for White Londoners (5 percent).[2] Additionally, London is suffering other severe economic ramifications from COVID-19 with business closures, falling expenditure, and lowered footfall meaning that London is faring worse than other areas of the UK. London's ultimate economic recovery trajectory will depend largely on the duration of current lockdown restrictions. The government had intended to remove all such restrictions in England from June 21, 2021, but due to the arrival of the Delta

A "Stay Home Save Lives" poster outside London's King's Cross station. The poster was designed to remind Londoners to only leave home for essential reasons during England's third national COVID-19 lockdown. (VVShots/Dreamstime.com)

COVID-19 variant, this unlocking was delayed to July 19, 2021. London's retail and hospitality sectors have been severely impacted by the large number of Londoners now working from home rather than entering the city center but it is hoped that once Londoners return to office working, the city's services sector will start to recover. While London's economy has recovered quickly from previous shocks, it will not necessarily do so again. Ultimately, economist expect the following industries to be the worst hit by the damage to London's economy: accommodation and food services, construction, manufacturing, education, arts and recreation, and the retail industries.

Overall, in the first quarter of 2020, in London all levels of business activity and employment registered a historic fall, consumer confidence was at its lowest level in seven years, and house prices fell. A reduction in London house prices experienced by the city's housing market in 2018 continued through 2019, with a slight recovery during the period December 2019 to March 2020. Property surveyors responding to the Royal Institution of Chartered Surveyors (RICS) Housing Market Survey in April 2020 reported, on balance, a reduction in London's house prices from August 2016 to November 2019, followed by a recovery at the start of 2020. Nonetheless, the prices fell to an all-time low in March and April 2020, with indicators suggesting that shortly thereafter, London house prices might fall further.[3] Indeed, London now has the UK's weakest performing house price growth, with London's annual price growth falling to 4.8 percent, down from 6.2 percent in the final quarter of 2020.[4] The fall in house prices reflects that many Londoners have moved out of the city, or plan to do so as they feel they will be able to work from home in future.

The introduction of a lockdown in the UK had a profound influence on consumer confidence. Data suggest that, in particular, London consumers view their household finances and economy in general over the next years very negatively: while the consumer confidence for London was positive for much of 2019, it became strongly negative in April 2020 and continued to be negative in May. However, it should be noted that consumer confidence in London is nonetheless significantly higher than that for the rest of the UK.[5]

London economists predict that some of London's local characteristics may prove advantageous in the city's economic recovery. In particular, some of London's main sectors—financial services, real estate, professional and technical activities, and information and communications—have suffered less during the UK's COVID-19 lockdown restrictions, as a relatively high proportion of London workers have been able to work from home.[6] At the same time, however, these advantages may be offset by other features, including the fact that many Londoners work in tourism and hospitality, the city's universities have seen a decrease in their numbers of international students, and the fact that many Londoners rely on public transport to get to work, with public transport likely to be limited in capacity for a years to come.

The long-term solution to London's ongoing economic shock will likely rely on the roll-out of COVID-19 vaccine. In short, it is probable that London's economy will not recover to its previous "normality" until the vaccine is administered to all Londoners. As of late June 2021, 58 percent of Londoners aged over 18 years had received one dose of a COVID-19 vaccine, a figure far lower than the 76 percent of people in the same age bracket living in the south west of England.[7] There were two main reasons for London's smaller take-up of the jabs. First, the multicultural makeup of London's population for numerous studies showed ethnic minorities in the UK were less likely to come forward to be vaccinated. Second, London has a younger population than the rest of the UK and so since much of the UK's vaccination rollout went through year groups (oldest first progressing through to youngsters) many Londoners were among the last to be jabbed.

The Purchasing Managers' Index (PMI) is a survey of London's private sector that shows the state of London's general business conditions as indicated by trends in such indicators as new businesses and employment. In

2019, the PMI data remained around 50.0, which indicated slightly expanding business conditions.[8] A small uptick occurred after the UK's general election in December 2019, as the election was seen as bringing some clarity to the subject of Brexit and the Brexit transition period. However, following the emergence of COVID-19, by March 2020, there had been a marked decline in the business indicators, with the key indicators of business activity, new businesses, and employment each at all-time lows.[9]

Aside from COVID-19, Brexit is another risk to London's economy, for the ongoing future trading relationship negotiations between the UK and the European Union (EU) have yet to be resolved. The EU as a whole receives the highest number of London exports, so the UK's relationship with the EU will significantly influence London's economic future. As well as potentially damaging the UK's reputation, leaving the EU could cause London to see a downturn in investment and a fall in the number of workers moving to the city.

London's economic future may also be jeopardized by global financial factors. An increase in global protectionism could damage the global flow of trade, while the UK government's borrowing during the pandemic may result in a reduction in much-needed investment. The intensification of regional conflicts around the world exacerbates global financial instability, and overall, the global economy remains highly volatile.

London's transport is central to both London's economic, social, and environmental future. The mayor of London has signaled his aim of pursuing economic policies that are socially and environmentally beneficial and hopes to create a sustainable economy focused on highly skilled employment. The London Infrastructure Plan (2015) asserts that up to £1 trillion of investment will be required by 2050 in order to fund necessary new London infrastructure that will ensure London remains both competitive in the global economy and resilient to climate change.[10] In particular, the mayor believes all such infrastructure will need to be designed and operated as an integrated and sustainable system that increases productivity, uses resources efficiently, and improves Londoners' quality of life. To this end, the mayor hopes that the funds needed to improve London life will come from direct public investment and from large-scale private investment of between £1 trillion and £1.7 trillion from firms in the City of London and other investors.[11] At present, however, London faces the prospect of city buildings lying empty because businesses are reconsidering how much office space they will require, given the looming UK recession and the risk of a resurgence of COVID-19. By delaying or canceling plans to relocate to London, companies can reduce their costs, so it is unknown how greatly firms will be willing to invest in London. The prospect of London offices remaining empty also means London's landlords will find it increasingly difficult to find tenants, leading the property market to readjust its rents and possibly offer businesses rent-free periods. At the start of 2020, London office landlords were enjoying a boom time resulting from the resounding UK general election victory in December that had lifted some Brexit uncertainty, and a shortage of office space had resulted in increased office prices. By the end of March 2020, however, lockdown came into force, resulting in 57 percent of London property developers interviewed at the end of March fearing that demand for office leases would become fall significantly.[12] This fear is borne out by a poll for the London Chamber of Commerce that found 13 percent of London businesses said working from home would become the norm and that they did not envisage having permanent offices in London.[13] Since then, the demand for London offices has fallen further, as many Londoners who had previously commuted to work started to enjoy working from home, along with mass unemployment starting to take effect.

The future of London's office use is particularly affected by newly constrained public transport capacity, with the Underground able to transport only 15 percent of its normal passenger numbers in order to comply with social distancing measures.[14] In reality, this means that some businesses have already ended their traditional office-based working model, thereby raising concerns over the future of office complexes such as Canary Wharf. As businesses look to reduce their costs, demand for office space could move from the center of London to emerging centers such as Battersea, Vauxhall, Stratford, and White City. However, recent figures suggest that even in emerging areas of London, there has been a widespread decrease in new construction.

It is not just businesses that are looking to relocate from London, however, for both London job hunters and home buyers have started to move to less densely populated areas of the UK in a mass relocation sparked by the COVID-19 pandemic. In June 2020, for example, there was a surge in the number of people wanting to find employment outside of London. This surge was mirrored by a rise in the number of Londoners looking for new homes in more isolated parts of the UK. Indeed, during this period, the number of people looking for employment outside of London was more than double that of the same period in 2019. Meanwhile, the proportion of London home buyers registering with realtors located outside of London virtually doubled in April 2020, with the destinations most popular with house hunters from London including the beach town of Worthing, in Sussex, on England's south coast; Ipswich in Suffolk, eastern England; and Milton Keynes in Buckinghamshire. All of these locations are areas where the population is at least twice as dispersed as in London.[15] In June 2020, London home buyers showed the greatest interest in Aylesbury Vale, in rural Buckinghamshire, southern England. In April 2019, only 28 percent of people wanting property viewings there came from London, but since the start of the COVID-19 pandemic, the number has risen to 44 percent. Part of the reason for this surge of interest in Aylesbury is that the area is approximately 30 times less populated than most areas of London. Similarly, other areas popular with Londoners wanting to leave the city include Tandridge, in Surrey, which is 22 times less populated than London; and Medway, in Kent, which is more than 5 times less densely populated than London.[16] As well as lower population densities, Londoners are looking to leave the city in order to try to avoid risks from traveling on public transport. Londoners' anxiety about traveling on public transport is reflected in mobile-phone tracking data that show people have been slower to return to the centers of the largest cities, such as London, than they have in smaller towns such as Worthing.

Academics warn that the flight of middle-class Londoners from London may exacerbate the inequalities evident in the city, for Londoners employed in low-paid jobs such as cleaning, transport provision, and café work in city centers will be left behind. If middle-class Londoners stop working, living, dining, and shopping in central London, then the city's hospitality and retail industries will suffer, and poorer workers will experience a downturn in employment. The belief that Londoners wish to work in areas other than London is borne out by Escape the City, a company that helps people find employment outside of London, which in June 2020 reported that of 1,000 people enlisting the company's services, 51 percent hoped to leave London, compared with 20 percent in the same period of 2019, thereby suggesting that a fundamental change in job seekers' preferences had occurred.[17] There is, however, some cause for optimism in London's employment levels, for technology, media, and telecommunication businesses have already started to drive demand for offices in London.

Since London takes the form of numerous settlements linked together, transport is of the utmost importance to many Londoners. Indeed, Londoners' public transport use is often considered an indicator of the current state of the city's economy. This is because when more people travel into London, it tends to be that the extra journeys reflect more people commuting to work or an increase in shopping and other leisure activities. In turn, an increase in shopping may indicate an increase in household spending. In March and April 2020, London public transport saw an unprecedented decline in both bus and Tube travel as a result of the pandemic. It is expected that demand for London's public transport will return to around 50 percent to 60 percent of pre-lockdown levels, though the figure drops to 40 percent to 50 percent for journeys into central London with more journeys occurring in Outer London than in Inner London Boroughs.[18]

Very recently, some London Boroughs have begun to implement so-called low-traffic neighborhoods (LTNs) in order to promote "active travel" (walking and cycling) as modes of transport. Some of the measures taken to allow LTNs include fairly innocuous moves such as widening pavements, providing outdoor seating, and improving cycle-lane safety, while other, more radical moves include limiting roads to residents only, thereby restricting through-traffic by introducing such road blockages as bollards and large planters. Some LTNs have benefited local residents by lowering air pollution and increasing the number of people walking and cycling for their everyday journeys. For example, Walthamstow Village, in East London, is considered one of London's most successful livable neighborhood plans (a TfL-funded program to improve the experiences of walkers, cyclists, and users of public transport), for researchers have found that due to the infrastructural changes wrought in Waltham Forest, residents now walk and cycle, on average, an extra 41 minutes a week.[19] Such programs are highly controversial, however. For example, in 2020, Ealing Council secured £400,000 of funding from TfL in order to introduce nine LTNs throughout the borough, with the aim of supporting the council's ongoing intention to make people walk and cycle more as well as maintain social distancing in the COVID-19 era.[20] The funding was used to widen footways and block roads with barriers. The transport changes were implemented using an experimental traffic order (ETO), which allows traffic authorities to impose changes without consultation. In many cases, Ealing residents were only given one week's notice of the introduction of LTNs in their neighborhoods, with some residents not informed of the changes at all. In theory, the LTNs are temporary, and their impact should be assessed in six months' time. The imposition of the LTNs without consultation caused much anger among residents, as evinced by innumerable irate posts on local Facebook groups and Twitter, arguing that the LTNs penalize the elderly, disabled, and those who needed regular medical treatment, start or finish work at times when public transport does not run, need to get their children to schools on opposite sides of the borough, or have to carry heavy equipment. Locals also pointed out that the changes occurred at a time when Londoners had been warned to avoid public transport due to COVID-19. Other residents fear that the roadblocks may impair the ability of emergency services to access properties quickly, for ambulances and fire trucks must unlock barriers using a special key in order to reach some properties. In addition, refuse trucks have difficulty negotiating the barriers. Some residents also argued that while congestion may be reduced on some streets, displaced traffic from newly blocked roads may shift to other streets, including those on which schools are located.

A report by the London Cycling Campaign and the pedestrianization campaign group London Living Streets states that 15 percent of displaced traffic reduces after the implementation of LTNs.[21] London Living Streets has also found that LTNs cause traffic to increase on main roads, though they argue such increases are acceptable as main roads—some with wider lanes or buildings set back farther from the road—are designed to absorb increases in traffic.[22] However, such claims have caused unprecedented discord among residents in London Boroughs that have introduced LTNs, for residents on roads onto which traffic is displaced wonder why they should experience higher traffic and pollution levels so that residents of other side streets, which are often already quiet in terms of traffic (due to speed bumps and width restrictions, for example) can experience a reduction in traffic. At the same time, some cyclists have claimed they now feel unsafe on Ealing's roads because the traffic levels on their regular routes increased. The discord in previously neighborly areas of Ealing included pro-LTN factions suggesting local businesses should be boycotted if they expressed concerns about the LTNs and some anti-LTN individuals likening the imposition of the traffic changes to living in an undemocratic police state. At the same time, local environmental activists further stoked anger on social media by likening drivers to monsters and rats. But then council leader was found to follow a Twitter account that parodied local residents critical of the LTNs. In August 2020, many of the concerns expressed by Ealing residents were echoed in a report on the LTN in Lee Green, South East London,[23] and in multiple news reports by homeowners in Greenwich, who feared extra traffic would be funneled down their narrow streets after the introduction of an LTN. Indeed, interviewees in Greenwich claimed they were considering selling their homes. The same month, Harrow Council, in North West London, scrapped plans to create low-traffic neighborhoods within the borough amid concerns the introduction of such a program might have a counterproductive impact on the environment.[24] Meanwhile, Bromley Council made news headlines when it started legal action against neighboring Croydon Council, when the introduction of an LTN within Croydon borough increased traffic within Bromley borough.[25] More recently many of London's LTNs and other active travel initiatives have been in a state of flux. In September 2020, the council in the London Borough of Wandsworth announced it would remove its LTNs as soon as possible. A few months later, in November 2020, the council of the Royal Borough of Kensington and Chelsea removed its controversial emergency cycle lanes just 7 weeks after their construction—a move that generated even greater controversy as it was the first time during the pandemic that costly cycle lanes introduced on main roads had been removed so soon after their installation. In May 2021, Ealing Council removed one of the borough's most controversial LTN zones. Around the same time, the leader of Ealing Council was ousted from his position by his own party having scraped through a vote of no confidence in September 2020 (by one vote and an abstention) amid concerns over his handling of the introduction of the LTNs that included his public declaration of his desire to take advantage of the COVID-19 crisis to push through traffic reforms.[26] In September 2021, Ealing Council announced it would scrap all but two of the borough's new LTNs.

Some LTNs also include the provision of so-called school streets, whereby roads are closed to all but residents during certain times on school days. The closures are intended to make parents and children walk or cycle to school rather than drive or take public transport. However, such measures are not universally popular, as some parents need to drop children at multiple locations before heading to work, and residents worry about disruption to deliveries and services. In April 2021, Harrow Council decided to remove two of its three LTNs but extended the use of school streets within the borough. Another measure to prevent overcrowding on buses in light of COVID-19 was announced in August 2020 ahead of the scheduled return to full-time school for the first time since the UK lockdown began. From September 1, 2020, many London buses will be dedicated to transporting schoolchildren exclusively. The buses will run on over 220 high-frequency routes designated as school services and will operate on school days between 7:30 a.m. and 9:30 a.m. and between 2:30 p.m. and 4:30 p.m.[27] The numerous school services buses will help allow social distancing, because fewer people will be able to ride on each individual bus. Although England's social distancing will wind down in England on July 19, 2021, the school bus service will remain in place though it will monitored to see if there is demand for such a service to continue.

A TIMELINE OF LONDON'S FUTURE

London's prospects—economic, social, political, and environmental—are unclear, but the following is a select timeline of the city's likely future.

2022: The COVID-19 pandemic has impacted the delivery of the new Elizabeth Line (Crossrail) train service, which is now expected to open in the first half of 2022, some two years later than scheduled. The delayed opening of Crossrail has added at least another £450 million to the project's total costs. The delay was blamed on the need to halve the normal number of workers who could be on-site at one time in order to maintain social distancing. Ironically, the extra capacity provided by Crossrail would have made it far easier for London commuters to social distance while traveling into the West End and the City of London without packing into crowded Tube cars. The latest estimated completion dates for the project mean that trains will not travel along the whole length of Crossrail from Berkshire to Essex until as late as May 2023.[28] The latest delay is a problem for TfL's already troubled finances, which have fallen sharply due to the slump in passenger revenues since the start of the UK's lockdown.

2022: The tallest building in the City of London, 22 Bishopsgate, is scheduled to open. Work on the building, which will be 62 stories tall with a floor space of 1.4 million square feet, was expected to conclude by June 2020 but was delayed due to the need to ensure site workers kept social distant during the COVID-19 pandemic. That meant the number of workers on the site at once fell from 1,200 to 25. The skyscraper has room for 12,000 office workers, and, despite the pandemic, around 60 percent of the office space has been leased.[29]

2023: The Museum of London will relocate to Smithfield. The museum plans to move from its present home within the Barbican to an abandoned indoor market space at Smithfield, next door to the famous meat market. It is hoped the relocation will double the museum's visitor numbers to more than 2 million per year.[30] It is proposed that in 2030, London's Centre for Music, a performance and educational facility, will open on the Museum of London's previous site.

2023: The V&A East is also expected to open in the Queen Elizabeth Olympic Park. This is a new branch of the Victoria and Albert Museum that will interconnect two sites in the Olympic Park, a brand-new museum on Stratford Waterfront and a new research center at the media center Here East, which is located within the Olympic Park and built specially for the 2012 London Olympics. The research center will hold 250,000 objects plus an additional 917 from the Victoria and Albert Museum's archives.[31]

2023: The Thames Tideway Tunnel is expected to be completed in 2023. The Tunnel will be 24 feet in diameter, up to 220 feet deep, up to 16 miles long, and able to provide enough deep sewage storage to avoid the need for other such tunnels to be built. Sewage will flow through the Tunnel under the force of gravity. This Tunnel will follow the route of the River Thames as far as Limehouse in London's Docklands, where it will then continue to Abbey Mills pumping station near Stratford, in East London. At Abbey Mills, the Tunnel links to the Lee Tunnel, which will carry sewage on to Beckton Sewage Treatment Works. The Thames Tideway Tunnel will connect to the 34 worst-polluting combined-sewer overflows (CSOs, overflow valves intended to reduce the risk of sewage overflowing during heavy rain) positioned along the Thames's riverbanks in London. Consequently, the Tunnel will capture about 15.5 million tons of the 18 million tons of untreated wastewater that enter the Thames annually.[32]

2024: In 2024, work is scheduled to begin on Crossrail 2. This is a new train route passing north-south through London and connecting the city to surrounding areas. Crossrail 2 is intended to prevent overcrowding on the Victoria, Piccadilly, Northern, Central, and District lines by providing Londoners with alternative routes. Crossrail 1 and 2 will intersect at Tottenham Court Road station. It is expected that the final plans for Crossrail

2 will be submitted to the UK parliament in 2021 or 2022, with construction to follow. It is hoped that Crossrail 2 will open in the early 2030s.

2025: 1 Undershaft, the tallest building in the City of London, should be completed by 2025. At 73 stories high, the skyscraper will rise to 1,016 feet and be located in the center of London's financial district, sandwiched between the "Cheesegrater" and "Gherkin" buildings.[33]

2025: In 2025, the House of Commons will leave the Palace of Westminster for at least six years at a cost of £4 billion so that renovation work can be carried out.[34] The new chamber will be in nearby Richmond House. However, the plans were designed before the COVID-19 pandemic threatened to drop the UK into recession, and there is speculation that politicians wish to backtrack on the idea of refurbishing Parliament in case the cost of the work causes a public backlash.

2028–2031: At some point between 2028 and 2031, the first phase of the High Speed 2 (usually referred to in the UK as simply HS2) rail route should open, linking London's Euston station to the city of Birmingham, in central England. HS2, which is highly controversial because it will cut through some of England's most precious ancient woodlands, is currently Europe's largest infrastructure project but has suffered delays and mounting concerns over its exact route and spiraling costs. At present, HS2 should run between London and Birmingham, carrying 1,300-foot trains fitted with as many as 1,100 seats per train. The line will allow trains to reach speeds of up to 250 miles per hour and would run up to 14 times per hour in each direction. As part of HS2, a new station may also be built next to Manchester Piccadilly station. Mayors in northern England are keen for the project to be delivered to help boost investment and productivity in the north. In 2015, the official cost of HS2 was set out at a little under £56 billion. However, since then, the government estimates the costs have risen to £106 billion.[35]

2029: The Bakerloo Tube line extension to Lewisham may be completed by 2029. A public consultation found strong support for a Tube extension beyond Elephant and Castle station, and the extension will include two new Underground stations at Old Kent Road and New Cross Gate. The new Tube stations will provide a direct route for commuters into central London while connecting transport links across South London, thereby reducing travel times and easing congestion. Work on the extension should begin in 2023 at an estimated cost of £3.1 billion.[36] Another Bakerloo line extension is expected to open in Bromley, South East London, in 2040.

2051: In 2051, London will mark the anniversaries of the Great Exhibition (in 1851) and Festival of Britain (in 1951).

2070: 2070 marks the end of the Thames Barrier's expected life span. A 2012 *Thames Estuary 2100* (TE2100) report confirmed that the barrier's life span has been extended from 2030 to 2070. However, it will be necessary to build replacement flood defenses to protect London from increases in sea level caused by climate change. The first proposed replacement for the Thames Barrier includes a new £6 billion barrier built across the Thames Estuary. A second proposal would be part of an ambitious infrastructure program that could include an airport as part of an urban regeneration plan. A third proposal is for a new barrier between Tilbury in Essex and the Hoo Peninsula in Kent, around 30 miles downstream from the current Thames Barrier. As well as preventing flooding, this barrier would be fitted with hydroelectric power generators capable of generating up to 525 gigawatt hours of energy per year (enough to power 76,000 households) with zero carbon emissions. The barrier would also include a new road as well as rail links that could form part of a fully integrated transport system, including a new orbital railway around London. This barrier would be located next to the new London Gateway Port, which will be one the world's biggest shipping ports. While the exact nature of the future Thames Barrier is unclear, the necessity for it is certain. According to a 2011 report, *Physical and Economic Consequences of Climate Change in Europe*, a predicted increase in global warming of around 3 to 5 degrees Celsius over the next 70 years will leave some 5.5 million people across Europe at risk of coastal flooding. The report highlighted London as one of the highest risk areas.[37]

LIFE IN THE CITY

THE NEW LONDON

London hasn't felt like London, really, since the start of the year.

I'm a doctor, living and working in London. It's been such an odd time. My working life has continued much the same as always, unlike so many others. Yes, the patients have been different (nothing quite prepares you for a patient with COVID-19), but working in emergency medicine has always been challenging.

But life outside of work, goodness that's changed so completely. There's a bit of a disconnect, to tell the truth. Hearing people talking about being furloughed and relaxing and enjoying the time they've had with their family, that's been hard. Watching them clap on Thursdays (a controversial Thursday evening ritual that emerged during the pandemic and saw people clap for key workers, including NHS staff), knowing it really meant nothing to them, knowing they had no conception of what so many of us have had to sacrifice to continue to work in the NHS, that's been hard.

Life outside the hospital has changed so much. The worry of carrying "the bug" home means I haven't hugged my mum since January. I wear a mask at home. Seeing all the people who don't have to worry about carrying home a deadly disease makes me almost envious. Watching the news and seeing crowds of people give me such a feeling of panic, knowing that they could be writing their own death sentence, knowing that they could be contributing to the NHS truly being overwhelmed.

I had the bug, right at the start of this whole thing. Just at the time when we were gearing up for battle, I ended up lying in bed for two weeks, feeling like death. The aftereffects of COVID haven't gone away completely, but at least I survived. Having had it myself, I'm at least able to empathize with patients and colleagues who are stricken. COVID is one of the worst illnesses I've seen, in the unpredictability of who will be affected and how badly they'll hurt.

I wonder if life in London will ever be "normal" again.
I don't think it will.

—Dr. N. Y. Suri

NOTES

1. Centre for Cities, "Cities Outlook 2021," January 25, 2021, https://www.cen treforcities.org/publication/cities-outlook-2021/.

2. GLA Economics, "COVID-19 and London's Economy. Impacts So Far and Economic Outlook," February 12, 2021, https://airdrive-secure.s3-eu-west-1.ama zonaws.com/london/dataset/covid-19-and-london-s-economy---impacts-and -economic-outlook/2021-02-12T13%3A59%3A27/COVID-19%20and%20the%20 London%20Economy%20final-published.pdf?X-Amz-Algorithm=AWS4-HMAC -SHA256&X-Amz-Credential=AKIAJJDIMAIVZJDICKHA%2F20210623%2Feu -west-1%2Fs3%2Faws4_request&X-Amz-Date=20210623T100104Z&X-Amz -Expires=300&X-Amz-Signature=8bcdf67de4b06b600a85300551c413e 4a0782c050a28ac9c124581b6f00118ad&X-Amz-SignedHeaders=hostP11.

3. *London's Economic Outlook*, 13.

4. Rupert Jones, "London Is Worst-Performing Region as UK House Prices Fall," *The Guardian*, March 31, 2021, https://www.theguardian.com/business /2021/mar/31/london-worst-performing-region-uk-house-prices-fall.

5. *London's Economic Outlook*, 10.

6. Ibid., 4.

7. "Covid Vaccine: How Many People in the UK Have Been Vaccinated So Far?" *BBC News*, June 22, 2021, https://www.bbc.co.uk/news/health-55274833

8. *London's Economic Outlook*, 11.

9. Ibid.

10. London Sustainable Development Commission, in association with UK100, *Financing for a Future London: How to Finance a Fair Transition to A Resilient, Circular, Zero Carbon London*, Greater London Authority, March 2020, https:// www.london.gov.uk/sites/default/files/green_finance_exec_sum_online_0.pdf, 13.

11. Ibid., 7.

12. Rachel Millard, "Home Working Puts Future of London Skyscrapers in Doubt," *The Telegraph*, May 19, 2020, https://www.telegraph.co.uk/business /2020/05/19/london-skyscrapers-face-critical-fall-demand-workers-stay-home.

13. Robert Booth, "Covid-19 Sparks Exodus of Middle-Class Londoners in Search of the Good Life," *The Guardian*, June 24, 2020, https://www.theguardian.com/uk-news/2020/jun/24/covid-19-sparks-exodus-of-middle-class-londoners-in-search-of-the-good-life.

14. Ibid.

15. Ibid.

16. Ibid.

17. Ibid.

18. Transport for London, "Travel in London. Report 13," 2020, https://content.tfl.gov.uk/travel-in-london-report-13.pdf P13-14.

19. "Low-Traffic Neighbourhoods," London Living Streets, https://londonlivingstreets.com/low-traffic-liveable-neighbourhoods.

20. "Low Traffic Neighbourhoods Planned for the Borough," *Ealing News Extra*, June 26, 2020, http://ealingnewsextra.co.uk/features/low-traffic.

21. London Cycling Campaign and London Living Streets, *A Guide to Low Traffic Neighbourhoods*, Https://Londonlivingstreets.Files.Wordpress.Com/2018/09/Lcc021-Low-Traffic-Neighbourhoods-Detail-V9.Pdf.

22. Emma Griffin, "Evaporating Traffic? Impact of Low-Traffic Neighbourhoods on Main Roads," London Living Streets, https://londonlivingstreets.com/2019/07/11/evaporating-traffic-impact-of-low-traffic-neighbourhoods-on-main-roads.

23. Grainne Cuffe, "Residents Speak Out about Lee Green LTN," News Shopper, August 4, 2020, https://www.newsshopper.co.uk/news/18627699.residents-speak-lee-green-ltn.

24. Adam Shaw, "Harrow Council Panel Rejects Low-Traffic Neighbourhoods," This Is Local London, August 11, 2020, https://www.thisislocallondon.co.uk/news/18643252.harrow-council-panel-rejects-low-traffic-neighbourhoods.

25. "Bromley in Legal Moves against Croydon over Road Closures," Inside Croydon, August 18, 2020, https://insidecroydon.com/2020/08/18/bromley-in-legal-moves-against-croydon-over-road-closures.

26. "Labour Council Leader Admits Plan to 'Take Advantage' of Covid," 247 News Around the World, September 28, 2020, https://247newsaroundtheworld.com/covid-19/labour-council-leader-admits-plan-to-take-advantage-of-covid/.

27. Becky Morton, "Coronavirus: Bus Journeys Will Be First Challenge of New School Year," BBC News, August 29, 2020, https://www.bbc.co.uk/news/uk-53894312.

28. Jonathan Prynn and Joe Murphy, "Crossrail Double Blow as It's Delayed until 2022 with £450 Million Extra Needed," *Evening Standard*, August 21, 2020, https://www.standard.co.uk/news/transport/crossrail-delayed-again-2022-a4530211.html.

29. George Hammond, "Will London's Newest Skyscraper Become a Monument to the Market Peak?" *Financial Times*, May 29, 2020, https://www.ft.com/content/9685e5e8-4669-4825-8ef3-a54c910d8864.

30. Maev Kennedy, "Off to Market: Museum of London Shows Off Its New Smithfield Site," *The Guardian*, May 20, 2016, https://www.theguardian.com/culture/2016/may/20/museum-of-london-to-relocate-to-smithfield.

31. "The V&A East Project," Victoria and Albert Museum, 2020, https://www.vam.ac.uk/info/va-east-project.

32. Department for Environment, Food and Rural Affairs, *Creating a River Thames Fit for Our Future: An Updated Strategic and Economic Case for the Thames Tideway Tunnel* (London: Crown, October 2015), 12, https://assets .publishing.service.gov.uk/government/uploads/system/uploads/attachment _data/file/471847/thames-tideway-tunnel-strategic-economic-case.pdf.

33. Oliver Wainwright, "1 Undershaft, the Tallest Skyscraper in the City of London, Revealed," *The Guardian*, December 7, 2015, https://www.theguardian .com/artanddesign/architecture-design-blog/2015/dec/07/1-undershaft-tallest -skyscraper-city-of-london-eric-parry#comment-64683726.

34. Brian Wheeler, "Coronavirus: Will £4bn Parliament Refurbishment Be Scrapped?" *BBC News*, May 22, 2020, https://www.bbc.co.uk/news/uk-politics -52682922.

35. "HS2: When Will the Line Open and How Much Will It Cost?" *BBC News*, February 11, 2020, https://www.bbc.co.uk/news/uk-16473296.

36. Rob Horgan, "Timeline Set for Bakerloo Line Extension to Lewisham," *New Civil Engineer*, September 13, 2018, https://www.newcivilengineer.com/latest /timeline-set-for-bakerloo-line-extension-to-lewisham-13-09-2018.

37. Ike Ijeh, "Thames Barrier: The Day after Tomorrow," *Building*, March 4, 2014, https://www.building.co.uk/focus/thames-barrier-the-day-after-tomorrow /5066708.article.

FURTHER READING

Bernal, Natasha. "The UK's Coronavirus Furlough Scheme, Explained by Experts." *Wired*, July 29, 2020. https://www.wired.co.uk/article/uk-furlough-scheme -job-protection.

Booth, Robert. "Covid-19 Sparks Exodus of Middle-Class Londoners in Search of the Good Life." *The Guardian*, June 24, 2020. https://www.theguardian .com/uk-news/2020/jun/24/covid-19-sparks-exodus-of-middle-class -londoners-in-search-of-the-good-life.

"Bromley in Legal Moves against Croydon over Road Closures." Inside Croydon, August 18, 2020. https://insidecroydon.com/2020/08/18/bromley-in-legal -moves-against-croydon-over-road-closures.

Cuffe, Grainne. "Residents Speak Out about Lee Green LTN." News Shopper, August 4, 2020. https://www.newsshopper.co.uk/news/18627699.residents -speak-lee-green-ltn.

Department for Environment, Food and Rural Affairs. *Creating a River Thames Fit for Our Future: An Updated Strategic and Economic Case for the Thames Tideway Tunnel*. London: Crown, October 2015. https://assets .publishing.service.gov.uk/government/uploads/system/uploads/attachment _data/file/471847/thames-tideway-tunnel-strategic-economic-case.pdf.

Griffin, Emma. "Evaporating Traffic? Impact of Low-Traffic Neighbourhoods on Main Roads." London Living Streets. https://londonlivingstreets.com /2019/07/11/evaporating-traffic-impact-of-low-traffic-neighbourhoods -on-main-roads.

Hammond, George. "Will London's Newest Skyscraper Become a Monument to the Market Peak?" *Financial Times*, May 29, 2020. https://www.ft.com /content/9685e5e8-4669-4825-8ef3-a54c910d8864.

Horgan, Rob. "Timeline Set for Bakerloo Line Extension to Lewisham." *New Civil Engineer*, September 13, 2018. https://www.newcivilengineer.com/latest /timeline-set-for-bakerloo-line-extension-to-lewisham-13-09-2018.

"HS2: When Will the Line Open and How Much Will It Cost?" *BBC News*, February 11, 2020. https://www.bbc.co.uk/news/uk-16473296.

Ijeh, Ike. "Thames Barrier: The Day after Tomorrow." *Building*, March 4, 2014. https://www.building.co.uk/focus/thames-barrier-the-day-after-tomorrow /5066708.article.

Kennedy, Maev. "Off to Market: Museum of London Shows Off Its New Smithfield Site." *The Guardian*, May 20, 2016. https://www.theguardian.com /culture/2016/may/20/museum-of-london-to-relocate-to-smithfield.

London's Economic Outlook: Spring 2020. Greater London Authority, 2020. https://www.london.gov.uk/sites/default/files/leo-spring-2020.pdf.

London Sustainable Development Commission, in association with UK100. *Financing for a Future London: How to Finance a Fair Transition to A Resilient, Circular, Zero Carbon London*. Greater London Authority, March 2020. https://www.london.gov.uk/sites/default/files/green_finance_exec _sum_online_0.pdf.

Millard, Rachel. "Home Working Puts Future of London Skyscrapers in Doubt." *The Telegraph*, May 19, 2020. https://www.telegraph.co.uk/business/2020/05 /19/london-skyscrapers-face-critical-fall-demand-workers-stay-home.

Morton, Becky. "Coronavirus: Bus Journeys Will Be First Challenge of New School Year." *BBC News*, August 29, 2020. https://www.bbc.co.uk/news/uk-5389 4312.

Prynn, Jonathan and Joe Murphy. "Crossrail Double Blow as It's Delayed until 2022 with £450 Million Extra Needed." *Evening Standard*, August 21, 2020. https://www.standard.co.uk/news/transport/crossrail-delayed-again -2022-a4530211.html.

Shaw, Adam. "Harrow Council Panel Rejects Low-Traffic Neighbourhoods." This Is Local London, August 11, 2020. https://www.thisislocallondon.co.uk /news/18643252.harrow-council-panel-rejects-low-traffic-neighbourhoods.

"The V&A East Project." Victoria and Albert Museum, 2020. https://www.vam .ac.uk/info/va-east-project.

Wainwright, Oliver. "1 Undershaft, the Tallest Skyscraper in the City of London, Revealed." *The Guardian*, December 7, 2015. https://www.theguardian .com/artanddesign/architecture-design-blog/2015/dec/07/1-undershaft -tallest-skyscraper-city-of-london-eric-parry#comment-64683726.

Select Bibliography

Barr, Charles. *Ealing Studios: A Movie Book*. 3rd ed. Berkeley: University of California Press, 1998.

Chalk, Peter, ed. *Encyclopedia of Terrorism: Volume 1: A–L*. Santa Barbara, CA: ABC-CLIO, 2013.

Clarke, Colin P., ed. *Terrorism: The Essential Guide*. Santa Barbara, CA: ABC-CLIO, 2018.

Corton, Christine L. *London Fog: The Biography*. Cambridge, MA: Belknap Press of Harvard University Press, 2015.

Cybriwsky, Roman Adrian. *Capital Cities around the World: An Encyclopedia of Geography, History, and Culture*. Santa Barbara, CA: ABC-CLIO, 2013.

Dingley, James. *The IRA: The Irish Republican Army*. Santa Barbara, CA: Praeger, 2012.

Jenkins, Simon. *A Short History of London: The Creation of a World Capital*. London: Penguin, 2019.

Jorgensen, Sara C. "London, United Kingdom: Facing the Challenges of Population Growth." In *Cities around the World: Struggles and Solutions to Modern Life. Volume 1*, edited by Jing Luo, 274–79. Santa Barbara, CA: ABC-CLIO, 2019.

Kynaston, David. *City of London: The History*. London: Vintage Books, 2012.

Linnane, Fergus. *London's Underworld: Three Centuries of Vice and Crime*. London: Robson Books, 2004.

Mason, Laura. "Great Britain." In *Food Cultures of the World Encyclopedia: Volume 4*, edited by Ken Albala, 147–59. Santa Barbara, CA: Greenwood, 2011.

Mount, Toni. *Everyday Life in Medieval London: From the Anglo-Saxons to the Tudors*. Stroud, UK: Amberley Publishing, 2014.

Nesser, Petter. *Islamist Terrorism in Europe*. Rev. ed. London: C. Hurst & Co., Ltd., 2018.

Oates, Jonathan. *Attack on London: Disaster, Rebellion, Riot, Terror & War*. Barnsley, UK: Wharncliffe Local History, 2009.

Porter, Roy. *London, a Social History*. Cambridge, MA: Harvard University Press, 1994.

Richardson, John. *The Annals of London: A Year-by-Year Record of a Thousand Years of History*. London: Cassell & Co., 2001.

Richardson, LeeAnne M. "The Journalist Who Exposed the Jeffrey Epsteins of Victorian London." The Conversation, August 12, 2019. https://the conversation.com/the-journalist-who-exposed-the-jeffrey-epsteins -of-victorian-london-121409.

Shelley, Fred M. *The World's Population: An Encyclopedia of Critical Issues, Crises, and Ever-Growing Countries*. Santa Barbara, CA: ABC-CLIO, 2015.

Travers, Tony. *The Politics of London: Governing an Ungovernable City*. London: Palgrave Macmillan, 2003.

Weinreb, Ben, Christopher Hibbert, John Keay, and Julia Keay. *The London Encyclopaedia*. 3rd ed. London: MacMillan, 2000.

Williams, Victoria. "Dickens' Use of the Fairy Tale in *Our Mutual Friend*." *Pennsylvania Literary Journal: British Literature* 2, no. 2 (Winter 2010): 47–75.

Williams, Victoria. "Great Expectations." In *Literary Geography: An Encyclopedia of Real and Imagined Settings*, edited by Lynn Marie Houston, 111–14. Santa Barbara, CA: Greenwood, 2019.

Williams, Victoria. "Murrow, Edward R. (1908–1965)." In *100 Entertainers Who Changed America: An Encyclopedia of Pop Culture Luminaries: Volume II: M–Z*, edited by Robert C. Sickels, 411–18. Santa Barbara, CA: ABC-CLIO, 2013.

Wilson, A. N. *London: A Short History*. London: Weidenfeld & Nicolson, 2015.

Wolfreys, Julian. *Dickens's London: Perception, Subjectivity and Phenomenal Urban Multiplicity*. Edinburgh: Edinburgh University Press, 2012.

Wright, John D. *Bloody History of London: Crime, Corruption and Murder*. London: Amber Books, 2017.

ELECTRONIC RESOURCES

Angel, Schlomo (Solly). "The Urban Expansion of London." Marron Institute of Urban Management *Blog*, September 14, 2012. https://marron institute.nyu.edu/blog/the-urban-expansion-of-london.

Archer, Ian W. "The Charity of Early Modern Londoners." *Transactions of the Royal Historical Society* 12 (2002): 223–44. Accessed February 7, 2020. https://www.jstor.org/stable/3679345?seq=1.

Arnold, Catharine. *Underworld London: Crime and Punishment in the Capital City.* London: Simon & Schuster, 2012.

Ash, Lucy. "London, France's Sixth Biggest City." BBC News, May 30, 2012. https://www.bbc.co.uk/news/magazine-18234930.

"Assessment of the GLA's Impact on Faith Inequality." Greater London Authority, December 2014. https://www.london.gov.uk/sites/default /files/assessment_of_the_glas_impact_on_faith_equality.pdf.

Barrett, Silviya, and Erica Belcher. "Components of Population Change." *London Intelligence*, issue 9, July 25, 2019: https://www.centrefor london.org/reader/the-london-intelligence-issue-9/demography /#components-of-population-change.

Bibby, Miriam. "London's Great Stink." Historic UK. Accessed July 8, 2021. https://www.historic-uk.com/HistoryUK/HistoryofBritain/Londons -Great-Stink.

Booth, Robert. "Covid-19 Sparks Exodus of Middle-Class Londoners in Search of the Good Life." *The Guardian*, June 24, 2020. https:// www.theguardian.com/uk-news/2020/jun/24/covid-19-sparks -exodus-of-middle-class-londoners-in-search-of-the-good-life.

Collinson, Alwyn. "How Bazalgette Built London's First Super-Sewer." Museum of London, March 26, 2019. https://www.museumoflondon .org.uk/discover/how-bazalgette-built-londons-first-super-sewer.

Cominetti, Nye, Laura Gardiner, and Hannah Slaughter. *The Full Monty: Facing Up to the Challenge of the Coronavirus Labour Market Crisis.* June 2020. https://www.resolutionfoundation.org/app/uploads/2020 /06/The-Full-Monty.pdf.

Department for Environment, Food and Rural Affairs. *Creating a River Thames Fit for Our Future: An Updated Strategic and Economic Case for the Thames Tideway Tunnel.* London: Crown, October 2015. https://assets.publishing.service.gov.uk/government/uploads /system/uploads/attachment_data/file/471847/thames-tideway -tunnel-strategic-economic-case.pdf.

Doherty, Rosa. "Golders Green: Clocking Up a Growth in Numbers." *Jewish Chronicle*, March 29, 2018. https://www.thejc.com/community /special-reports/golders-green-clocking-up-a-growth-in-numbers -1.461649.

Douglass, Gordon, and Eduardo Orellana. "Outlook for London's Economy Remains Gloomy as Lockdown Is Eased." *London's Economy Today*, issue 214, June 2020. https://www.london.gov.uk/sites/default/files /londons_economy_today_no214_250620.pdf.

Environment Agency. "Surface Water: The Biggest Flood Risk of All." Speech by Sir James Bevan KCMG, chief executive, Environment Agency, CIWEM Surface Water Management Conference, October 17, 2018. https://www.gov.uk/government/news/surface-water-the -biggest-flood-risk-of-all.

Estimation of Changes in Air Pollution in London during the COVID-19 Outbreak. Response to the UK Government's Air Quality Expert Group Call for Evidence. Greater London Authority, April 2020. https://www.london.gov.uk/sites/default/files/london_response _to_aqeg_call_for_evidence_april_2020.pdf.

"The Evacuation of Children during the Second World War." History Press, 2020. https://www.thehistorypress.co.uk/articles/the-evacuation -of-children-during-the-second-world-war.

Geology of London." London Natural History Society, June 27, 2020. http:// lnhs.org.uk/index.php/articles-british/249-geology-of-london.

Girardi, Aaron, and Joel Marsden. *A Description of London's Economy.* GLA Economics Working Paper 85, March 2017. https://www.london .gov.uk/sites/default/files/description-londons-economy-working -paper-85.pdf.

Goebel, Stefan, and Jerry White. "London and the First World War." *London Journal* 41, no. 3 (2016): 199–218. https://www.tandfonline.com /doi/full/10.1080/03058034.2016.1216758.

"Great Plague of 1665–1666." National Archives. Accessed July 8, 2021. https://www.nationalarchives.gov.uk/education/resources/great -plague.

"The Great Storm of 1987." Met Office. Accessed July 8, 2021. https://www .metoffice.gov.uk/weather/learn-about/weather/case-studies/great -storm.

Griffin, Emma. "Evaporating Traffic? Impact of Low-Traffic Neighbour- hoods on Main Roads." London Living Streets. Accessed July 8, 2021. https://londonlivingstreets.com/2019/07/11/evaporating-traffic -impact-of-low-traffic-neighbourhoods-on-main-roads.

Hammond, George. "Will London's Newest Skyscraper Become a Monu- ment to the Market Peak." *Financial Times*, May 29, 2020. https:// www.ft.com/content/9685e5e8-4669-4825-8ef3-a54c910d8864.

Hardach, Sophie. "How the River Thames was Brought Back from the Dead." BBC, November 12, 2015. http://www.bbc.co.uk/earth /story/20151111-how-the-river-thames-was-brought-back-from -the-dead.

"Health and Exposure to Pollution." Greater London Authority, 2020. https://www.london.gov.uk/what-we-do/environment/pollution -and-air-quality/health-and-exposure-pollution.

Hill, Kate. "How Many Pubs in London." Estate Agents London News, August 31, 2018. https://www.greaterlondonproperties.co.uk/how -many-pubs-in-london.

Hill, Kate. "How Many Sex Shops in Soho?" Estate Agents London News, June 21, 2018. https://www.greaterlondonproperties.co.uk/how-many -sex-shops-in-soho.

Hope, Mike. *The Economic Impact of Brexit on London.* Greater London Authority, October 2019. https://www.london.gov.uk/sites/default /files/brexit-analysis-final.pdf.

"HS2: When Will the Line Open and How Much Will It Cost?" BBC News, February 11, 2020. https://www.bbc.co.uk/news/uk-16473296.

Husband, Stuart. "Little Istanbul." *Evening Standard,* June 27, 2002. https:// www.standard.co.uk/news/little-istanbul-7223100.html.

Ijeh, Ike. "Thames Barrier: The Day after Tomorrow." *Building,* March 4, 2014. https://www.building.co.uk/focus/thames-barrier-the-day-after -tomorrow/5066708.article.

Inman, Phillip. "London's 19% Economic Surge Underlines Divide with Rest of England." *The Guardian,* September 5, 2019. https://www.theguardian .com/business/2019/sep/05/londons-19-economic-surge-underlines -divide-with-rest-of-england.

Leeser, Rachel. "Poverty in London 2018/19." Greater London Authority, March 27, 2020. https://data.london.gov.uk/blog/poverty-in-london-2018-19.

London Environment Strategy. London: Greater London Authority, May 2018. https://www.london.gov.uk/sites/default/files/london _environment_strategy_0.pdf.

"London Plagues 1348–1665." Museum of London: Pocket Histories, 2011. https://www.museumoflondon.org.uk/application/files/5014/5434 /6066/london-plagues-1348-1665.pdf (site discontinued).

London Resilience Partnership. *London Risk Register.* Version 8.1, January 2019. https://www.london.gov.uk/sites/default/files/london_risk _register_2019.pdf.

London Resilience Partnership. *Severe Weather and Natural Hazards: Response Framework.* Version 1, June 2017. https://www.london.gov.uk /sites/default/files/severe_weather_and_natural_hazards_framework _v1.0.pdf.

London Sustainable Development Commission, in association with UK100. *Financing for a Future London. How to Finance a Fair Transition to a Resilient, Circular, Zero Carbon London.* Greater London Authority, March 2020. https://www.london.gov.uk/sites/default/files/green _finance_exec_sum_online_0.pdf.

London's Economic Outlook: Spring 2020. Greater London Authority, 2020. https://www.london.gov.uk/sites/default/files/leo-spring-2020.pdf.

London's Foundations: Protecting the Geodiversity of the Capital. Greater London Authority, March 2009. http://londongeopartnership.org .uk/wp/wp-content/uploads/2018/08/Londons-Foundations-2009 .pdf.

"Low-Traffic Neighbourhoods." London Living Streets. Accessed July 8, 2021. https://londonlivingstreets.com/low-traffic-liveable-neighbourhoods.

Mayor of London/London Assembly. "Chapter One: Context and Strategy." 2020. https://www.london.gov.uk/what-we-do/planning/london -plan/past-versions-and-alterations-london-plan/london-plan -2016/london-plan-chapter-one-context-and-strategy-6.

"Michelin-Star Restaurants in London." TimeOut London, November 20, 2019. https://www.timeout.com/london/restaurants/michelin-star -restaurants-in-london.

Myers, Rebecca. "General History of Women's Suffrage in Britain." *The Independent*, May 28, 2013. https://www.independent.co.uk/news/ uk/home-news/general-history-of-women-s-suffrage-in-britain -8631733.html.

"Overview of the Thames Basin." British Geological Survey, 2020. https:// www.bgs.ac.uk/research/groundwater/waterResources/thames /overview.html.

Pirie, Madsen. "When a Killer Smog Hit London." Adam Smith Institute, December 4, 2019. https://www.adamsmith.org/blog/when-a-killer -smog-hit-london.

Potential Impacts of Immigration Policies Based on Skills and Salary Thresholds in London. Greater London Authority, July 2019. https:// www.london.gov.uk/sites/default/files/executive-summary-cin58 -59.pdf.

Robinson, Bruce. "London: Brighter Lights, Bigger City." BBC, February 17, 2011. http://www.bbc.co.uk/history/british/civil_war_revolution /brighter_lights_01.shtml.

Sanders-McDonagh, Erin. *Immoral Geographies and Soho's Sex Shops: Exploring Spaces of Sexual Diversity in London.* 2018. https://bura .brunel.ac.uk/bitstream/2438/19272/1/FullText.pdf.

"Tate Modern Overtakes British Museum as Top UK Visitor Attraction." BBC News, March 27, 2019. https://www.bbc.co.uk/news/entertainment -arts-47711540.

Transport for London and Mayor of London. *SUDS in London: A Guide.* November 2016. http://content.tfl.gov.uk/sustainable-urban-drainage -november-2016.pdf.

Webber, Esther. "The Rise and Fall of the GLC." BBC, March 31, 2016. https://www.bbc.co.uk/news/uk-england-london-35716693.

"What Happened in the Great Fire of London?" Museum of London: Pocket Histories, 2011. https://www.museumoflondon.org.uk/application

/files/6514/5511/5493/what-happened-great-fire-london.pdf (site discontinued).

What Londoners Tell Us around Knife Crime and Violence. January 2019. https://www.london.gov.uk/moderngovmb/documents/s63353 /Appendix%20B%20-%20MOPAC%20Surveys%20presentation.pdf.

"What Was Life Like in Medieval London?" Museum of London: Pocket Histories, 2011. https://www.museumoflondon.org.uk/application /files/1614/5442/8566/what-was-life-like-medieval-london.pdf (site discontinued).

Wieshmann, Handan, Matthew Davies, Ollie Sugg, Sophie Davis, and Simon Ruda. *Violence in London: What We Know and How to Respond.* Mayor of London's Violence Reduction Unit, January 28, 2020. https://www.london.gov.uk/sites/default/files/bit_london_violence _reduction_final_28_january_2020.pdf.

Index

About the Author

Victoria R. Williams, PhD, is an independent writer and researcher living in London. She is the author of ABC-CLIO's *Weird Sports and Wacky Games around the World: From Buzkashi to Zorbing* (winner of the 2016 RUSA Outstanding Reference Sources Award); *Celebrating Life Customs around the World: From Baby Showers to Funerals*; and *Indigenous Peoples: An Encyclopedia of Culture, History, and Threats to Survival.* She is also the coeditor of ABC-CLIO's *Etiquette and Taboos around the World: A Geographic Encyclopedia of Social and Cultural Customs.* Williams has written on a variety of other subjects, including Hollywood film, human sacrifice, Mesoamerican mythology, Victorian literature, and British folk customs.

www.ingramcontent.com/pod-product-compliance
Lightning Source LLC
Chambersburg PA
CBHW070608270326
41926CB00013B/2463